T0319879

Accessibility, Equity and Efficiency

NECTAR SERIES ON TRANSPORTATION AND COMMUNICATIONS NETWORKS RESEARCH

Series Editor: Aura Reggiani, *Professor of Economic Policy, University of Bologna, Italy*

NECTAR (Network on European Communications and Transport Activities Research) is an international scientific, interdisciplinary association with a network culture. Its primary objective is to foster research collaboration and the exchange of information between experts in the fields of transport, communication and mobility.

NECTAR members study the behaviour of individuals, groups and governments within a spatial framework. They bring a wide variety of perspectives to analyse the challenges facing transport and communication, and the impact these challenges have on society at all levels of spatial aggregation.

This series acts as a companion to, and an expansion of, activities of NECTAR. The volumes in the series are broad in their scope with the intention of disseminating some of the work of the association. The contributions come from all parts of the world and the range of topics covered is extensive, reflecting the breadth and continuously changing nature of issues that confront researchers and practitioners involved in spatial and transport analysis.

Titles in the series include:

Accessibility, Equity and Efficiency

Challenges for Transport and Public Services

Edited by

Karst T. Geurs

Professor of Transport Planning, University of Twente, the Netherlands

Roberto Patuelli

Associate Professor of Economic Policy, University of Bologna, Italy

Tomaz Ponce Dentinho

Professor of Regional, Environmental and Agricultural Economics, University of the Azores, Portugal

NECTAR SERIES ON TRANSPORTATION AND COMMUNICATIONS NETWORKS RESEARCH

Edward Elgar
PUBLISHING

Cheltenham, UK • Northampton, MA, USA

© Karst T. Geurs, Roberto Patuelli and Tomaz Ponce Dentinho 2016

All rights reserved. No part of this publication may be reproduced, stored in a retrieval system or transmitted in any form or by any means, electronic, mechanical or photocopying, recording, or otherwise without the prior permission of the publisher.

Published by
Edward Elgar Publishing Limited
The Lypiatts
15 Lansdown Road
Cheltenham
Glos GL50 2JA
UK

Edward Elgar Publishing, Inc.
William Pratt House
9 Dewey Court
Northampton
Massachusetts 01060
USA

A catalogue record for this book
is available from the British Library

Library of Congress Control Number: 2015952674

This book is available electronically in the **Elgar**online
Economics subject collection
DOI 10.4337/9781784717896

ISBN 978 1 78471 788 9 (cased)
ISBN 978 1 78471 789 6 (eBook)

Typeset by Servis Filmsetting Ltd, Stockport, Cheshire
Printed and bound in Great Britain by TJ International Ltd, Padstow

Contents

Contributors

Paulo Rui Anciães is a Research Associate at the Centre for Transport Studies, University College London, United Kingdom.

Benjamin Büttner is a Research Associate and Lecturer at the Chair of Urban Structure and Transport Planning, Technische Universität München, Munich, Germany.

Kenneth Button is a University Professor in the School of Policy, Government and International Affairs, Virginia, United States.

Zhenhua Chen is a Postdoctoral Research Associate of the University of Southern California, CREATE Homeland Security Center, United States.

Panayotis Christidis is Principal Researcher in the Institute for Prospective Technological Studies (IPTS), Joint Research Centre (JRC), European Commission, Seville, Spain.

Hande Demirel is Associate Professor at the Istanbul Technical University, Department of Geomatics, Turkey.

Tomaz Ponce Dentinho is Professor in Regional, Environmental and Agricultural Economics at the University of Azores, Portugal; Executive Director of the Regional Science Association International (RSAI); and President of the Portuguese Association for Regional Development (APDR).

Jordan Evans is Research Assistant at the Chair of Urban Structure and Transport Planning, Technische Universität München, Munich, Germany.

Karst T. Geurs is Full Professor of Transport Planning at the Centre for Transport Studies, faculty of Engineering Technology, University of Twente, Enschede, the Netherlands.

Mert Kompil is a researcher in the Institute for Environment and Sustainability (IES), Joint Research Centre (JRC), European Commission, Ispra, Italy.

Kevin J. Krizek is Professor of Transport in the Programs of Environmental

Design and Environment Studies at the University of Colorado, Boulder, United States.

Lissy La Paix is Assistant Professor at the Centre for Transport Studies, faculty of Engineering Technology, University of Twente, Enschede, the Netherlands.

David Levinson is Professor in the Department of Civil, Environmental, and Geo-Engineering at the University of Minnesota, United States; and directs the Networks, Economics, and Urban Systems (NEXUS) research group, United States.

Elena López is Senior Researcher of the Transport Research Centre (TRANSyT), Technical University of Madrid, Spain.

David Philip McArthur is Lecturer in Transport Studies at the School of Social and Political Sciences, University of Glasgow, United Kingdom.

Paul Mogush is Principal City Planner of the City of Minneapolis, United States.

Andrés Monzón is Director of the Transport Research Centre (TRANSyT) and Professor of Transport at the Civil Engineering Department, Technical University of Madrid, Spain.

Rui Neiva is the NextGen Fellow and is the main researcher for Eno's NextGen working group, Eno Center for Transportation, Washington, DC, United States.

Emilio Ortega is Researcher of the Transport Research Centre (TRANSyT) and Assistant Professor of GIS at the Environmental and Forestry Engineering Department, Technical University of Madrid, Spain.

Liv Osland is Professor in Economics, Department of Economics and Business Administration, Stord/Haugesund University College, Haugesund, Norway.

César Pakissi is Professor, Department of Natural Sciences, Higher Institute for Educational Sciences (ISCED), Huambo, Angola.

Roberto Patuelli is Associate Professor of Economic Policy at the Department of Economics, University of Bologna, Italy.

Boris A. Portnov is Full Professor at the Department of Natural Resources and Environmental Management, Graduate School of Management, University of Haifa, Israel.

Inge Thorsen is a Professor at the Department of Economics and Business Administration, Stord/Haugesund University College, Haugesund, Norway.

Jan Ubøe is Professor at the Department of Business and Management Science, Norwegian School of Economics, Norway.

Gebhard Wulfhorst directs the Department for Urban Structure and Transport Planning, Technische Universität München, Munich, Germany.

Preface and acknowledgements

This book presents the seventh volume in the Edward Elgar NECTAR Series on Transportation and Communications Networks Research. NECTAR (Network on European Communications and Transport Activities Research) is a European-based scientific association with the primary objective to foster research collaboration and exchange of information between experts in the field of transport, communication and mobility from all European countries and the rest of the world. It is a multidisciplinary social science network gathering a wide variety of perspectives on transport and communication problems and their impacts on society in an international perspective. This book clearly addresses these objectives by presenting chapters linking accessibility to social equity and economic efficiency analysis, incorporating a wide variety of perspectives.

Several contributions originate from the 12th NECTAR International Conference at the São Miguel Island, Azores (Portugal), in 2013. We then amplified the list of chapters by recruiting other internationally renowned authors active in accessibility research to share their work. We appreciate the authors' contributions and the attentiveness with which they addressed the peer reviewers' comments.

The quality of the chapters benefited from the timely and constructive comments received from the peer reviewers and we thank them for their efforts. Elisabete Martins from the University of the Azores provided invaluable editing support. Finally, we thank Alan Sturmer (Executive Editor, Edward Elgar Publishing) for his unwavering support to help organize this effort. We are excited to contribute with another book in the high-quality NECTAR series.

Karst T. Geurs, Roberto Patuelli and Tomaz Ponce Dentinho

PART I

Introduction

1. Accessibility, equity and efficiency

Karst T. Geurs, Tomaz Ponce Dentinho and Roberto Patuelli

The tension between efficiency and equity has been the focus of major debate since equity aspects started to be considered as part of project evaluation procedures (Thomopoulos et al. 2009). In this book, we contribute to the debate by focusing on the links and trade-offs between accessibility, economic efficiency and equity in both the developed and developing country contexts. Accessibility is a concept that has been central to physical planning and spatial modelling for more than 50 years. Accessibility can be viewed as a product of the land use and transport systems, and describes the extent to which land use and transport systems enable (groups of) individuals to reach activities or destinations by means of a (combination of) transport mode(s) (Geurs and van Wee 2004). From the literature it is clear that accessibility is linked to economic efficiency and equity. In general, increased accessibility resulting from a transport project is considered an important user benefit for people and firms. A traveller can make a trip at less cost or greater convenience; there might be less congestion, and more destinations may be reached in the same time. For firms, firstly, a reduction in interaction cost may increase efficiency of production (that is, time saved can be used in productive activities), and may become more competitive and attract more customers. Secondly, improved commuting conditions may improve the labour market, giving rise to improved productivity. However, the linkage between accessibility and spatial economic development is not straightforward. The economic effects are the result of a complex pattern of effects leading in different directions, not all of which are intuitively obvious. For example, improved accessibility between two countries, cities, areas or regions may sometimes benefit one of them to the disbenefit of the other (SACTRA 1999; Banister and Berechman 2001). There are thus also equity issues at stake.

In recent years, there has been growing attention to the equity impacts of transport developments and transport projects, and in particular to using accessibility indicators to capture equity impacts. However, equity analysis is not straightforward. Firstly, the term is often not well defined and 'fairness' and 'justice' are usually used interchangeably, depending on the context. Within transport infrastructure appraisal additional terms are used, including 'solidarity' or (territorial or spatial) 'cohesion' (Thomopoulos et al. 2009), adding a further degree of ambiguity. Secondly, transportation equity analysis can be difficult because there are several types of equity, various ways to categorize people for equity analysis, numerous impacts to consider, and various ways of measuring these impacts (Litman 2002; van Wee and Geurs 2011). Often a distinction is made between equity of opportunity, or process equity (the extent to which there is fair access to the planning and decision-making process), and equity of the outcome, or result equity (the extent to which consequences of a decision are considered just) (Levinson 2010).

Within outcome equity analysis related to transport and accessibility there are several dimensions across which equity can be quantified, for example horizontal equity, vertical equity, social and spatial or territorial equity, and generational equity (see, for literature overviews, Thomopoulos et al. 2009; Levinson 2010). Horizontal equity is the extent to which individuals within a class (for example, income, gender, ability, race) are treated similarly. Vertical equity is the extent to which members of different classes are treated similarly. Social equity refers to the distribution of impacts by population segments that differ in abilities and needs, for example by income, social class, age or ability to travel. Spatial equity refers to the spatial distribution of impacts, for example by region or city. In social equity it is often assumed that everyone should enjoy at least a basic level of access, even if people with special needs require extra resources and subsidies. A basic level of access implies that people can obtain goods, services and activities that are considered valuable to society, such as emergency services, medical care, education, employment, food and clothing.

To quantify outcome equity, statistical indicators are often used. Well-known indicators are the Gini, Theil and Atkinson indices. These have, for example, been used to measure the effects of changes in accessibility measures resulting from road pricing strategies (e.g., Ramjerdi 2006; Souche et al. 2016). These studies show that different inequality indicators produce contrasting and sometimes contradictory results, and results may differ at different geographical scales.

Reducing equity and promoting economic efficiency are often conflicting goals. For example, to provide all individuals and relevant population groups a basic level of access by providing public transport services to remote areas and/or giving public transport subsidies to specific population groups (the elderly, disabled and so on) is often not economically efficient. There is thus an ethically relevant discussion as to what a basic level of accessibility constitutes, or a minimum level of participation in society, below which a problem exists that legitimates or necessitates policy. This at least to some extent is a political issue, a political choice. The choice may vary over place and time, and between persons with different political preferences (van Wee and Geurs 2011). Concerns about equal rights of access to various services or other fundamental aspects of human life have been researched for many years, and from the time of Aristotle several theories have emerged. Two fundamental theories seem to dominate in *ex ante* transport and accessibility evaluations in practice (Thomopoulus et al. 2009; van Wee and Roeser 2013). Utilitarianism theory most dominated in practice as it reflects the backbone of welfare economics and cost–benefit analysis (CBA), but at the same time utilitarianism and CBA have been heavily debated by social scientists and philosophers. Alternatively, several egalitarian theories have been developed emphasizing that everyone has equal rights or benefits for a particular service or scheme. The approaches by John Rawls, Amartya Sen and Martha Nussbaum are the most well-known egalitarian theories (see e.g., Van Wee and Geurs 2011; Van Wee 2011), but other less well-known theories such as Michael Walter's 'Spheres of Justice' are also used in the academic literature to provide theoretical foundations for a distributive approach to transport (Martens et al. 2012). In the planning practice, however, there seems to be fairly little attention for justice-oriented accessibility analyses and planning. This also holds for countries such as the United States and the United Kingdom which are at the forefront of countries with policy attention for the equity implications of transport. In the US transport-related environmental justice regulations were introduced in the 1990s. Martens et al. (2012) review the US transport planning practice and conclude that only a few metropolitan planning organizations in the United States actually measure or invoke the distribution of access. These authorities, even those with the most sophisticated analysis techniques, however, fail to define a well-founded goal against which to assess the results of the analysis. In the UK, transport-related social equity policies and guidelines have been developed, driven by a social exclusion policy agenda. Local transport authorities have been required to undertake strategic and local accessibility planning since 2006 (Lucas 2012). The lack of well-founded goals and indicators also seems problematic in the UK planning practice. Halden (2011) reviews the UK accessibility planning process and states that because of the flexibility offered within accessibility planning and the plethora of potential measures which can be deployed, many local authorities have yet to find an optimal balance in the range, choice and calculation approach for indicators. Moreover, Lucas (2012) concludes that accessibility mapping tools used in planning practice have tended to underplay the complexity of the lived travel experiences of socially excluded individuals, and overlooked other important barriers for social exclusion.

Part II of the book comprises a set of chapters linking population accessibility and equity issues. In Chapter 2 Boris Portnov investigates whether accessibility factors tend to grow or decrease over time in terms of development and population priorities. He looks at the evolution of the relation between municipal development in Switzerland, taken as a relative measure of population size, and accessibility of Swiss municipalities, from 1950 to 2000, and concludes that relative lack of access limits relative growth, and that private accessibility to public infrastructures has an increasing role in that. Summing up, accessibility still matters for development. Chapters 3 and 4 focus on the issue of rural depopulation and accessibility. Paulo Anciães (Chapter 3) studies the population decline in the interior of Portugal and concludes that accessibility can act either as a push or a pull factor in the countryside areas, and that this can be seen in indicators that capture different components of the effects. For Norway, David McArthur and his colleagues (Chapter 4) use a numeric model to look at the iterative and cumulative effects that relate population changes not only to migration of basic employment but also to housing prices and labour market accessibility, that interfere with the process; they accomplish the interesting result that local accessibility and housing prices do have a role on location population patterns at regional and national levels. From this it seems that local accessibility, and related housing prices, appear to play an important role on the effects of overall accessibility in regional development.

The issues addressed in Part III are related to measuring equity in access to daily activities and services. Chapter 5 explores the impact of local accessibility in development and welfare, looking into the impact of mobility costs – connected with oil prices – on the different segments of an urban population, focusing on the case of the Munich urban area. Benjamin Büttner and his co-authors conclude by making some recommendations on how households can become less exposed to oil shocks by having access to different types of accessibility alternatives: public transportation, car sharing and teleworking. The allocation of public services is complementary to the provision of infrastructural accessibility and, for developing countries, important issues that influence the spatial patterns of growth and, necessarily, the sustainability of development and accessibility; this is the theme exploited by César Pakissi and Tomaz Dentinho in Chapter 6, where they focus on the impacts of the equity of different patterns of rational spatial allocation of public services.

Part IV of the book focuses on the efficiency of railway systems. In many countries, government policies aim to improve accessibility by subsidies or public investments. The liberalization of the US railroad system led to considerable increases in its economic efficiency, and thereby transferred traffic from the roads, producing wider transportation and environmental benefits. Chapters 7 and 8 highlight that the performance of passenger rail transport depends upon the quality of local transport to access the stations. The argument is proved in Chapter 7, by Andrés Monzón and colleagues, for the high speed route of Madrid–Cuenca–Valencia–Alicante where it is shown that the quality of the accessibility at local level reflects the potential of the accessibility of the modern railway because access and egress to the station play a crucial role in the overall accessibility. This same theme is addressed in the work of Lissy La Paix and Karst Geurs (Chapter 8), who present discrete choice models based on joint revealed preference and stated preference data to identify the main components of access and egress mode choice to train stations in the Netherlands. They examine the effectiveness of different types of measures to increase station access (for example, bicycle parking pricing, 'liveliness' of railway stations in terns of cafés, restaurants and so on) for increasing train ridership. The results show that train ridership strongly depends on the quality of feeder modes and station facilities. In addition, the freight sector is subject to economic regulation by national governments because of the monopolistic tendency and strategic importance of the industry. Kenneth Button and colleagues in Chapter 9 examine the effects of deregulation on the efficiency of the US freight railroads.

Part V of the book includes contributions for the evaluation of transport investment and implications for accessibility. In Chapter 10, Paul Mogush and co-authors provide some clarifying input for investments in bicycle trails. They show that trails must be adapted to the type of neighbourhood to get the optimal solution for bicycle trails, because some of these trails can reduce the value of houses. Finally, Chapter 11, written by Mert Kompil and his colleagues, proposes and applies transport accessibility measures for Europe; the aim is to develop a framework to assess impacts of various policy options and transport infrastructure investments on accessibility at the European level. Daily accessibility was found to be the most suitable and effective measure to assess transport investments paid by European Cohesion Funds, revealing once more the importance of local accessibility.

In summary, the contributions in this book from researchers show that accessibility models, firstly, help to explain spatial and transport developments in developed and developing countries; and secondly, are powerful tools to explain the equity and efficiency impacts of urban and transport policies and projects.

REFERENCES

Banister, D. and Y. Berechman (2001), 'Transport investment and the promotion of economic growth', *Journal of Transport Geography*, **9** (3), 209–218.

Geurs, K.T. and B. van Wee (2004), 'Accessibility evaluation of land-use and transport strategies: Review and research directions', *Journal of Transport Geography*, **12** (2), 127–140.

Halden, D. (2011), 'The use and abuse of accessibility measures in UK passenger transport planning'. *Research in Transportation Business & Management*, **2**, 12–19.

Levinson, D. (2010), 'Equity effects of road pricing: A review', *Transport Reviews: A Transnational Transdisciplinary Journal*, **30**, 33–57.

Litman, T. (2002), 'Evaluating transportation equity', *World Transport Policy and Practice*, **8** (2), 50–65.

Lucas, K. (2012), 'A critical assessment of accessibility planning for social inclusion', in K.T. Geurs, K. Krizek and A. Reggiani (eds), *Accessibility Analysis and Transport Planning: Challenges for Europe and North America*, Cheltenham, UK and Northampton, MA, USA: Edward Elgar, pp. 228–242.

Martens, K., A. Golub and G. Robinson (2012), 'A justice-theoretic approach to the distribution of transportation benefits: Implications for transportation planning practice in the United States', *Transportation Research Part A: Policy and Practice*, **46** (4), 684–695.

Ramjerdi, F. (2006), 'Equity measures and their performance in transportation', *Transportation Research Record*, **1983**, 67–74.

SACTRA (1999), 'Transport and the economy', Standing Advisory Committee on Trunk Road Assessment, Department of the Environment, Transport and the Regions, London.

Souche, S., A. Mercier and N. Ovtracht (2016), 'The impacts of urban pricing on social and spatial inequalities: The case study of Lyon (France)', *Urban Studies*, **53** (2), 373–399.

Thomopoulos, N., S. Grant-Muller and M.R. Tight (2009), 'Incorporating equity considerations in transport infrastructure evaluation: Current practice and a proposed methodology', *Evaluation and Program Planning*, **32** (4), 351–359.

Van Wee, B. (2011), *Transport and Ethics. Ethics and the Evaluation of Transport Policies and Projects*, Cheltenham, UK and Northampton, MA, USA: Edward Elgar.

Van Wee, B. and K.T. Geurs (2011), 'Discussing equity and social exclusion in accessibility evaluations', *European Journal of Transport and Infrastructure Research*, **11** (4), 350–367.

Van Wee, B. and S. Roeser (2013), 'Ethical theories and the cost–benefit analysis-based ex ante evaluation of transport policies and plans', *Transport Reviews*, **33**, 743–760.

PART II

Equity issues in population accessibility

2. Does accessibility still matter? Evidence from Swiss municipalities

Boris A. Portnov

2.1 INTRODUCTION

The relative importance of location attributes may change over time, as postulated by the locational relativity hypothesis (Portnov and Schwartz 2008). This hypothesis proposes that in the initial stages of economic development, connectivity, and proximity to basic resources (such as fresh water and mineral deposits or train tracks and all-weather roads) tend to dominate location decision-making. However, while economy and society develop, new location-related elements may gain prominence. These new elements include climatic differentials, environmental attractiveness and proximity to unique urban functions (such as cultural facilities and educational services), which few major population centres may provide (Glaeser et al. 1992; Glaeser et al. 2001). In addition, average road travel time may dwindle as infrastructure improves, new all-weather highways are constructed, the quality of vehicles improves, and average travel speed and motorization levels rise (Knowles 2006; Banister 2011; Portnov et al. 2011).

Location is a fundamental concept underlying most early studies in urban geography, which emphasized the role of transport costs, commuting limits and geographic barriers to trade (von Thünen 1996 [1826]; Christaller 1966 [1933]; Lösch 1971 [1938]; Isard 1967 [1956]; Beckmann 1968; Geurs and van Wee 2004; Knowles 2006). However, in the more recent urban debate, the effect of location on urban performance has not been viewed as either obvious or straightforward. In fact, proponents of a non-spatial approach to urban development deny any natural growth advantage to individual urban locations. According to them, while people of similar backgrounds, incomes and environmental preferences flock together, location differences emerge (Gotlieb 1996). That point of view is essentially shared by the proponents of the so-called new economic geography, which assumes that concentration and deconcentration forces create multiple equilibria, which may exist in several geographic loci simultaneously, unrelated to the place's geographic attributes (Krugman 1993, 1995; Fujita et al. 2001).

Concurrently, the neo-cultural growth approach emphasizes the role of so-called second-nature factors, such as cultural diversity, human capital, innovation and creativity, as determinants of urban development, placing less emphasis on first-nature factors attributed to location and geography (Florida 2002). A similar approach is advocated by the endogenous growth theory, which postulates that cities develop because of the production factors they host, and that urban growth (or the lack thereof) has little to do with cities' geographic environment (Jacobs 1969; Henderson et al. 1995; Dosi et al. 2010; Ang and Madsen 2011).

Despite a wealth of studies carried out to date and focusing on urban location, only a handful of studies have attempted to look into a change in the association between location and urban performance, and how this link changes over time. In one such study, Portnov and Schwartz (2008) investigated the effect of urban location on population growth in Europe and pointed out that urban location is a relative attribute, with the evolution of urban places resolving itself into a simple process of accumulating or losing location advantages (compared with other urban places) and gaining (or losing) comparative disadvantages. The authors also raised the possibility that, in addition to the above cross-sectional relativity of location attributes, the relative significance of such attributes may also change over time, reflecting the diminishing importance of proximity to basic resources (essential in the early phases of industrialization), and increasing population mobility and improving infrastructure; however, the authors of this study did not investigate such a possibility empirically.

In another study, Portnov et al. (2011) looked into how location affected the population growth of municipalities in Switzerland in the second half of the twentieth century. The analysis demonstrated the temporal relativity of location attributes, even for small territorial divisions such as the Swiss cantons. Although the present chapter builds on this paper by Portnov et al. (2011), it focuses on a more specific task, aiming to determine whether accessibility factors tend to gain strength or dwindle over time in response to development changes and potential changes in population priorities.

The rest of the chapter is organized as follows. It starts with a brief discussion of local growth and accessibility in Switzerland. Next, it analyses how the relative importance of individual location attributes for the population employment growth of Swiss municipalities changed over time, using multilevel/multivariate analysis tools. As the chapter shows, the importance of accessibility by public transport as a factor of local growth clearly weakened over time, whereas the importance of accessibility by private transport rose constantly during the studied period. This trend is attributed to improved infrastructure and increased mobility, along with changes in population preferences towards more environmentally favourable geographic areas.

2.2   SWITZERLAND AS A CASE STUDY

Switzerland has seen a massive transformation since the early 1950s. Since then, the country's population increased by more than 70 per cent, from 4.2 million residents in 1950 to 7.2 million residents in 2000, and real incomes rose by 225 per cent (Swiss Statistics 1951–2008).

The majority of the country's population lives between the Alps in the south and the Jura mountains in the north-west. The Mittelland region is located between the Alps and Jura mountains and includes four major conurbations: Zürich, Bern, Lausanne and Geneva. Only Basel lies north of the Jura (see Figure 2.1). A large number of mid-sized cities complement the Swiss network of major population centres; many of them host highly specialized manufacturing and service industries.

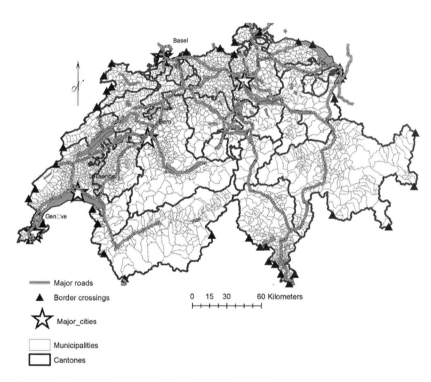

Source: Base maps obtained from Axhausen et al. (2006).

Figure 2.1   Relevant geographical elements of Switzerland: municipal, cantonal divisions, major roads, water bodies, population centres and international border crossings

Motorway construction in Switzerland started relatively late in comparison with neighbouring countries and proceeded rather slowly. While most originally planned motorways were completed in the 1980s, the full-scale motorway construction programme is still under way. Various regional connectors augment the network and connect all but the smallest cantons with the network (Portnov et al. 2011).[1]

2.2.1   Growth and Accessibility Data

Studying temporal variations in the spatial relativity of location attributes requires information on changes in population, employment and accessibility, both across individual territorial units (municipalities and cantons) and over a substantial time period. A database including these variables was collated in an earlier project by Tschopp et al. (2003a, 2003b; Tschopp and Keller 2003a) and discussed in detail by Portnov et al. (2011). The present chapter uses a coherent data set generated for the 2889 municipalities, covering the period 1950 till 2000. The specific variables used in the analysis are briefly discussed hereafter.

The central access variable was calculated as the aerial (shortest path) distance between the municipality and the closest of Switzerland's five major urban centres: either Zürich, Bern, Geneva, Basel or Lausanne (see Figure 2.1). Additional explanatory variables covered by the analysis were: the distance from the nearest motorway, aerial distance from the nearest river; the (shortest road) distance to the nearest international border crossing; and weather conditions. The importance of these variables as potential growth predictors is outlined below in brief.

Distance to the nearest major urban centre captures access to national foci of education, services and employment. Distance to motorways implies both the access of local residents to the high-quality road network, facilitating daily and periodical commuting (Levinson 1998; Paez 2006; Reggiani et al. 2011; Rodríguez et al. 2011), and may potentially increase the visibility of a municipality for families in search of a suburban residence (Portnov et al. 2011).

Given Switzerland's alpine and sub-alpine mountainous topography, distance from a major river or lake is a rough indicator of the availability of flat land for settlement and of fertile land for agriculture. Moreover, riverside locations (and the enticing views they tend to offer) may be especially attractive to residents, developers and tourists, enhancing the development potential of a municipality and helping to diversify its employment base.

Distance to international border crossings reflects potential benefits that a municipality may achieve by exploiting the economic opportunities of border proximity (such as transshipment, border processing, tourism, cross-border shopping and the availability of seasonal labour). Due to development differentials between countries, proximity to an international border crossing may attract labour migrants as well as enable cross-border shopping for cheaper goods and services in neighbouring countries (Soysal 1994; Timothy 2005).

Favourable weather conditions in localities are likely to reflect their attractiveness to migrants and tourists, thus affecting a municipality's economic performance and population growth. The weather conditions in the municipalities were assessed by three indicators: the average temperature in January, the average annual number of hours of sunshine, and annual precipitation (mm). The values are the latest available estimates provided by Swiss-Meteo, the national meteorological office. It was assumed that their relative positions have not changed in a systematic way over the last 50 years. All else being equal, Swiss municipalities with more sunny days and less precipitation were expected to be more attractive to migrants and more successful in retaining residents than less favourably located places.

Aschauer (1989), Vickerman (1991), Levinson (1998), Banister and Berechman (2000), Geurs and Ritsema van Eck (2001) and Geurs and van Wee (2004) reviewed a substantial amount of literature on the measurement of accessibility.

The total benefit (consumer surplus) available was chosen from a set of spatial alternatives measured through the log-sum term of the minimally specified discrete destination choice model (Williams 1977; Ben-Akiva and Lerman 1985):

$$A_i = \ln \sum_{\forall j} X_j f(c_{ij}), \qquad (2.1)$$

where A_i stands for accessibility of location I, X_j represents opportunities at location j, c_{ij} is the generalized cost of travel between locations i and j as measured by travel time. $f()$ is the weighting function for the generalized costs of travel (here $e^{-\lambda c_{ij}}$) and λ is the parameter set to 0.2, estimated empirically by Schilling (1973; cited in Axhausen et al. 2006) using consumer surplus (rent) in a destination and mode/route choice context (Schilling 1973; cited in Axhausen et al. 2006).

The travel time estimates for the five consecutive decades were calculated for both road and public transport, separately for each municipality (Axhausen et al. 2008; Erath and Fröhlich 2004). The public transport travel times were based on the summer timetables of the Swiss railways in the relevant year, plus calibrated estimates for the scheduled bus travel times for municipalities without a railway station. In the road networks, new alignments of high-capacity roads opened after 1950 were included. In the absence of demand matrices for the decades preceding 2000, the speed differences on different road types were captured through a set of average speed assumptions, based on an extensive review of the literature (Erath and Fröhlich 2004).

In the analysis, the accessibility measurements were represented by two variables – *Ac_pub* and *Ac_priv* – reflecting access by public and private transport, respectively.[2] To calculate the values of these variables, the following three parameters – the total number of residents in a locality, employment in manufacturing (Sector 2) and employment in services (Sector 3) – were chosen as proxies for the opportunities a municipality offers.

In addition, five decennial time periods – 1950–60, 1960–70, 1970–80, 1980–90 and 1990–2000 – and 26 individual cantons were represented in the analysis by their fixed effects, that is, dichotomous variables taking on the value 1, if data are relevant for a specific time period or if a municipality is in a given canton, and 0 otherwise. (Regression coefficients for cantonal dummies are not reported in the following discussion, for brevity's sake.) Table 2.1 contains descriptive statistics of selected research variables.

2.2.2 Statistical Methods

As mentioned previously, the main objective of the analysis was to determine time-related changes in the strength of association between the development performance of municipalities and various accessibility indices. Therefore, multilevel regression models with time period dummies and accessibility–time period interaction effects were used as a tool. The main reason for using multilevel fixed effects models was twofold: to determine whether the rates of population and employment growth changed significantly across different time periods, and whether the accessibility variables took on different values for the investigated decennial periods (as indicated, respectively, by different statistical significance of time period dummies and time period accessibility interaction terms).

In the analysis, the dependent variables were estimated as the natural logarithm of the ratio between a municipality's population size (or the size of its employment sector) at the end of decennial period t and its population size (or employment sector size, depending on the model) at the beginning of the corresponding decennial period $t - 1$:

$$CH_{ij(t,\,t-1)} = ln(P_{ij(t)}/P_{ij(t-1)}) = ln(P_{ij(t)}) - ln(P_{ij(t-1)}), \qquad (2.2)$$

where $CH_{ij(t,\,t-1)}$ is the change in either population size or employment sector size of municipality i between the start $(t - 1)$ and the end (t) of decennial period j; $P_{ij(t)}$ and $P_{ij(t-1)}$ are corresponding performance

Table 2.1 Descriptive statistics of selected research variables

Variable	Minimum	Maximum	Mean	Std. Dev.	Skewness	Kurtosis
Ac_pub	16.00	400 508.00	2380.22	9599.60	24.82	773.29
Ac_priv	124.00	2 344 552.00	13 814.28	46 224.76	31.54	1214.06
D_cities	0.00	174 261.00	47 113.69	38 743.27	1.52	1.49
D_rivers	2.00	43 232.00	5885.19	6088.24	1.94	5.45
D_borders	277.00	83 724.00	33 667.82	18 589.80	0.37	−0.56
T_january	−0.50	1.50	0.42	0.41	−0.01	−0.39
D_roads	0.00	29 494.00	4046.06	4121.77	1.72	3.77
D_autoban	4.00	508 384.00	5853.53	11 665.24	28.51	1191.22
D_newborders	277.00	508 690.00	28 740.85	19 551.31	5.48	124.16
Altitude	204.00	998.00	583.37	165.14	0.67	−0.31
Sunshine	1500.00	2200.00	1651.90	159.64	1.44	1.59
Precipitation	0.00	2415.00	1155.83	417.26	−0.93	2.19
Emp_sector2_1950	0.00	108 437.00	401.07	2745.31	26.81	922.06
Emp_sector3_1950	0.00	94 388.00	187.31	2200.72	32.27	1243.80
Population_1950	24.00	390 020.00	1631.49	9575.45	28.73	1024.28
Ac_pub_1950	35.00	316 950.00	1729.70	8284.45	26.98	869.95
Ac_priv_1950	139.00	1 514 227.00	7988.90	35 028.04	33.17	1280.17
Pop_growth_1950–60 (ln)	−1.61	1.65	0.03	0.20	0.82	9.78
Emp_sector2_2000	0.00	42 953.00	357.66	1367.99	19.10	511.89
Emp_sector3_2000	0.00	296 576.00	907.19	7263.19	28.83	1033.81
Population_2000	22.00	363 273.00	2512.07	9762.91	23.26	730.12
Ac_pub_1990	25.00	400 508.00	3071.03	10 989.67	23.66	717.27
Ac_priv_1990	124.00	2 344 552.00	19 514.58	56 567.46	30.20	1096.25
Pop_growth_1990–2000 (ln)	−0.74	0.81	0.10	0.12	0.17	3.20

Notes: Number of cases, 2890; see text for the description of the variables' names.

measures of municipality i estimated for the end and the start of study period j, respectively.

The generic model used in the analysis is given by the following equation:

$$CH_{ij(t,\,t-1)} = a + \beta P_{ij(t-1)} + \partial \boldsymbol{LOC}_i + \eta \boldsymbol{ENV}_i + \theta \delta_j \boldsymbol{ACCESS}_{ij(t-1)}$$

$$+ \delta_j + \mu_n + \varepsilon. \tag{2.3}$$

Here, $\boldsymbol{ACCESS}$, $\boldsymbol{LOC}$ and $\boldsymbol{ENV}$ are vectors of variables that represent: (1) accessibility of municipality i by either public or private transport (see subsection 2.2.1 on growth and accessibility data) at the start of decennial period j; (2) locational attributes (namely, proximity of a municipality to the closest main city of the country, proximity to the nearest border crossing, and so on); and (3) environmental attributes (for example, elevation above sea level, number of sunny days per year, amount of precipitation and so on), respectively. a, β, λ, θ, δ, μ and η are regression coefficients; δ_j and μ_n are fixed effects that account for common factors for a given decennial time period (j) and fixed cantonal effects that account for similarities among municipalities located in canton n ($n = 26$), respectively. The values $\delta_j \boldsymbol{ACCESS}_{ij(t-1)}$ are time period accessibility interaction terms, and ε is a random error term.

2.3   RESULTS

Tables 2.2 and 2.3 give lists of variables affecting population growth rates of municipalities and employment sector changes, for models estimated without cantonal dummies and models including cantonal fixed effects, respectively. In addition, Table 2.4 reports five additional models, estimated separately for the time periods under investigation (1950 through 2000).

Model 1: Dependent variable – natural logarithm of population growth rates, $Ln(P_t) - Ln(P_{t-1})$; cantonal dummies not included.
Model 2: Growth in the employment Sector 2 (manufacturing), $Ln(S2_t) - Ln(S2_{t-1})$; cantonal dummies not included.
Model 3: Growth in the employment Sector 3 (services), $Ln(S3_t) - Ln(S3_{t-1})$; cantonal dummies not included; t and $t - 1$ are the end and the start of a given time period, respectively.
Model 4: Dependent variable – natural logarithm of population growth rates, $Ln(P_t) - Ln(P_{t-1})$; cantonal dummies added.

Table 2.2   Factors affecting population and employment growth across Swiss municipalities in 1950–2000

Variables	Model 1		Model 2		Model 3	
	B^a	t^b	B^a	t^b	B^a	t^b
Constant	−0.194	−8.527**	−0.315	−4.410**	−0.154	−3.218**
Population size (or employment base, $t − 1$) ($\times10^{-6}$)^c	0.257	0.861	−3.270	−1.069	−12.052	−5.896**
D_cities ($\times10^{-6}$)	−1.412	−21.898**	−1.000	−4.919**	−2.135	−15.729**
D_rivers ($\times10^{-6}$)	−4.272	−16.043**	−3.877	−4.624**	−4.850	−8.669**
D_borders ($\times10^{-6}$)	−1.309	−15.259**	−1.236	−4.675**	−1.040	−5.787**
T_january ($\times10^{-3}$)	−73.502	−13.754**	−82.083	−4.920**	−99.145	−8.832**
D_autoban ($\times10^{-6}$)	−2.002	−8.446**	−0.997	−1.342	−1.930	−3.893**
Sunshine ($\times10^{-6}$)	232.671	15.598**	236.109	5.054**	213.497	6.824**
Precipitation ($\times10^{-6}$)	13.331	3.758**	19.002	1.638	17.128	2.261*
Period dummies:^{d}						
1960–70 (P2)	0.040	8.445**	0.136	9.323**	0.450	45.878**
1970–80 (P3)	0.014	3.014**	0.364	24.845**	0.705	70.837**
1980–90 (P4)	0.094	19.724**	0.148	10.007**	0.282	27.548**
1990–2000 (P5)	0.071	14.978**	−0.114	−7.699**	0.004	0.352
Interaction terms:						
Ac_pub*P2 ($\times10^{-6}$)	6.009	4.293**	−4.807	−1.134	−0.359	−0.126
Ac_pub*P3 ($\times10^{-6}$)	−7.330	−6.323**	−23.474	−6.773**	−11.889	−5.030**
Ac_pub*P4 ($\times10^{-6}$)	−9.594	−9.599**	−9.415	−3.145**	1.385	0.651
Ac_pub*P5 ($\times10^{-6}$)	−6.526	−7.113**	−10.448	−3.811**	2.363	1.173
Ac_priv*P2 ($\times10^{-6}$)	−1.329	−4.112**	1.071	1.092	1.139	1.683
Ac_priv*P3 ($\times10^{-6}$)	1.173	5.245**	3.949	5.820**	3.221	6.819**

19

Table 2.2 (continued)

Variables	Model 1		Model 2		Model 3	
	B[a]	t[b]	B[a]	t[b]	B[a]	t[b]
Ac_priv*P4 ($\times 10^{-6}$)	1.589	8.168**	1.652	2.791**	0.850	2.040*
Ac_priv*P5 ($\times 10^{-6}$)	0.934	5.428**	1.765	3.374**	1.030	2.768**
Cantonal dummies	no		no		no	
No. of cases	14442		14442		14442	
R^2	0.138		0.098		0.384	
R^2-adjusted	0.137		0.097		0.383	
SEEw[e]	0.173		0.523		0.360	
F[f]	115.408**		73.16**		441.049**	

Notes:
Method: multilevel regression analysis with time-period fixed effects; absolute measures of proximity; cantonal dummies are not included.
[a] unstandardized regression coefficient; [b] t-statistic and its two-tailed significance level; [c] depend on the model type (that is, population size in population growth models, and size of the corresponding employment sector in the sectorial growth model; [d] reference category – years 1950–60 (P1); [e] Standard error of the estimate; [f] F-statistic.
*Indicates a 0.05 significance level; **Indicates a 0.01 significance level.
D_cities = distance to the nearest major urban centre, km (Zürich, Bern, Geneva, Basel or Lausanne); D_rivers = areal distance from municipality to a major river or lake, km; $D\_borders$ = distance to the nearest international border crossing, km; $T\_january$ = average temperature in January, centigrade; $D\_autoban$ = distance to the nearest highway, km; $Sunshine$ = the average annual number of hours of sunshine; $Precipitation$ = the annual precipitation (mm); Ac_pub and Ac_priv = accessibility by public and private transport, respectively (see text for explanations); P[period]1 = years 1950–60; P[period]2 = years 1960–70; P[period]3 = years 1970–80; P[period]4 = years 1980–90; P[period]5 = years 1990–2000.

Table 2.3   Factors affecting population and employment growth across Swiss municipalities in 1950–2000

Variables	Model 4		Model 5		Model 6	
	B^a	t^b	B^a	t^b	B^a	t^b
Constant	−0.351	−10.022**	−0.430	−3.805**	−0.458	−6.153**
Population size (or employment base, $t − 1$) ($\times10^{-6}$)^c	0.180	0.608	−2.886	−0.933	−10.711	−5.232**
D_cities ($\times10^{-6}$)	−1.056	−8.142**	−1.320	−3.181**	−1.617	−5.882**
D_rivers ($\times10^{-6}$)	−4.378	−13.101**	−2.979	−2.818**	−5.214	−7.344**
D_borders ($\times10^{-6}$)	−1.032	−7.119**	−1.923	−4.217**	−0.821	−2.677*
T_january ($\times10^{-3}$)	−29.548	−3.404**	−64.956	−2.350*	−17.505	−0.952
D_autoban ($\times10^{-6}$)	−1.980	−7.720**	−1.513	−1.837	−1.528	−2.822**
Sunshine ($\times10^{-6}$)	315.607	15.072**	296.654	4.421**	365.329	8.225**
Precipitation ($\times10^{-6}$)	2.370	0.617	33.004	2.591*	21.111	2.559*
Period dummies:^{d}						
1960–70 (P2)	0.040	8.567**	0.135	9.327**	0.451	46.230**
1970–80 (P3)	0.014	3.102**	0.364	24.894**	0.707	71.341**
1980–90 (P4)	0.094	20.058**	0.148	9.986**	0.284	27.871**
1990–2000 (P5)	0.071	15.271**	−0.114	−7.754**	0.006	0.586
Interaction terms:						
Ac_pub*P2 ($\times10^{-6}$)	5.308	3.833**	−5.953	−1.404	−0.825	−0.289
Ac_pub*P3 ($\times10^{-6}$)	−7.768	−6.776**	−24.497	−7.061**	−12.288	−5.204**
Ac_pub*P4 ($\times10^{-6}$)	−10.104	−10.214**	−10.441	−3.480**	0.750	0.353
Ac_pub*P5 ($\times10^{-6}$)	−6.985	−7.694**	−11.282	−4.107**	1.600	0.796

Table 2.3   (continued)

Variables	Model 4		Model 5		Model 6	
	B^a	t^b	B^a	t^b	B^a	t^b
$Ac\_priv*P2$ ($\times10^{-6}$)	−1.183	−3.696**	1.338	1.362	1.123	1.660
$Ac\_priv*P3$ ($\times10^{-6}$)	1.235	5.575**	4.145	6.100**	3.159	6.690**
$Ac\_priv*P4$ ($\times10^{-6}$)	1.659	8.602**	1.848	3.113**	0.782	1.874
$Ac\_priv*P5$ ($\times10^{-6}$)	0.992	5.817**	1.912	3.648**	0.971	2.605*
Cantonal dummies	yes		yes		yes	
No. of cases	14442		14442		14442	
R^2	0.165		0.105		0.392	
R^2-adjusted	0.162		0.102		0.390	
SEE[e]	0.170		0.521		0.358	
F[f]	63.029**		35.237**		202.521**	

Notes: See notes to Table 2.2. Method: multilevel regression analysis with time-period fixed effects; absolute measures of proximity; cantonal dummies are included

Model 5: Growth in the employment Sector 2 (manufacturing), $Ln(S2_t) - Ln(S2_{t-1})$; cantonal dummies added.
Model 6: Growth in the employment Sector 3 (services), $Ln(S3_t) - Ln(S3_{t-1})$; cantonal dummies added; t and $t - 1$ are the end and the start of a given time period, respectively.

As Tables 2.2 and 2.3 show, in nearly all the estimated models and especially in the models without cantonal effects (Table 2.3), time period dummies emerged as positive and statistically significant, implying that the rates of population and employment growth in the municipalities rose during the studied period, except for the 1990–2000 decade. In that decade, these growth rates appeared to slow down, even became negative for manufacturing employment (P5: $t = -7.699$; P < 0.01; Model 2, Table 2.2 and $t = -7.754$; P < 0.01; Model 5, Table 2.3).

It is also noteworthy that access by public transport was positively associated with population growth during the years 1960–70 (Ac_pub*P2: $t = 4.293$; P < 0.01; Model 1, Table 2.2 and $t = 3.833$; P < 0.01; Model 4, Table 2.3, but then became negatively associated with growth, in both the employment and the manufacturing sector (see Models 1–2, Table 2.2 and Models 4–5, Table 2.3). By contrast, the strength of association between the accessibility by private transport on the one hand, and population and employment growth (Ac_priv*P2-5) on the other hand were on the rise, increasing from significantly negative to significantly positive in the models estimated for population growth (see Model 1 and Model 4), and from positive but insignificant values for the 1960–70 period to strongly positive values, as observed in both Sector 2 and Sector 3 employment growth models (see Models 2–3, Table 2.2 and Models 5–6, Table 2.3). Figure 2.2 illustrates the diminishing effect of accessibility by public transport and the rise in the importance of accessibility by private transport, featuring *t*-statistics of the corresponding accessibility variables reported in Tables 2.2 and 2.3.

The explanation for these trends may be fairly straightforward: rising motorization levels and improved road networks reduced the dependency of the population on public transport, turning municipalities with good access for private car travellers into the main *foci* of in-country migration, thus triggering changes in the employment sector as well.

Table 2.4 and Figure 2.3 help to shed additional light on these time-related changes. While the reversal of the importance of public versus individual accessibility factors, illustrated by Figure 2.3a, generally coincides with the trend observed in results of the multilevel modelling (Figures 2.2a, 2.2b and Tables 2.2–2.3), Figure 2.3b also highlights time-related changes in other growth determinants. In particular, as

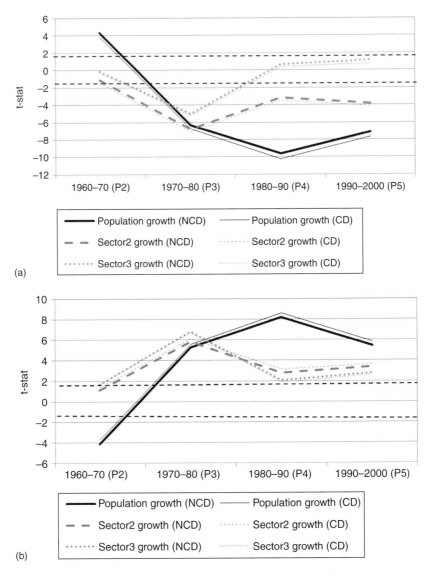

Notes: The values of *t*-statistics are based on the *t*-statistics of accessibility * period
interaction terms reported in Tables 2.2 and 2.3. Horizontal dotted lines indicate a 0.05
significance threshold.

Figure 2.2   *Changes in the statistical significance of accessibility factors
across different time periods (as indicated by multilevel models
with accessibility interaction terms) by public transport (a)
and private transport (b)*

Table 2.4 Factors affecting population growth in municipalities across different time periods

Variables	Model 9 1950–60 B^a	Model 9 1950–60 t^b	Model 10 1960–70 B^a	Model 10 1960–70 t^b	Model 11 1970–80 B^a	Model 11 1970–80 t^b	Model 12 1980–90 B^a	Model 12 1980–90 t^b	Model 13 1990–2000 B^a	Model 13 1990–2000 t^b
Constant	-0.075	-1.343	-0.561	-7.872**	-0.496	-8.601**	0.004	0.084	-0.080	-2.069*
Population size (×10^{-6})	-0.249	-0.076	10.303	2.959**	-0.889	-0.398	-7.869	-4.656**	-7.869	-2.870**
Employment sector 2 (×10^{-6})	29.016	4.643**	-7.271	-0.946	-6.668	-1.157	5.793	1.387	5.793	-0.238
Employment sector 3 (×10^{-6})	-85.706	-7.044**	-71.335	-5.985**	2.871	0.511	11.578	4.578**	11.578	4.187**
Ac_pub_start (×10^{-6})	15.476	7.163**	5.169	2.109*	-5.694	-3.351**	-6.912	-6.108**	-6.912	-6.651**
Ac_priv_start	-0.230	-0.487	0.944	1.820	1.094	3.724**	1.039	5.563**	1.039	5.212**
D_cities (×10^{-6})	-1.298	-8.119**	-2.159	-10.531**	-2.148	-12.701**	-0.977	-7.388**	-0.977	-7.591**
D_rivers (×10^{-6})	-1.106	-1.623	-1.667	-1.917	-3.142	-4.439**	-4.421	-8.030**	-4.421	-3.195**
D_borders (×10^{-6})	-0.439	-2.082*	-0.688	-2.564*	-1.224	-5.616**	-0.825	-4.859**	-0.825	-4.784**
T_january (×10^{-3})	-112.845	-8.471**	-171.920	-10.105**	-104.597	-7.535**	-30.116	-2.783**	-30.116	-6.116**
D_roads (×10^{-6})	-3.081	-2.133*	-2.704	-1.467	-0.641	-0.426	1.374	1.173	1.374	0.355
D_autoban (×10^{-6})	-5.280	-3.873**	-9.010	-5.185**	-7.992	-5.644**	-3.966	-3.593**	-3.966	-3.977**
Altitude (×10^{-6})	-297.514	-12.476**	-303.831	-9.972**	-26.509	-1.067	15.193	0.786	15.193	-1.139
Sunshine (×10^{-6})	217.167	5.922**	597.745	12.764**	459.020	12.020**	156.964	5.275**	156.964	7.724**
Precipitation (×10^{-6})	59.064	6.253**	65.019	5.407**	39.813	4.070**	-6.626	-0.870	-6.626	-2.051*
Cantonal dummies	no		no		no		no		no	
No. of cases	2889		2889		2889		2889		2889	
R^2	0.283		0.249		0.177		0.141		0.124	
R^2-adjusted	0.278		0.245		0.172		0.135		0.119	
SEE	0.160		0.204		0.166		0.129		0.111	
F	63.319**		53.432**		34.551**		26.335**		22.819**	

Notes: See notes to Table 2.2. Method: multiple regression analysis without time-period fixed effects; cantonal dummies not included.

25

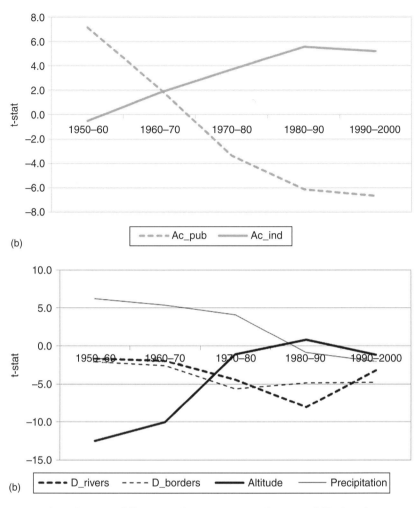

Notes: Ac_pub = accessibility by public transport; Ac_priv = accessibility by private transport; D_rivers = distance to the closest river; D_borders = distance to the nearest international border crossing; Altitude = altitude above the sea level; Precipitation = average annual amount of precipitation (mm). (The values of *t*-statistics are based on the *t*-statistics of accessibility * period interaction terms reported in Tables 2.2–2.3. Horizontal dotted lines indicate a 0.05 significance threshold).

Figure 2.3   Changes in the statistical significance of accessibility measures (a), and environmental and locational attributes (b), affecting population growth of municipalities (period-specific models without interaction effects)

Figure 2.3b shows, high altitude significantly impeded the population growth of municipalities in the 1950s and 1960s, but this was no longer so from the 1970s onwards. Possible reasons behind this change may include infrastructure improvements, making highland areas more accessible, as well as the increasing attractiveness of elevated places due to the potentially attractive views and the clean air they offer. Furthermore, though high amounts of precipitation were concomitant with high rates of population growth during the 1950s, 1960s and 1970s, lower amounts of precipitation gradually became associated with higher growth rates of municipalities from the 1980s onwards. This change is likely to reflect a switch from agriculture-oriented development towards a preference for living in urban areas with clear skies and less precipitation. The increasing importance of proximity to the main rivers, often entailing attractive views, and proximity to international border crossings, with the possibilities of cross-border exchanges this enables, is further indicative of the ongoing locational priority changes.

2.4 CONCLUSIONS

The development-fostering effect of any given location attribute is likely to depend on whether other places possess that attribute as well (Portnov and Schwartz 2008). The relative importance of location attributes may also vary across different time periods. In particular, as witnessed in the present analysis, the statistical significance of accessibility by public transport as a determinant of local growth appeared to weaken over time. The explanation may be fairly straightforward: if connectivity and proximity to basic resources are likely to dominate location decision-making during the initial stages of economic development, new location-related elements may gain importance when an economy develops. These elements may include a preference for living in areas with both transit and pedestrian accessibility (Rodríguez et al. 2011) and a preference for job-rich areas, which are associated with shorter commutes (Levinson 1998). The importance of infrastructure proximity may be also influenced by societal changes and population ageing. As the elderly, people with low incomes and single-parent households tend to be less geographically mobile, they often prefer to live in densely populated urban areas saturated with social and cultural opportunities near their homes (Mercado and Paez 2009; Morency et al. 2011). Moreover, when roads and railroads improve and motorization levels rise, fractional effects of distance quite naturally decline, especially if accessibility improves in both core and peripheral regions (Knowles 2006; Kotavaara et al. 2011).

This present analysis built on a study by Portnov et al. (2011) that aimed to demonstrate how the importance of accessibility by private and public transport changes over time. The present chapter furthers the results of that previous analysis in several respects. First, it analyses both population growth and employment performance of Swiss municipalities (in both secondary and tertiary sectors), not only population growth as in the former study. It also uses more advanced statistical techniques, based on interaction terms between time periods and accessibility that help to explore changes in the effect of accessibility on municipalities' growth and economic performance more thoroughly.

In addition, although the results of the former study point out that accessibility factors and location attributes as local growth predictors tend to weaken over time, the present analysis provides additional insights into this complex process. The importance of accessibility by public transport, as a factor of local growth, indeed appeared to weaken over time, whereas the importance of accessibility by private transport rose during the study period, apparently owing to growing motorization levels as well as to changes in population priorities as factors of locational choice. The present chapter also demonstrates that environmental attributes (such as attractive views, potentially associated with higher altitudes, and low amounts of precipitation) gained greater prominence in the past decades as local growth predictors, compared with their relative importance during earlier periods. The conclusion is that limited accessibility still hinders local growth, even in a small and highly developed country such as Switzerland, although specific reasons for the accessibility persistence tend to change from one time period to another.

In urban development literature, it is hypothesized that the effect of location attributes depends on how much they stand out in their regional or national contexts. This location relativity hypothesis was raised by Felsenstein and Portnov (2005) and tested by Cheshire and Magrini (2006), who investigated how climatic differentials affect population growth in Western Europe. In another recent study, Portnov and Schwartz (2008) demonstrated that the relativity concept is applicable to several location-related indicators, not climate alone, and that location parameters appear more important than absolute ones in explaining the geographical distribution of population growth. The main contribution of this chapter to the location relativity hypothesis is in demonstrating the *temporal relativity* of location attributes for population growth but also for employment change in local areas; this was less thoroughly investigated in previous studies on municipal growth.

It is also necessary to acknowledge that the study was made possible by a detailed historical population database available for Swiss municipalities.

To the best of my knowledge, no database of such scope and quality is available for any other European country.

To conclude, several limitations of the study should be mentioned. There are several alternative measures of accessibility commonly used in empirical research, including infrastructure-based, activity-based and utility-based accessibility measures (for a detailed review of different measures of accessibility see, for example, Geurs and Ritsema van Eck 2001). The present chapter is based on one accessibility measure only, estimated as the generalized cost of travel measured by travel time (see Axhausen et al. 2006 for more details). Therefore the possibility cannot be discounted that the results might be slightly different if other accessibility measures, other functional forms, and/or other parameters for the accessibility calculation had been used. In addition, it is fairly clear that in the 2000s, people did not value travel time in the same way that they valued it in the 1950s and even in the 1970s. However, as the present analysis is based on a fixed Shilling parameter estimate calculated in the framework of an earlier project (see Axhausen et al. 2008; Erath and Fröhlich 2004), this assumption could not be verified empirically. Further studies may be required to verify time-related changes in the travel time attitude and to assess the performance of different functional forms of accessibility measures.

ACKNOWLEDGEMENTS

The chapter is based in part on: Portnov, B.A., Axhausen, K.W., Tschopp, M. and M. Schwartz (2011), 'Diminishing effects of location? Some evidence from Swiss municipalities, 1950–2000', *Journal of Transport Geography*, **19**, 1368–1378. However, in the preparation of this chapter, the original study was revised considerably and the chapter features the results of new analyses of additional performance and accessibility measures and analytical tools that were not a part of the earlier analysis. The author also acknowledges, with gratitude, that the data for this study were collated and generated at the Institute for Transport Planning and System (IVT), ETH Zürich funded by the Swiss National Fund (SNF) and the Bundesamt für Verkehr (BAV) in Bern, Switzerland.

NOTES

1. The Swiss cantons have the authority to tax incomes and set spending priorities, even for social services. In that respect, the cantons resemble US states more than German *Länder*.

2. In the initial stages of the analysis, proximity to railroad lines was used as an additional explanatory variable. However, later on, this variable was excluded from the analysis due to the relatively low statistical significance and strong co-linearity with other explanatory variables, especially with proximity to highways.

REFERENCES

Ang, J.B. and J.B. Madsen (2011), 'Can second-generation endogenous growth models explain the productivity trends and knowledge production in the Asian miracle economies?', *Review of Economics and Statistics*, **93** (4), 1360–1373.

Aschauer, D. (1989), 'Is public expenditure productive?', *Journal of Monetary Economics*, **23** (2), 177–200.

Axhausen, K.W., Dolci, C., Fröhlich, P., Scherer, M. and A. Carosio (2008), 'Constructing time scaled maps: Switzerland 1950–2000', *Transport Reviews*, **28** (3), 391–413.

Axhausen, K.W., Fröhlich, P. and M. Tschopp (2006), Changes in Swiss accessibility since 1850, *Arbeitsberichte Verkehr und Raumplanung*, 344, IVT, ETH Zürich, Zürich.

Banister, D. (2011), 'The trilogy of distance, speed and time', *Journal of Transport Geography*, **18** (4), 950–959.

Banister, D. and J. Berechman (2000), *Transport Investment and Economic Development*, London: UCL Press.

Beckmann, M. (1968), *Location Theory*, New York: Random House.

Ben-Akiva, M.E. and S.R. Lerman (1985), *Discrete Choice Analysis: Theory and Application to Travel Demand*, Cambridge, MA: MIT Press.

Cheshire, P.C. and S. Magrini (2006), 'Population growth in European cities: Weather matters – but only nationally', *Regional Studies*, **40** (1), 23–37.

Christaller, W. (1966 [1933]), *Central Places in Southern Germany*, Englewood Cliffs, NJ: Prentice Hall.

Dosi, G., Fagiolo, G. and A. Roventini (2010), 'Schumpeter meeting Keynes: A policy-friendly model of endogenous growth and business cycles', *Journal of Economic Dynamics and Control*, **34** (9), 1748–1767.

Erath, A. and P. Fröhlich (2004), 'Geschwindigkeiten im PW-Verkehr und Leistungsfähigkeiten von Strassen über die Zeit', *Arbeitsbericht Verkehrs- und Raumplanung*, 183, IVT, ETH Zürich, Zürich.

Felsenstein, D. and B.A. Portnov (eds) (2005), *Regional Disparities in Small Countries*, Heidelberg: Springer Verlag.

Florida, R.L. (2002), *The Rise of the Creative Class and How it's Transforming Work, Leisure, Community, and Everyday Life*, New York: Basic Books.

Fujita, M., Krugman, P. and A.J. Venables (2001), *The Spatial Economy: Cities, Regions, and International Trade*, Cambridge, MA: MIT Press.

Geurs, K.T. and J.R. Ritsema van Eck (2001), 'Accessibility measures: review and applications', RIVM report, 408505006, National Institute of Public Health and the Environment, Bilthoven.

Geurs, K.T. and B. van Wee (2004), 'Accessibility evaluation of land-use and transport strategies: review and research directions', *Journal of Transport Geography*, **12** (2), 127–140.

Glaeser, E.L., Kallal, H.D., Scheinkman, J.A. and A. Shleifer (1992), 'Growth in cities', *Journal of Political Economy*, **100** (6), 1126–1152.

Glaeser, E.L., Kolko, J. and A. Saiz (2001), 'Consumer city', *Journal of Economic Geography*, **1**, 27–50.

Gotlieb, Y. (1996), *Development, Environment, and Global Dysfunction: Toward Sustainable Recovery*, Delray Beach, FL: St Lucie Press.

Henderson, V., Kuncoro, A. and M. Turner (1995), 'Industrial development in cities', *Journal of Political Economy*, **103**, 1067–1090.

Isard, W. (1967 [1956]), *Location and Space-economy; A General Theory Relating to Industrial Location, Market Areas, Land Use, Trade, and Urban Structure*, 5th edn, Cambridge, MA: MIT Press.

Jacobs, J. (1969), *The Economy of Cities*, New York: Random House.

Knowles, R.D. (2006), 'Transport shaping space: Differential collapse in time–space', *Journal of Transport Geography*, **14** (6), 407–425.

Kotavaara, O., Antikainen, H. and J. Rusanen (2011), 'Population change and accessibility by road and rail networks: GIS and statistical approach to Finland 1970–2007', *Journal of Transport Geography*, **19** (4), 926–935.

Krugman, P. (1993), 'First nature, second nature, and metropolitan location', *Journal of Regional Science*, **33** (2), 129–144.

Krugman, P. (1995), *Development, Geography and Economic Theory*, Cambridge, MA: MIT Press.

Levinson, D.M. (1998), 'Accessibility and the journey to work', *Journal of Transport Geography*, **6** (1), 11–21.

Lösch, A. (1971 [1938]), *The Economics of Location*, New Haven, CT, USA and London, UK: Yale University Press.

Mercado, R. and A. Paez (2009), 'Determinants of distance travelled with a focus on the elderly: A multilevel analysis in the Hamilton CMA, Canada', *Journal of Transport Geography*, **17** (1), 65–76.

Morency, C., Paez, A., Roord, M.J., Mercado, R. and S. Farber (2011), 'Distance travelled in three Canadian cities: Spatial analysis from the perspective of vulnerable population segments', *Journal of Transport Geography*, **19** (1), 39–50.

Paez, A. (2006), 'Exploring contextual variations in land use and transport analysis using a probit model with geographical weights', *Journal of Transport Geography*, **14** (3), 167–176.

Portnov, B.A., Axhausen, K.W., Tschopp, M. and M. Schwartz (2011), 'Diminishing effects of location? Some evidence from Swiss municipalities, 1950–2000', *Journal of Transport Geography*, **19**, 1368–1378.

Portnov, B.A. and M. Schwartz (2008), 'On the relativity of urban location', *Regional Studies*, **42** (4), 605–615.

Reggiani, A., Bucci, P., Russo, G., Haas, A. and P. Nijkamp (2011), 'Regional labour markets and job accessibility in City Network systems in Germany', *Journal of Transport Geography*, **19** (4), 528–536.

Rodríguez, D.A., Levineb, J., Weinstein Agrawal, A. and J. Song (2011), 'Can information promote transportation-friendly location decisions? A simulation experiment', *Journal of Transport Geography*, **19** (2), 304–312.

Schilling, H.R. (1973), 'Kalibrierung von Widerstandsfunktionen', *Studienunterlagen*, Lehrstuhl für Verkehrsingenieurwesen, ETH Zürich, Zürich.

Soysal, Y. (1994), *The Limits of Citizenship: Migrants and Post-National Membership in Europe*, Chicago, IL: University of Chicago Press.

Swiss Statistics (1951–2008), *Statistical Yearbook of Switzerland*, Neuchatel: Swiss Federal Statistical Office FSO.

Timothy, D.J. (2005), *Shopping Tourism, Retailing and Leisure (Aspects of Tourism)*, Tonawanda, NY: Multilingual Matters, Limited.

Tschopp, M. and P. Keller (2003), 'Raumstruktur-Datenbank: Gemeinde-Zuordnungstabelle', *Arbeitsberichte Verkehrs- und Raumplanung*, 170, IVT, ETH Zürich, Zürich.

Tschopp, M., Keller, P. and K.W. Axhausen (2003a), 'Raumnutzung in der Schweiz: Eine historische Raumstruktur-Datenbank', *Arbeitsberichte Verkehrs- und Raumplanung*, 165, IVT, ETH Zürich, Zürich.

Tschopp, M., Sieber, R., Keller, P. and K.W. Axhausen (2003b), 'Demographie und Raum in der Schweiz', *DISP*, **153**, 25–32.

Vickerman, R.W. (1991), *Infrastructure and Regional Development*, London: Pion.

Von Thünen, J.H. (1996 [1826]), *The Isolated State*, Oxford: Pergamon Press.

Williams, H.C.W.L. (1977), 'On the formation of travel demand models and economic evaluation measures of user benefits', *Environment and Planning A*, **9** (2), 285–344.

3. Population decline and accessibility in the Portuguese interior

Paulo Rui Anciães

3.1 INTRODUCTION

Improvements in accessibility increase the attractiveness of a place, as they increase the number of opportunities that can be reached by its population (Wachs and Kumagai 1977). While this idea is generally valid in the case of urban areas, in rural contexts improvements in the ease of access of distant places can also contribute to population decline, as they may induce people to move to those other places and then travel regularly to their home towns to visit friends and family.

More broadly, the role of transport as a pull or push factor for migration in rural areas depends on the type of accessibility it improves. It is important to identify the type of destinations that are made accessible. For example, different populations place a different value on access to national, regional or local centres, and on access to jobs or services (Farrington and Farrington 2005). The mode of transport is also relevant. While improvements in private transport accessibility are directly linked with the reduction of travel times on the road network, improvements in public transport accessibility also depend on the suitability of services and schedules and on levels of access to transport nodes such as train or bus stations (Ochojna and Brownlee 1977; Nutley 1985; Martin et al. 2002; Martin et al. 2008). Empirical research can only capture the relationships between accessibility and population dynamics if the measures of accessibility used reflect the changes to the options that are considered as feasible by the populations.

The links between accessibility and population dynamics may also differ from prior expectations in the cases where accessibility deteriorates (for example, when public transport services are withdrawn). There is only a small amount of evidence on the effects of railway line closures on the communities living in the affected areas (Whitelegg 1987; Taylor 2006). Very few of the available studies investigate the effect on population change. In order to assess the social relevance of line closures, more research is needed on their impacts on accessibility and on population change. However, this assessment is not straightforward, as there are different possibilities for evaluating levels of access to railway services and the lost potential in terms of diversity of travel destinations or severed access to opportunities in those destinations.

The objective of this chapter is to assess the influence of changes in accessibility on the population decline in the Portuguese countryside in the two last decades. The analysis compares two types of accessibility changes: those related to the investment in the road network and those related to the disinvestment in the railway network. The relationships are controlled for changes in local (non-motorized) accessibility and control variables measuring characteristics of the population and of the natural and social environment.

The chapter also addresses methodological issues related to the selection and measurement of indicators of accessibility. The analysis compares the effects of alternative indicators, measuring access to the motorway and railway networks, the number of places that can be accessed, and the number of opportunities existing in those places. The construction of the indicators also incorporate detail regarding different frequencies (daily or weekly), departure and arrival times (morning, afternoon or evening) and travel time thresholds for trips to work. The analysis of rail trips takes into account the availability of services for return trips, connection times between different services, and public transport options and times for accessing stations.

The chapter proceeds as follows. The next section briefly reviews the literature on the multiple relationships between accessibility and population change and on the way those relationships depend on the specification of accessibility indicators. Section 3.3 is an overview of the population decline in the Portuguese interior in the last 20 years and of the large-scale investment in the motorway network and disinvestment in the rail network occurring in that period. The variables and model specifications are presented in section 3.4. Section 3.5 presents the findings of these models, and section 3.6 concludes the chapter with some reflections on the policy and research implications of this study.

3.2   TRANSPORT AND RURAL POPULATION CHANGE

There is a large amount of empirical evidence on the relationships between accessibility and population change at the local level (Voss and Chi 2006; Kotavaara et al. 2011; Mojica and Martí-Henneberg 2011; Chi 2010, 2012; Koopmans et al. 2012; Ji et al. 2014). A wide diversity of impacts has been identified, usually specific to the geographic context in which they were found. The effects of accessibility on population change in rural areas tend to be different from those in suburban and urban areas (Chi 2010, 2012). The populations in these three types of areas differ in terms of accessibility needs as they also differ in terms of age, marital status, employment status and sector of employment. In addition, factors such as geographic isolation and dependence in relation to local and regional centres are more relevant in rural areas than in urban and suburban areas, where the geographic distribution of population and employment is less concentrated. On the other hand, the negative effects of the transport system (such as congestion and pollution) have a higher influence on the patterns of residence location in urban and suburban areas than in rural areas.

In general, improvements in accessibility have a positive impact on population change, although it is not always easy to disentangle the chain of causes and effects leading to that impact. Usually, the relationship between accessibility and population change is mediated by economic factors (Button 1995; Rietveld and Bruinsma 1998). Accessibility attracts investment and improves local economic conditions and job prospects, which in turn lead to population increase. In contrast, geographic isolation tends to be linked with out-migration, sometimes independently of economic or employment factors (McNabb 1979).

The general hypothesis above applies to different types of investment in transport infrastructure such as road (Voss and Chi 2006) and rail networks (Mojica and Martí-Henneberg 2011), which tend to be positively related to rural population change, contributing to population growth in the areas served and, in some cases, to the depopulation of the areas that are not served. Studies including the two types of investment in the same empirical model have also found that they have independent effects on population change (Kotavaara et al. 2011).

However, accessibility may also have a negative effect on population change as it allows people to migrate to the areas that are made more accessible, a phenomenon usually identified as one of the negative spillovers from transport infrastructure (Boarnet 1998). The reduction of travel times induces people to relocate to areas with better employment prospects, while maintaining social relationships in their home towns through regular visits. A negative relationship between accessibility has been found, for example, in the study of Vaturi et al. (2011), who found that in suburban areas within reach of a large city, access to railway contributes to a negative migration balance.

A case with far less empirical evidence is that of the disinvestment in the transport infrastructure. A few studies of railway closures have shown that the withdrawal of passenger services has effects on economic activity and social structures in rural areas (Whitelegg 1987; Taylor 2006). However, railway closures may not have a negative effect on either economic activity or population change, when the withdrawal of services is combined with the positive impacts of other forms of economic rationalization (Parolin et al. 1993).

The empirical analysis of the links between changes in accessibility and population dynamics also depends on the type of accessibility that is measured. Different conclusions about spatial variations in accessibility can be reached for different measures (Vandenbulcke et al. 2009). Moreover, each measure is linked to a specific normative aspect (Páez et al. 2012). Parameters that are not obtained through the modelling of people's actual behaviour (which is often the case of travel time thresholds) reflect a certain judgement about their well-being. While the use of a diversity of accessibility measures is welcomed, in practice policy-makers tend to use a small number of relatively simple indicators. This is because complex measures are not always easy to make operational (Geurs and van Wee 2004).

The set of indicators found in studies relating accessibility to population dynamics is large. Some studies provide general measures of the travel possibilities available at one place, such as the density of roads (Voss and Chi 2006), or the presence of a station in the vicinity of that place (Koopmans et al. 2012). Other studies focus on the separation between a place and specific destinations, measured by the distance or travel time to centres (Millward 2005), the distance or travel time to the nearest access point to the private or public transport networks (Kotavaara et al. 2011), and maximum time thresholds to travel destinations (Ribeiro et al. 2010). Potential accessibility measures have also been found to have a good explanatory power in the modelling of population density (Song 1996). These measures assume that accessibility depends positively on the number of opportunities in each destination and negatively on travel time. While the range of possible indicators is large, it should be noted that they measure dimensions of accessibility that are at least partially independent from each other. Empirical studies can then include several measures of accessibility in the same models.

In the definition of a suitable indicator, options must be taken, however, regarding the nature of the destinations that people need to access. Models relating population change with potential accessibility measures tend to use population size as an indicator of the attractiveness of that destination. However, the distribution of the population may not be related to the distribution of workplaces and the services and facilities people need to access. In the case of ageing rural populations, the spatial distribution of health facilities is a special case of concern (Escalona-Orcao and Díez-Cornago 2007).

Recent advances in accessibility studies have also shown the importance of time constraints in the definition of accessibility and the need to consider aspects such as the set of available transport options, trip chaining and opening times of facilities (Weber and Kwan 2003; Dong et al. 2006). This is especially relevant in the case of public transport accessibility, which depends to a large extent on factors such as departure times (Ochojna and Brownlee 1977) and frequency of services (Nutley 1985). An examination of the availability and frequency of connections between different places, and of bus access to rail or coach stations, may reveal that services fail to meet the accessibility needs of the populations. The withdrawal of these services may then have little impact on population change, as they may have ceased to be considered as a viable transport alternative.

3.3   POPULATION DECLINE, ROAD INVESTMENT AND RAILWAY DISINVESTMENT IN PORTUGAL

The spatial patterns of population change in Portugal reflect the traditional divide between the economically dynamic coastal strips and the lagging regions of the interior. The overall Portuguese population has remained stable over the last decades, at around 10 million. However, Figure 3.1 shows that the population declined throughout most of the interior and grew (or decreased less) in the coastal areas. In addition, the population in the areas with highest decline in the 1991–2001 period continued to decrease during the 2001–2011 period. The black line in Figure 3.1 shows the delimitation of the study area of this chapter. In this area, there are only a few places where the population increased in the periods of concern, in most cases corresponding to municipal capitals.

The two last decades have also seen large-scale investment in the road infrastructure, and especially in the motorway network (left side of Figure 3.2). During the 1990s, this investment was facilitated by the relatively high economic growth and influx of funds from the European Union. However, the expansion of the network accelerated during the 2000s, despite the deterioration of macroeconomic conditions. Some of the new motorways have duplicated the capacity that already existed in the main central coast corridor and others have extended the service to all the regional centres in the interior. As a result of this massive investment, the motorway density in Portugal is now almost double the average density in the European Union.

In contrast, public transport services shrank dramatically during the same periods. The most striking example is the reduction of passenger railway

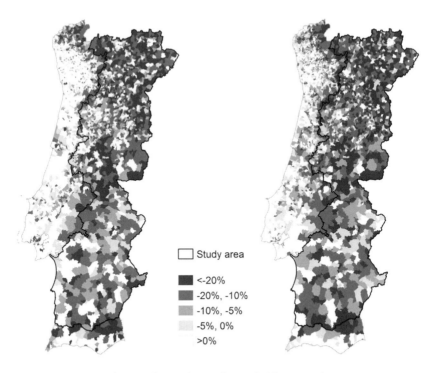

☐	Study area
■	<-20%
■	-20%, -10%
■	-10%, -5%
	-5%, 0%
	>0%

Figure 3.1   Population change by civil parish (freguesia)

services, following two waves of line closures, in the periods 1988–92 and 2008–2012 (Figure 3.2). The first wave of closures occurred as a part of the restructuring of the railway sector, which gave priority to the parts of the system with higher economic viability: suburban and intercity transport in the main axes. A large part of the less viable lines (790 km) was closed, mainly in the most isolated parts of the interior: the north-east and southern regions. After a steady reduction of rail services since 1992, the ongoing economic crisis triggered a new wave of line closures, justified as an essential part of the restructuring of the Portuguese public sector. Since 2009, a total of 490 km of railway lines were closed to passenger services, including most of the remaining lines in the north-east and southern regions, while the future of a few other lines remains uncertain. In 2013, only one third of the stations that once served the interior provinces were in operation. Bus replacements for the lines closed, provided by the railway operator, proved to be short-lived.

There is a growing need for the assessment of the links between the three patterns described above. One of the reasons is that there is evidence that the improvement of the road system was insignificant in explaining either

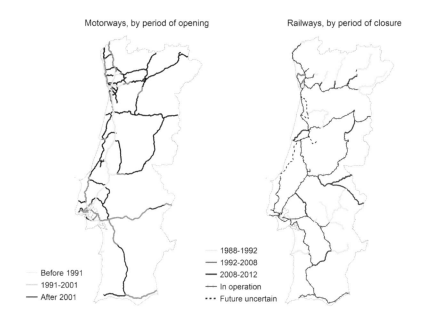

Motorways, by period of opening

Railways, by period of closure

1988-1992
1992-2008
2008-2012
In operation
Future uncertain

Before 1991
1991-2001
After 2001

Figure 3.2   Road investment and railway disinvestment in Portugal

population or economic dynamics in the period 1991–2001 in part of the regions of concern (Ribeiro et al. 2010). This suggests that the large-scale investment in road accessibility is not achieving the desired objective of convergence between those regions and the more dynamic Portuguese and European regions. At the same time, recent studies have shown that railways have had a positive effect on population growth and economic vitality in small places in Portugal (Mojica and Martí-Henneberg 2011), and that some of the railway lines closed could be economically viable if their service was improved (Tão 2011).

3.4   VARIABLES AND MODELS

3.4.1   Study Area and Dependent Variables

The study is conducted at the level of the civil parish (*freguesia*), the smallest administrative unit in Portugal. The study area is defined at the level of NUTS 3 regions, and includes the *freguesias* in the regions in continental Portugal where the population decreased at an average of at least 10 per cent in the 2001–2011 period (See Figure 3.1).

The *freguesias* corresponding to the capitals of municipalities are excluded from the analysis, as they have distinct population dynamics, acting as local centres attracting population from the surrounding villages. The study area is then formed by 1640 *freguesias*, with an average of 740, 674 and 602 people in 1991, 2001 and 2011, respectively. Changes in administrative borders were accounted for by assigning to the new *freguesias* and those with changed borders a proportional part of the population of the *freguesias* from which they originated. The analysis refers to a representative point of the main population agglomeration in each *freguesia*; the locations of which are given by data from the Portuguese Geographic Institute (IGP).

The dependent variables are the ratio of the population at the end and beginning of each period. These variables are explained by accessibility measures and control variables (the characteristics of the population and of the natural and social environment). Descriptive statistics for these variables are provided in Table 3.1.

3.4.2   Explanatory Variables: Accessibility

The first set of accessibility variables measure geographic isolation, defined in relation to local centres. The first variable is the road network distance to the capital of the municipality to which the *freguesia* belongs. The second is a dummy variable for the *freguesias* located along roads that directly link municipal capitals. A distinction is then made between the opportunities (jobs) located inside each *freguesia*, assumed to be accessible by non-motorized transport (walking or cycling), and those located outside, accessible by motorized transport (car or public transport).

Local accessibility is measured in terms of the change in the number of places that can be accessed by non-motorized modes of transport, considering jobs, businesses and services. These variables can also be interpreted as indicators of local economic vitality. Each *freguesia* is also assigned the number of places in *freguesias* within 15 minutes walking or cycling from its representative point. The numbers of jobs, businesses and services were calculated from a database compiling all the companies registered in each *freguesia*, which is updated every other year by the Portuguese National Statistics Institute (INE). It should be noted that in both periods, the number of jobs, businesses and services are only weakly correlated (correlations of less than 10 per cent between jobs and the other two variables, and of around 35 per cent between businesses and services).

Road and rail accessibility are expressed as changes in the periods concerned. An adjustment is made in the case of the calculation of rail accessibility in order to account for the concentration of the majority of changes

Table 3.1   Descriptive statistics

	Units	1991–2001		2001–2011	
		Mean	SD	Mean	SD
Population (change)	relative change	−0.130	0.145	−0.148	0.167
Geographic isolation					
Distance to municipal capital	km	9.428	5.186	=	=
Along road linking capitals	dummy	0.004	0.004	=	=
Local accessibility (change)					
Jobs	change	−0.347	0.368	−0.578	0.278
Businesses	change	0.994	1.852	0.665	1.051
Services	change	0.563	1.589	0.403	1.022
Road accessibility (change)					
Time to motorway	change (minutes)	−81.928	30.242	−37.86	34.42
Places accessible (daily)	change	1.527	1.982	1.985	2.686
Places accessible (weekly)	change	7.263	6.381	11.57	9.261
Jobs accessible (daily)	1000 change	0.00001	0.00002	19.12	25.1
Jobs accessible (weekly)	1000 change	0.00041	0.00029	833.7	387.3
Rail accessibility (change)					
Time to station	change (minutes)	8.300	16.25	1.013	7.610
Places accessible (daily)	change	−0.029	0.249	−0.006	0.148
Places accessibility (weekly)	change	−0.654	3.331	−0.162	1.746
Jobs accessible (daily)	1000 change	0.00001	0.00024	0.049	0.781
Jobs accessible (weekly)	1000 change	0.00087	0.00654	3.441	22.741
Natural and social environment					
Temperature	°C	13.11	2.150	=	=
Slope	% points	7.172	5.768	=	=
Water	prop. agricultural area	0.009	0.046	=	=
Good soil	prop. agricultural area	0.170	0.172	=	=
Forest fires	rel. to forested area	0.019	0.075	0.006	0.039
Heritage	number of sites	0.796	1.098	=	=
Old businesses	change	0.325	1.117	0.407	1.126
Population (initial)					
Population (initial)	1000	0.046	0.061	0.043	0.068
Young (initial)	prop. population	0.135	0.035	0.122	0.032
Low-qualified (initial)	prop. adults	0.732	0.075	0.398	0.066
Graduates (initial)	prop. adults	0.014	0.018	0.024	0.019
Unemployment (initial)	prop. active	0.068	0.064	0.082	0.062
Agriculture employment (initial)	prop. employment	0.433	0.219	0.279	0.188

Notes: =: same value as in the 1991–2001 period.

in the rail network in two short periods that overlap with the census periods. The changes between 1988 and 1992 are assigned to the period 1991–2001 and the changes between 2008 and 2012 are assigned to the period 2001–2011. This may introduce or reduce distortion in the analysis, depending on the time lag in which population dynamics respond to past or planned changes in rail accessibility. It should be noted that the changes between 2008 and 2012 may affect population growth in the 2001–2008 period because the closure of railway lines was in all cases preceded by a steady reduction in the availability of railway services. The closures in the period 2008–2012 are therefore an indicator of the reduction of services during the preceding years.

Two dimensions of road and rail accessibility are considered: the level of access to the transport network and the options provided by the network. The changes in the access to the network are defined as the changes in the travel times to nearest motorway junction or nearest railway station. These times are measured on the road network and assume that private or public transport is available for accessing rail services, an assumption that is only lifted in the indicators of the options provided by the network, explained below. The road and motorway network and the location of railway stations in 1991, 2001 and 2011 are modelled in a geographic information system based on data from road maps and official rail timetables. The speeds imputed to the road and motorway links were based on speed limits for each type of road and location in each year and on slopes. Dummies are calculated for time thresholds under 15 and 30 minutes. Figure 3.3 shows the proportion of the *freguesias* in the data set under these time thresholds, revealing the convergence between levels of access to motorways and railway stations since 1991.

The changes in the options provided by the transport network are identified as the change in the number of places that are accessible or in the number of opportunities (jobs) available in those places. The distinction between the two sets of variables is made in order to isolate the effect of changes in transport from changes in the number of opportunities in each location.

The set of possible places includes all the *freguesias* in continental Portugal. Time impedance is not considered; that is, places are classified as either accessible or not. While the inclusion of this element would add relevant detail to the measure, it would also require an estimation of parameters measuring the rate of decay of accessibility with travel times, the calibration of which requires unavailable data about population mobility.

Assumptions are placed on the frequency and day of the week that trips are made: individuals commute daily to the workplace, or live near the workplace and return on weekends to the place where they have their

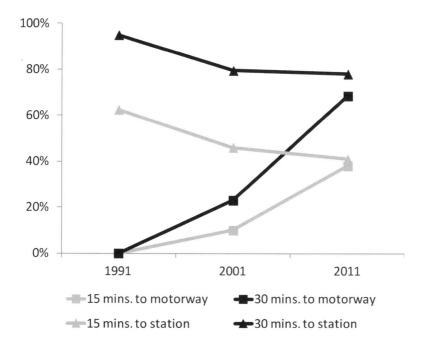

Figure 3.3   *Proportion of freguesias served by the motorway and railway networks*

permanent residence or have family or social ties. A place is defined as accessible on the road network if the private transport travel times to that place are below a given threshold, which depends on the trip frequency. The thresholds are assumed to be one hour for daily trips to work and four hours for weekly trips to work. The identification of places accessible by rail requires further assumptions, related to the level of access to stations, time thresholds for different sections of the trip, and the suitability of existing services in relation to the times of day the trips need to be made.

A database was built in Microsoft Access containing: (1) the travel times by non-motorized mode and by bus from each *freguesia* and each place to the nearest train station; and (2) the pairs of stations connected by services that allow for trips arriving at a given time of day and returning at another given time of day. The total travel times and interchange times between services were also registered. The data were obtained by analysing the rail schedules in the three years of analysis (1991, 2001, and 2011).

The sets of places considered as accessible for daily and weekly trips to work were obtained by selecting the records in this database that fulfil certain criteria, based on certain assumptions, as described below. It is assumed that bus services only connect rail stations with municipal capitals. At the origins and destinations other than municipal capitals, stations are accessed by non-motorized mode (walking or cycling). The bus or walk/cycle trips at either end are restricted to 15 minutes for daily trips to work and 30 minutes for weekly trips to work. Daily return trips to work also require arrival at the workplace between 8:00 and 9:30 and departure between 17:30 and 19:30 on all weekdays, restricting the rail section of the trip to a maximum of one hour. Weekly return trips require departure from the workplace on Friday after 17:30 and arrival at the hometown before 24:00, returning on Sunday after 14:00. A restriction of a maximum 30 minutes is placed on the waiting time at any intermediate station, to account for the disutility usually associated with this time (De Keizer et al. 2012). A set of eight variables is then produced: the number of places accessible by daily and weekly trips by road and rail, and the number of jobs in the places accessible by those trips.

3.4.3   Control Variables

Two sets of control variables were considered. The first set measures the characteristics of the natural and social environment. The second set measures the characteristics of the population. In a preliminary analysis, a large number of theoretically relevant variables were considered. The variables that were strongly correlated with other variables and that showed high post-estimation variance inflation factors (an indicator of multicollinearity in ordinary least squares regression) were excluded from the final set of explanatory variables.

The characteristics of the natural environment are assessed by a series of variables calculated from the *Environmental Atlas* published by the Portuguese Environmental Agency (APA). It is expected that outmigration (and population decline) is lower in places with warmer climates and with better conditions for agricultural activities.

The average temperature is an indicator of general climatic comfort and is included to account for the high variation among the northern and the southern parts of the Portuguese interior. A series of variables measure the suitability of the local environment for agricultural activities, including the average slope, the ratio between the area covered with water and agricultural area, and the proportion of soils classified as having no limitations to agriculture. The final variable is an indicator of forest fires and is expressed as the burnt area at the end of each period as a proportion of the total forested area at the beginning, using data from the CORINE ('coordination of information on the environment') land cover maps compiled by the European Union. This variable is included to control for the incidence of forest fires in the Portuguese countryside and their effects on the vulnerability of the local economy and society.

The social environment is assessed by two indicators of cultural capital and 'sense of place'. These are the number of places with historical or cultural importance, calculated from data in the *Environmental Atlas*, and the number of old businesses (more than 20 years old), which is estimated from the business database. It is expected that places with lower cultural capital and established businesses have higher out-migration and population decline.

A second set of control variables accounts for the characteristics of the population at the beginning of each period, calculated from census data. The set includes population size, the proportion of young people (15–24 years old), the proportions of low-qualified (four or less years of schooling) and graduates in the adult population, the unemployment rate, and the proportion of employment in the primary sector.

3.4.4 Models

Six models are estimated in each of the two periods, differing on the indicators of road and rail accessibility included. Each model includes indicators of ease of access to the transport network and indicators of the places accessible by the network. Models 1–3 include the number of places that can be accessed by road and rail transport and models 4–6 include the number of jobs at those places. Access to the network is measured alternatively as the time to the nearest access point to the motorway and rail networks (models 1 and 4) and as dummy variables for times to nearest access point of less than 15 minutes (models 2 and 5) and 30 minutes (models 3 and 6).

A spatial lag is included in all models, as preliminary estimations revealed that the model residuals were autocorrelated. The lag is the average of the population change in the neighbouring *freguesias*, based on the criterion of queen-type contiguity (shared borders). This variable accounts for the factors that are not captured in the control variables but affect population dynamics in the region where the *freguesias* are located, or alternatively, for the interrelationships among population dynamics in neighbouring *freguesias* via diminished economic opportunities and social networks.

3.5 RESULTS

The results of the model estimation are presented in Tables 3.2 and 3.3. The distance to the municipal capital is negatively and significantly related

Table 3.2   Regressions of population change, 1991–2001

	(1)	(2)	(3)	(4)	(5)	(6)
dist. capital	−0.003 ***	−0.003 ***	−0.003 ***	−0.003 ***	−0.003 ***	−0.003 ***
road capitals	−0.001	−0.002	−0.001	−0.002	−0.003	−0.002
jobs	0.055 ***	0.055 ***	0.055 ***	0.055 ***	0.055 ***	0.055 ***
businesses	0.004 ***	0.004 ***	0.005 ***	0.004 ***	0.005 ***	0.005 ***
services	0.007 ***	0.007 ***	0.007 ***	0.008 ***	0.008 ***	0.007 ***
time junction	0.0003 ***			0.0004 ***		
time < 15		−0.024 **			−0.022 **	
time < 30			−0.002			−0.003
places (day)	0.002	0.002	0.002	513.8 ***	601.7 ***	577.4 ***
places (week)	0.0002	0.001	0.001	−31.84 ***	−26.76 **	−24.55 **
time station	0.0004*			0.0003		
time < 15		−0.014 **			−0.012 *	
time < 30			−0.013 *			−0.010
places (day)	−0.002	−0.000	−0.004			
places (week)	0.001	0.000	0.001			
jobs (day)				−10.18	−10.99	−12.41
jobs (week)				−0.515	−0.367	−0.379

temperature	0.0003	−0.001	−0.001	0.001	−0.0001	0.0001
slope	−0.002 ***	−0.002 ***	−0.002 ***	−0.002 ***	−0.002 ***	−0.002 ***
water	0.100 *	0.118 **	0.113 *	0.088	0.107 *	0.103 *
good soil	−0.012	−0.011	−0.011	−0.015	−0.009	−0.009
burnt	0.047	0.040	0.042	0.043	0.033	0.035
heritage	−0.002	−0.003	−0.003	−0.003	−0.004	−0.004
old businesses	0.009 ***	0.009 ***	0.009 ***	0.009 ***	0.009 ***	0.009 ***
population	−0.005	−0.003	−0.003	−0.004	−0.001	−0.002
young	0.341 ***	0.347 ***	0.338 ***	0.258 ***	0.282 ***	0.275 ***
low-qualified	−0.158 ***	−0.152 ***	−0.141 ***	−0.160 ***	−0.151 ***	−0.142 ***
graduate	1.407 ***	1.421 ***	1.393 ***	1.378 ***	1.382 ***	1.363 ***
unemployed	−0.055	−0.054	−0.059	−0.061	−0.064	−0.067
agriculture	−0.095 ***	−0.090 ***	−0.093 ***	−0.113 ***	−0.108 ***	−0.108 ***
spatial lag	0.246 ***	0.253 ***	0.259 ***	0.235 ***	0.257 ***	0.261 ***
constant	0.071	0.051	0.044	0.105 **	0.074 *	0.067
R²	0.365	0.364	0.361	0.372	0.369	0.366

Notes: ***, **, *: significant at the 1%, 5% and 10% levels.

Table 3.3 *Regressions of population change, 2001–2011*

	(1)	(2)	(3)	(4)	(5)	(6)
dist. capital	−0.003 ***	−0.003 ***	−0.003 ***	−0.003 ***	−0.003 ***	−0.003 ***
road capitals	−0.016 ***	−0.016 ***	−0.016 ***	−0.016 ***	−0.016 ***	−0.016 ***
jobs	0.071 ***	0.071 ***	0.071 ***	0.072 ***	0.072 ***	0.072 ***
businesses	0.005 *	0.005 *	0.005 *	0.005 **	0.005 **	0.005 **
services	0.006 **	0.006 **	0.006 **	0.006 **	0.006 **	0.006 **
time junction	−0.0001			−0.0001		
time < 15		0.001			0.005	
time < 30			−0.001			0.001
places (day)	0.004 **	0.003 **	0.004 **			
places (week)	−0.001	−0.001	−0.001			
jobs (day)				0.267 **	0.214 *	0.228 **
jobs (week)				−0.016 **	−0.014 *	−0.013 *
time station	−0.001 *			−0.0003		
time < 15		0.014			0.012	
time < 30			0.030 ***			0.029 ***
places (day)	−0.022	−0.020	−0.021			
places (week)	−0.0006	0.0006	0.0007			
jobs (day)				−0.002	−0.001	−0.002
jobs (week)				0.0002	0.0001	0.0001

48

	(1)		(2)		(3)		(4)		(5)		(6)	
temperature	−0.002		−0.003	**	−0.002	*	−0.002		−0.003	**	−0.003	**
slope	−0.002	***	−0.002	***	−0.002	***	−0.002	***	−0.002	***	−0.002	***
water	0.079		0.075		0.081		0.077		0.070		0.075	
good soil	0.035	**	0.031	*	0.032	*	0.032	*	0.027		0.027	
burnt	−0.078		−0.078		−0.073		−0.086		−0.089		−0.086	
heritage	−0.0005		−0.0004		−0.001		−0.001		−0.001		−0.001	
old businesses	0.006	***	0.006	**	0.006	***	0.007	***	0.007	***	0.007	***
population	0.015	***	0.015	***	0.015	***	0.016	***	0.015	***	0.015	***
young	0.089		0.079		0.079		0.039		0.028		0.027	
low-qualified	−0.041		−0.043		−0.041		−0.050		−0.053		−0.052	
graduate	0.547	***	0.558	***	0.550	***	0.535	***	0.559	***	0.556	***
unemployed	−0.061		−0.057		−0.059		−0.078	*	−0.071	*	−0.073	*
agriculture	−0.046	***	−0.043	***	−0.045	***	−0.056	***	−0.049	***	−0.052	***
spatial lag	0.245	***	0.242	***	0.241	***	0.244	***	0.240	***	0.239	***
constant	−0.003		0.006		0.006		0.018		0.031		0.029	
R^2	0.301		0.300		0.303		0.302		0.301		0.303	

Notes: ***, **, *: significant at the 1%, 5% and 10% levels.

to population change, which is consistent with the theory that geographic isolation is a pull factor for migration. However, the dummy for the location of the *freguesias* along roads linking municipal capitals is also negatively and significantly related to population change in the 2001–2011 period, suggesting that the existence of direct links with central places may also facilitate out-migration.

The coefficients of the three measures of local accessibility are positive and significant in both years, confirming prior expectations. The changes in the times to the nearest motorway junction are only significant in the 1991–2001 period. The coefficient is positive, which means that the higher the reduction in time to motorways, the higher the population decline. The results of the variables measuring access to the railway network in the same period are consistent with that pattern: the higher the increase in the time to railway stations, the lower the population decline is. The changes in the dummies for the time thresholds are also significant. The loss of a station within a radius of either 15 or 30 minutes is linked with population decline. The results differ in the 2001–2011 period, where the coefficient for the time to the nearest station is negative and the coefficient for the change in the 30-minutes station dummy is positive. In other words, the increase in time to the nearest station and the loss of access to a station increase population decline.

In both years, the coefficient of the change in the number of jobs accessible by day trips by car is significant and positive (the higher the change in the number of jobs, the lower the population decline in a given *freguesia*). However, the coefficient of the change in the number of jobs accessible by weekly trips by car is negative (the higher the change in the number of jobs, the higher the population decline). None of the rail accessibility variables were found to be statistically significant.

The natural and social environment control variables that are significant tend to have the expected sign: the population decline is higher in areas with lower temperature, higher slopes, poorer soils, less water and fewer old business. The demographic control variables are also significant in almost all cases and confirm that population decline is higher in areas with smaller population, with higher proportion of older and less qualified people, and in areas with higher unemployment and share of agricultural employment.

The influence of the spatial lag variable is always positive and significant. This result is consistent with those of other studies on the relationship between rural accessibility and population change (Voss and Chi 2006; Ribeiro et al. 2010; Koopmans et al. 2012).

3.6   DISCUSSION AND CONCLUSIONS

This chapter tested the existence of links between three patterns observed in the Portuguese interior regions in the last two decades: population decline, investment in the road network and disinvestment in the railway network. The study contributes to the accessibility literature by comparing the impact of access to the road and rail networks and to nearby and distant places, accessible on a daily or weekly basis. The impact of accessibility on population change is controlled for the natural, social and demographic context. The findings show that population decline is significantly associated with several accessibility measures in different periods, including the location of the *freguesias* along roads linking municipal capitals, the changes in the times to the nearest motorway junction and rail station, the existence of a rail station in the vicinity of a place, and the change in the number of jobs accessible.

The results suggest that the investment in the road infrastructure does not promote territorial cohesion, at least when cohesion is assessed by population dynamics. The improvement of access from rural areas to regional or national centres can in fact contribute to population decline as it creates conditions for out-migration. This is an effect specific to the nature of transport infrastructure, in contrast with other types of public investment and policies, such as the promotion of employment or the provision of services in rural areas. Changes in the number of jobs and services were indeed found to be significantly and positively related to population change in all models estimated.

The models also show that the closures of railway lines are not necessarily linked with population decline. This link was found in the period 2001–2011 but not in 1991–2001, when population decline was associated with the absence of closures. Moreover, these links were found for the dummy variable indicating the existence of a station in the vicinity of a *freguesia*, but not for the accessibility measures that incorporate the suitability of railway services in meeting the travel needs of the populations. The absence of significant links for these measures may be due to the fact that the existing services before the lines were closed were no longer considered as valid options by the population, as they did not allow return trips to the relevant destinations on the required days of the week and at the required times of day. The increase in the number of places connected by the network (through rescheduling of direct services or creating of bus feeder lines) may improve rail accessibility and have a significant positive impact in population dynamics.

In the context of accessibility research, this chapter confirms the relevance of isolating the impacts of different aspects of accessibility on population change. These aspects are related to the types of destinations people need to access, and to the modes of transport they consider as options. In each period, and possibly in each study area, only some aspects will be significantly related to population change, as the accessibility needs of the populations are different and change over time. The analysis of other contexts may require the inclusion of dimensions that were not tested in this chapter, such as the accessibility of students and access by coach services.

Other methodological questions still require further development. Causality is one of these questions, as the links between road and population change tend to be bidirectional (Voss and Chi 2006). For example, decisions about railway closures may be based on the lack of economic viability of the closed lines, due to low demand, which in turn is caused in part by population decline. The closure of the lines may then contribute to further population decline. The possible endogeneity of the accessibility variable may explain the relatively low goodness of fit of the models estimated in this chapter. The correction of this issue is complex as it is difficult to model the determinants of changes in accessibility. This is especially true in the case of railway closures, which depend on factors that are difficult to measure, such as the political context, the political power of the local populations living along the lines closed, and relationships between central and local governments.

Another important question is the time scale of effects. The links between accessibility and population change may operate with a certain time lag. This aspect can be incorporated in the analysis by using autoregressive models (Koopmans et al. 2012) or explanatory variables for the number of years since access to the network started or was cut (Voss and Chi 2006).

Finally, it is important to notice that population change is in fact a composite variable, the sum of the natural population change and net migration. The two components may respond differently to changes in accessibility and should then be modelled separately. However, this may not always be feasible, as birth, death and migration statistics may not be available for researchers at a sufficiently disaggregated level.

REFERENCES

Boarnet, M.G. (1998), 'Spillovers and the locational effects of public infrastructure', *Journal of Regional Science*, **38** (3), 381–400.

Button, K. (1995), 'What can meta analysis tell us about the implications of transport?', *Regional Studies*, **29** (6), 507–517.

Chi, G. (2010), 'The impacts of highway expansion on population change: an integrated spatial approach', *Rural Sociology*, **75** (1), 58–89.

Chi, G. (2012), 'The impacts of transport accessibility on population change across rural, suburban and urban areas: A case study of Wisconsin at sub-county levels', *Urban Studies*, **49** (12), 2711–2731.

De Keizer, B., Geurs, K.T. and G.H. Haarsmanv (2012), *Interchanges in Timetable Design of Railways: A Closer Look at Customer Resistance to Interchange between Trains*, Proceedings of the European Transport Conference, Glasgow, 8–10 October, Glasgow; available at http://abstracts.aetransport.org/paper/download/id/4049.

Dong, X., Ben-Akiva, M.E., Bowman, J.L. and J.L. Walker (2006), 'Moving from trip-based to activity-based measures of accessibility', *Transportation Research A*, **40** (2), 163–180.

Escalona-Orcao, A.I. and C. Carmen Díez-Cornago (2007), 'Accessibility to basic services in one of the most sparsely populated areas in Europe: The province of Teruel (Spain)', *Area*, **39** (3), 295–309.

Farrington, J. and C. Farrington (2005), 'Rural accessibility, social inclusion and social justice: Towards conceptualisation', *Journal of Transport Geography*, **13** (3), 1–12.

Geurs, K.T. and B. van Wee (2004), 'Accessibility evaluation of land-use and transport strategies: Review and research directions', *Journal of Transport Geography*, **12** (2), 127–140.

Ji, W., Wang, Y., Zhuang, D., Song, D., Shen, X., Wang, W. and G. Li (2014), 'Spatial and temporal distribution of expressway and its relationships to land cover and population: A case study of Beijing, China', *Transportation Research D*, **32**, 86–96.

Koopmans, C., Rietveld, P. and A. Huijg (2012), 'An accessibility approach to railways and municipal population growth, 1840–1930', *Journal of Transport Geography*, **25**, 98–104.

Kotavaara, O., Antikainen, H. and J. Rusanen (2011), 'Population change and accessibility by road and rail networks: GIS and statistical approach to Finland 1970–2007', *Journal of Transport Geography*, **19** (4), 926–935.

Martin, D., Jordan, H. and P. Roderick (2008), 'Taking the bus: Incorporating public transport timetable data into health care accessibility modelling', *Environment and Planning A*, **40** (10), 2510–2525.

Martin, D., Wrigley, H., Barnett, S. and P. Roderick (2002), 'Increasing the sophistication of access measurement in a rural healthcare study', *Health and Place*, **8** (1), 3–13.

McNabb, R. (1979), 'A socio-economic model of migration', *Regional Studies*, **13** (3), 297–304.

Millward, H. (2005), 'Rural population change in Nova Scotia, 1991–2001: Bivariate and multivariate analysis of key drivers', *Canadian Geographer*, **49** (2), 180–197.

Mojica, L. and J. Martí-Henneberg (2011), 'Railways and population distribution: France, Spain, and Portugal, 1870–2000', *Journal of Interdisciplinary History*, **42** (1), 15–28.

Nutley, S.D. (1985), 'Planning options for the improvement of rural accessibility: use of the time–space approach', *Regional Studies*, **19** (1), 37–50.

Ochojna, A.D. and A.T. Brownlee (1977), 'Simple indices for diagnosing rural public transport problems', *Traffic Engineering and Control*, **18**, 482–485.

Páez, A., Scott, D.M. and C. Morency (2012), 'Measuring accessibility: Positive and normative implementations of various accessibility indicators', *Journal of Transport Geography*, **25**, 141–153.

Parolin, B.P., Filan, S.J. and A. Ilias (1993), 'Impact assessment of rail branch line closure', *Australian Geographical Studies*, **31** (2), 189–200.

Ribeiro, A., Antunes, A.P. and A. Páez (2010), 'Road accessibility and cohesion in lagging regions: Empirical evidence from Portugal based on spatial econometric models', *Journal of Transport Geography*, **18** (1), 125–132.

Rietveld, P. and F. Bruinsma (1998), *Is Transport Infrastructure Effective? Transport Infrastructure and Accessibility: Impacts on the Space Economy*, New York: Springer.

Song, S. (1996), 'Some tests of alternative accessibility measures: A population density approach', *Land Economics*, **72** (4), 474–482.

Tão, M.M. (2011), 'O exemplo alemão – Subsídios para um novo caminho-de-ferro na região do Alentejo' (The German example: subsidies for a new railway in the Alentejo region), *Transportes em Revista*, **8** (90), 40–69.

Taylor, Z. (2006), 'Railway closures to passenger traffic in Poland and their social consequences', *Journal of Transport Geography*, **14** (2), 135–151.

Vandenbulcke, G., Steenberghen, T. and I. Thomas (2009), 'Mapping accessibility in Belgium: A tool for land-use and transport planning?', *Journal of Transport Geography*, **17** (1), 39–53.

Vaturi, A., Portnov, B.A. and Y. Gradus (2011), 'Train access and financial performance of local authorities: Greater Tel Aviv as a case study', *Journal of Transport Geography*, **19** (2), 224–234.

Voss, P.R. and G. Chi (2006), 'Highways and population change', *Rural Sociology*, **71** (1), 33–58.

Wachs, M. and T.G. Kumagai (1973), 'Physical accessibility as a social indicator', *Socio-Economic Planning Sciences*, **7** (5), 437–456.

Weber, J. and M-P. Kwan (2003), 'Bringing time back in: A study on the influence of travel time variations and facility opening hours on individual accessibility', *Professional Geographer*, **54** (2), 226–240.

Whitelegg, J. (1987), 'Rural railways and disinvestment in rural areas', *Regional Studies*, **21** (1), 55–63.

4. Rural depopulation, labour market accessibility and housing prices

**David Philip McArthur, Liv Osland,
Inge Thorsen and Jan Ubøe**

4.1 INTRODUCTION

In Norway, as in the other Nordic countries, there has been an increasing tendency to centralization (Nivalainen 2003). The typical situation in Norway is that major cities and their surrounding suburban areas have in the long run captured a large proportion of the total population. According to Statistics Norway (Brunborg 2009) the proportion of people living in the most central municipalities increased steadily from 61 per cent to 67 per cent from 1980 to 2009. There are many possible reasons for this tendency. One obvious reason is the relocation of jobs in favour of urban areas, giving these areas better job opportunities.

For example, some peripheral towns in western Norway developed many decades ago due to the presence of low-cost hydroelectricity, which attracted power-intensive industries. The comparative advantage of such locations lost significance as the transportation costs of power fell. This resulted in reduced employment in manufacturing, leading to a process of economic decline and depopulation. In general, the relocation of jobs in favour of urban areas may be due to combinations of Marshall's three sources of agglomeration economies: knowledge spillovers, non-traded local input and local skilled labour pool (McCann 2013).

Traditionally, spatial variation in unemployment has been considered to be an important driver of migration (Meen 2001). Based on Norwegian data, McArthur et al. (2010) found a marked tendency for unemployment rates to be lower in rural labour market areas as compared to urban areas. Hence, it seems like a more reasonable hypothesis that increased centralization in a country like Norway is due to the fact that compared to more rural areas of the country, on average urban residents have better access to *inter alia* education, health care and a range of other urban amenities, in addition to the benefits of a more diversified labour market.

In general, commuting represents one possible, and important, counterforce towards increased centralization. Renkow (2007), Sandow (2008) and Partridge et al. (2009) emphasize the importance of commuting flows in adjusting to a changed regional labour market situation. In this respect, investments in road infrastructure represent one possible policy action to preserve a decentralized residential location pattern, and to make rural settlements less vulnerable to various types of negative shocks. Depending on distances, commuting could be a substitute for migration, or it could be the other way around (Reitsma and Vergoossen 1988). If commuting costs decline, longer commutes are more likely to be preferred to migration.

However, different types of rural areas face different challenges. Accordingly, whether transportation will be a suitable policy action to support rural settlements is not always clear. See McArthur et al. (2014) for a discussion of this point. According to Partridge et al. (2010) it depends *inter alia* on the distance to larger centres of employment. If distances are relatively short, an integration policy – based on, for example, shortening travelling time – is recommended. If distances are relatively long, they argue that a sufficient supply of jobs will be the preferred rural development policy action. It is worth noting that spatial separation may change over time due to factors such as congestion, fuel prices, transport infrastructure investment or technology. Policy responses may therefore need to vary accordingly.

Other counterforces to centralization may be wage mechanisms and housing market effects. In this chapter, we focus on the interdependence between housing prices and centralization. There exist relatively few papers studying how housing prices affect residential settlements and vice versa. One exception is Millington (1994). This paper provides an overview of some possible modelling approaches when studying the interactions between migration, wages, unemployment and housing markets. Johnes and Hyclak (1999) is another one, focusing on the linkages between housing and labour markets. Using data from the UK, they found that relatively higher housing prices in certain areas caused increased migration from these areas. This result is also confirmed by Rabe and Taylor (2012). Hämäläinen and Böckerman (2004) focus on the effect of housing market in an interregional Finnish setting. They found that increased housing prices, in addition to a larger proportion of owner-occupants, contribute to reduce net migration into a region. Based on US data, Potepan (1994) also found that the causality goes in both directions: higher net migration raises metropolitan housing prices, whereas higher housing prices discourage further net migration. The effects of house prices on migration may also vary with the direction of moves. In line with this Hämäläinen and Böckerman (2004) found that out-migration does not respond to the same degree to changes in housing market conditions as in-migration.

The complex interactions and interdependencies between house prices and population dynamics make it difficult to study the topic either empirically or analytically. Plantinga et al. (2013), for example, highlight some of the difficulties which can and have arisen in empirical studies of this topic. In our chapter, we perform numerical simulations using the model presented in McArthur et al. (2014). We build on that modelling framework by incorporating house prices and allowing them to influence the probabilities that people migrate out of a zone within a region.

The chapter is structured as follows. A presentation of the model is provided in section 4.2. Section 4.3 considers how the distribution of jobs and workers between a number of zones in a geography depends on the spatial configuration of those zones. Section 4.4 demonstrates how under certain circumstances the complex non-linearities of the modelling framework can lead to dramatic changes for even small perturbations in the prevailing conditions. The model is extended in section 4.5 to account for house prices. The effect of house prices on the model outcomes is analysed in sections 4.6 and 4.7. The dynamics of the adjustment between equilibria are examined in section 4.8. An empirical example from western Norway is presented in section 4.9. Some concluding remarks are given in section 4.10.

4.2   A DESCRIPTION OF THE MODEL

The model applied in this chapter is an extension of the model presented in detail in McArthur et al. (2014). We present a mostly non-technical description of the model here, closely following the description given in McArthur et al. (2014). Figure 4.1 offers an illustration of the key mechanisms in the model. Both the technical and non-technical descriptions of the model closely follow McArthur et al. (2014).

The model splits a region up into zones, each containing a number of jobs and workers. Migration, commuting and job creation/destruction occurs until an equilibrium state is reached where the number of jobs and people in each zone stabilizes. At the core of the model is the relationship between the supply of and demand for labour. The spatial equilibrium model utilizes the idea of economic base (Goldner 1971; Lowry 1964). Jobs are therefore split between the basic and local sector. Economic activity in the basic sector is generally export oriented and therefore determined by factors exogenous to the region, for example local innovativity and competitiveness, reflecting for instance agglomeration economies, the wage

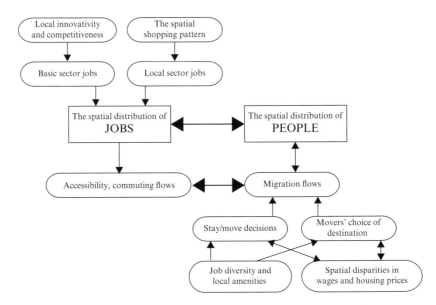

Figure 4.1   Basic mechanisms in the modelling framework

level, transport costs and the local entrepreneurial spirit. This is shown in the upper-left portion of Figure 4.1. In our model, these jobs are distributed according to an exogenously given pattern.

The size of the local sector in a zone will depend on the population of that zone, its location relative to other zones and the non-work travel behaviour of the population. The incorporation of this aspect is based on Gjestland et al. (2006). This chapter highlights the fact that factors such as agglomeration and economies of scale often give firms located in the centre of a region an advantage. These firms can often offer a wider selection of goods and services at a lower price. Co-locating in the centre also makes it easier for consumers to conduct multi-purpose trips. However not all non-work trips will be made towards the centre of a region. Consumers will compare the benefits of accessing services in the centre to the travel costs associated with making the trip. People in zones close to the city centre will tend to make more trips into the centre, while those located further away will tend to make more intra-zonal trips.

The net effect is that the density of local sector activity will tend to be highest in the centre, lowest in the suburbs and then approaching the regional average for the more peripheral zones. Gjestland et al. (2006) present this reasoning along with empirical support from Norway. It is worth noting that one consequence of this is that situations may arise where improving the connectivity of a zone to the centre of the region may damage employment in the peripheral zone.

Residential location choices are framed as two-step choices. In the first stage of the process, the decision in one of whether to stay or move from the zone. An important feature of the model is that people are less likely to move out of a zone which has good commuting opportunities; that is, one which has good accessibility. Accessibility has been found to be a desirable attribute in the location decision in several studies (e.g., Eliasson et al. 2003; Lundholm 2010; Van Ham and Hooimeijer 2009). Such locations offer flexibility for both individuals and dual-earner households. The model also accounts for the fact that people's decisions about whether to stay or leave may be interdependent. For instance, if a large number of people leave a rural zone, it may lose local amenities such as a library, grocery store or school. This makes the zone less attractive to the people left behind and increases the chance that they will choose to leave.

Accessibility is included in the migration decision using a generalized distance measure. A weighted average distance to jobs in all other zones is calculated. The weights are adjusted to account for varying competition for jobs at different locations (measured as jobs per local job seeker). Disproportionate weight is given to zones which are located at a short distance to reflect the benefits of living in a cluster of zones. In the migrate/remain decision, the accessibility measure is combined with information on the balance between the supply of and demand for labour in each zone. This is to capture the fact that a zone with unemployment and poor accessibility is particularly unattractive as a residential location.

When a worker decides to migrate, they search outward in the network for a zone which is satisfactory. Upon finding such a zone, the search terminates. Migration is therefore deterred by both distance and intervening opportunities (Stouffer 1940).

Commuting flows are implicitly included in the model through the accessibility measure in the migration decision. However we also calculate the explicit flows between zones using a gravity model (Sen and Smith 1995).

Figure 4.1 accounts for different kinds of interdependencies. One such interdependency which we introduce in this chapter as an extension to the model presented in McArthur et al. (2014) is that migration decisions may affect house prices, and house prices may affect migration decisions. The transportation network and the spatial distribution of jobs determine the labour market accessibility of the different residential location alternatives. Osland and Thorsen (2008) show that accessibility capitalizes into house prices, reflecting the fact that people are willing to pay a premium to locate in an area with high accessibility.

House prices in the model therefore vary between zones depending on the distance of the zone from the central business district (CBD) and the zone's labour market accessibility. Both of these effects have been found to be important in explaining the spatial variation in house prices (Osland and Thorsen 2008). Labour market accessibility in this context is measured using a Hansen-style measure (Hansen 1959):

$$A_i = \sum_j^n E_j^{\rho_H} \exp(\sigma_H * d_{ij}),$$

where E_j is total employment in zone j, $\rho_H = 1.1$ and $\sigma_H = -0.1$. House prices in zone i, HP_i, are then calculated using the hedonic house price equation:

$$HP_i = \exp(13.4311 - 0.1 * \log(d_{i, CBD}) - 0.01 * \log(d_{i, CBD})^2$$
$$+ 0.08 * \log(A_i)).$$

The parameters stated above are based on values estimated in Osland and Thorsen (2008).

Given the mechanisms in the model, the development of the different zones can be understood using the concept of the economic base multiplier. For example, assume a new basic sector firm decides to locate in a zone. The new jobs attract new workers. When workers choose to live in a region they stimulate intra-zonal demand for goods and services. This increases the local sector density and employment in the zone. This improvement in the zone's internal economy deters people from leaving and attracts new migrants into the zone, further increasing demand in the local sector. An increase in the basic sector can therefore lead to several rounds of improvements. The reverse is also true.

4.3   A CASE WHERE BASIC SECTOR JOBS ARE EVENLY SPREAD BETWEEN NON-CBD ZONES

In this section we study how the number of jobs and workers in a zone depends on the location of the zone relative to the CBD and the other zones of the region. This is done through simulations, where the distance between a zone and the CBD is systematically varied.

4.3.1   A Simple, Illustrative Geography

Consider the very simple five-node network illustrated in Figure 4.2. The CBD is assumed to be located in zone B. The distances from the CBD to

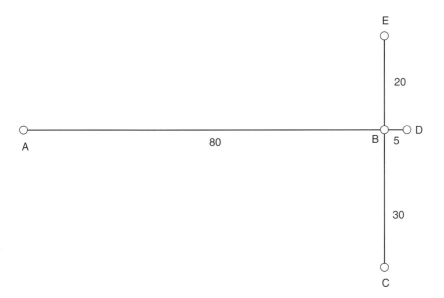

Figure 4.2 A five-node network of zones

the other zones are indicated in the figure. We interpret them as distances, although we could also consider them to be travelling time or generalized mobility costs. The suburban zone D is located only 5 km from zone B, while the zones C and E are located within a reasonable commuting distance from the CBD of the geography: 30 and 20 km, respectively. In Figure 4.2 zone A appears to be a peripheral rural location, 80 km from the CBD. The distance between the zones A and B, d_{AB}, will be systematically varied, however, to study the impact of this distance on the equilibrium employment and population in zone A. Reductions in distances may be due to investments in road infrastructure, for instance by removing the effect of topographical barriers through the construction of tunnels and/ or bridges. Alternatively, d_{AB} can be interpreted as travelling times, and reduced travelling times can result from better road standards, higher speed limits and more efficient traffic management.

Finding an equilibrium spatial distribution of population and workers of course calls for a parameterization of the model. The parameter values chosen for what we will refer to as the standard case of the numerical experiments are presented in McArthur et al. (2014). According to numerical experiments, the equilibrium solution is in particular sensitive to variations in the parameter β, which represents the distance deterrence effect in the migration decision. In the experiments reported in this section, β = −0.5.

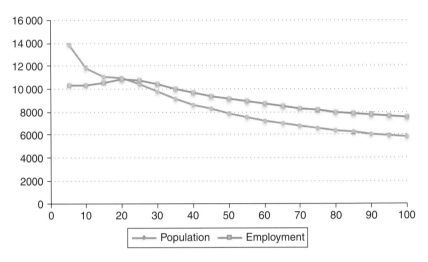

Note: Equilibrium population and employment in zone A are shown on the vertical axis against different values of distance on the horizontal axis; β = −0.5

Figure 4.3   *Equilibrium population and employment when zone A is located at various distances from the CBD (standard case)*

4.3.2   The Impact of Variations in the Distance from the CBD

In this section, there is a concentration of basic sector jobs (E_b) in the CBD, while the basic sector jobs that are not located in the CBD are assumed to be evenly spread between the zones A, C, D and E: $E_b^B = 10\,000$, $E_b^A = E_b^C = E_b^D = E_b^E = 3000$. The discussion to follow focuses primarily on the location of zone A relative to the CBD and the rest of the system. As mentioned previously, the distance and travelling time between the zones A and B can be reduced through road infrastructure investments. This affects residential location decisions, commuting behaviour and non-work travel behaviour. Hence, the equilibrium spatial distribution of jobs and people will also be affected.

Consider first the possibility that zone A is located very close to the CBD, as illustrated in Figure 4.3, where zone A appears as a suburban zone with a high population and a relatively low number of local sector jobs. The zone is attractive for commuters, while the people living here tend to direct their non-work trips to the CBD.

The equilibrium employment and population is in particular sensitive to variations in distance at low levels of d_{AB}. If, for instance, d_{AB} was 10 km rather than 5 km, zone A gets less attractive as an origin of commuting, causing a reduced population. On the other hand, more people do their shopping locally, which means that the zone gets more attractive for local sector activities. Hence, there are two forces pulling the equilibrium level of population in different directions. In the case illustrated by Figure 4.3 the force explained by commuting attractiveness dominates for $d_{AB} < 15$, while the two forces are approximately balancing each other out for $15 < d_{AB} < 25$. For $d_{AB} > 25$, non-work travel decisions and local sector activities are only marginally affected by variations in distance. Hence, the effect on labour market accessibility dominates, explaining why both population and local sector employment are declining functions of the distance from the CBD for $d_{AB} > 25$.

4.4 THE EXISTENCE OF A BIFURCATION POINT

Assume that zone A has 200 rather than 3000 basic sector jobs, and that the difference of 2800 jobs is proportionally distributed among the other zones in the geography. Assume in addition that workers are less willing to move, corresponding to a higher value of $\beta = -1.5$ (Figure 4.4). The impact of this distance deterrence parameter on the equilibrium solution

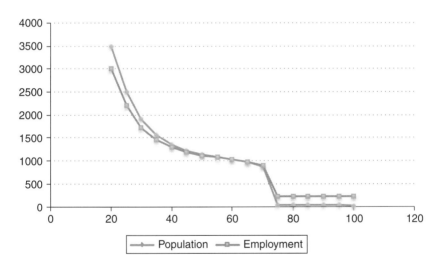

Note: A bifurcation point with $E_b^A = 200$ and $\beta = -1.5$. Equilibrium population and employment in zone A are shown on the vertical axis against different values of d_{AB} on the horizontal axis.

Figure 4.4 *Equilibrium population and employment in zone A at various distances from the CBD: Illustration of a bifurcation point*

is discussed in McArthur et al. (2014). As equilibrium solutions are calculated for increasing values of d_{AB}, a situation eventually emerges where a process of interdependent migration decisions comes into action. This takes the zone into a very different kind of equilibrium solution, with a dramatically lower level of population and local sector jobs.

In Figure 4.4, the bifurcation point is located at $d_{AB} \approx 70$. The figure illustrates how the character of the equilibrium solution differs dramatically if zone A is located at a distance of 75 km rather than 70 km from the CBD. The time dynamics, and potential transition problems, involved if changes in the road network bring the relevant distance beyond the bifurcation point are discussed in McArthur et al. (2014).

The results of the experiments presented above are based on a critical population threshold of 800 in the model. Below this population threshold, the rate of out-migration increases. This very simple function determining interdependency in migration decisions serves more as an example of what impact this kind of mechanism might have on the equilibrium spatial configuration of population and employment. This approach with numerical experiments also gives an opportunity to study how the existence and location of a bifurcation point depends on aspects of migration, non-work travel and labour market behaviour.

4.5   HOUSE PRICES AND MIGRATION DECISIONS

It is a very reasonable hypothesis that house prices contribute to explaining residential location choices. The most widely accepted theory that links residential location to the price of housing is given by standard urban economic theory represented by the monocentric city model (Alonso 1964). The household chooses the residential location so that utility is maximized, balancing *inter alia* the increased costs of commuting and the advantages of lower unit price of land or housing with increased distance from the CBD. Residential location choices and travelling costs are, hence, closely integrated.

In the housing market literature accessibility has traditionally been accounted for by the single-dimension measure of distance to CBD (Dubin 1992; Waddell et al. 1993). Osland and Thorsen (2008) have expanded this approach. In their regression model spatial variation in housing prices is explained by urban attraction and labour market accessibility effects as explained in section 4.2. In this chapter average house prices will therefore vary systematically between the zones A, B, C, D and E in accordance with these two variables. Budget considerations affect the choice of residential location for households who move, and they affect the probability of moving from the current residential location. As a spatial interaction counterpart, migration and commuting appear as substitutes in labour market decisions. In this first set of experiments, the probability of staying at the current residential location is assumed to depend on house prices within the zone. The decision to stay or to move from a zone depends on the labour market accessibility of the zone. The probability of staying can be argued to increase if house prices become very low, due to an unwillingness to experience capital losses.

The housing market is introduced into the model in a simplified way. The house prices in each zone are a function of the zone's distance to the CBD and the zone's labour market accessibility. We assume that if house prices in a zone drop below some threshold, then it begins to reduce the probability of out-migration. The threshold is a simplified way of representing an average price below which a mover may experience a capital loss. The implicit assumption here is that it will be difficult for a person to obtain a house in another zone for less than this sum. The lower the price goes below this threshold, the greater the expected capital loss and the greater the probability of staying in the zone. The probability of staying in the zone then increases in proportion to how far house prices fall below the threshold. If, for instance, the threshold is NOK 1 million (around €120 000), and the price of a (homogeneous) house is NOK 500 000, then the probability of staying is doubled compared to a situation where house prices are at or above the threshold.

4.6   HOUSE PRICES, PERIPHERAL POPULATION AND COMMUTING IN THE STANDARD CASE

Figure 4.3 illustrates how sensitive population and local sector employment in zone A are to variations in the distance between the zone and the CBD. If zone A is located far from the CBD, however, both the urban attraction effect and the labour market effect contribute to explain low local house prices. Due to the unwillingness to move from a low-priced house this may induce more workers to stay in the zone, despite an unfortunate labour market accessibility situation. Commuting may substitute migration for many workers.

Assume that the probability of moving from zone A is unaffected by changes in house prices, unless they are below a threshold of NOK 1.2 million. Figure 4.5 illustrates the impact of this effect on how the equilibrium population in zone A depends on the distance d_{AB}. Also shown in the figure for comparison is a curve showing a situation where house prices do not affect migration behaviour. This is equivalent to assuming a threshold equal to zero.

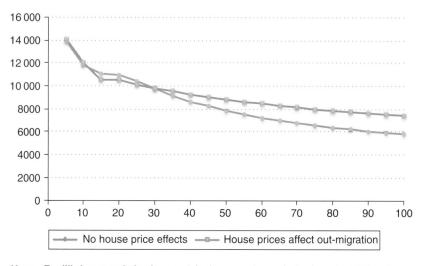

Note: Equilibrium population in zone A is shown on the vertical axis against different values of d_{AB} on the horizontal axis. The population is shown both with and without an effect whereby the probability of staying in a zone is negatively related to variations in house prices below NOK 1.2 million; $\beta = -0.5$

Figure 4.5   *The relationship between equilibrium population in zone A and distance from the CBD, when accounting for and when not accounting for spatial variation in housing prices*

It follows from Figure 4.5 that equilibrium population in the peripheral zone is less sensitive to the distance from the CBD in a case where out-migration is affected by house prices. This illustrates that house prices may contribute to prevent a depopulation from peripheral areas, and to maintain a decentralized spatial population pattern. More workers choose to live in zone A and commute to jobs elsewhere in the system, but the main effect in terms of spatial interaction is that considerably more jobs in zone A are occupied by workers with a residence in this zone. This is illustrated in Figure 4.6.

The fact that equilibrium population in zone A is higher in cases where outmigration is affected by house prices means that labour market accessibility is slightly higher in this case. This is because fewer people choose to leave the zone, and hence there is greater employment in the local sector. This further means that house prices in zone A are higher in this case than in the case where migration flows are invariant to house prices. This expectation is confirmed by the results from the spatial equilibrium model. In this particular case, however, the effect on housing prices is very marginal, and hardly visible in Figure 4.7. A situation where house prices have a more marked effect is presented in section 4.7.

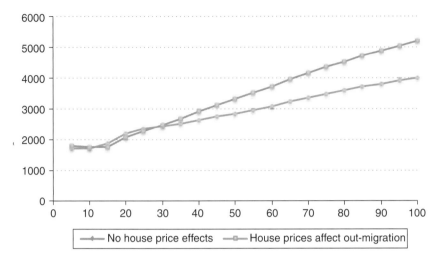

Note: The number of workers who work and live in zone A increases with d_{AB}, and this tendency is enhanced when the probability of staying in a zone is negatively related to variations in house prices below NOK 1.2 million; $\beta = -0.5$. Population is shown on the vertical axis and the distance d_{AB} on the horizontal axis.

Figure 4.6   The number of people who work and live in zone A changes with house prices and the distance from the CBD

4.7   HOUSE PRICES AND THE POSSIBILITY OF RURAL DEPOPULATION

It was illustrated in section 4.4 that the equilibrium solution may change substantially at a specific distance from the CBD in a case where the peripheral zone has a low number of basic sector jobs and/or the distance deterrence effect in the migration decision is high. From a theoretical point of view, this dramatically different equilibrium solution may not appear if account is taken of the possibility that falling house prices contribute to preventing workers from moving. Figure 4.8 demonstrates how the equilibrium solution may be affected by the influence of house prices on out-migration. In this figure, the effect of falling house prices is to prevent a process of total rural depopulation, unless $d_{AB} > 100$. This corresponds to a case where there are only 200 basic sector jobs in zone A, and the distance deterrence effect in the migration decision is -1.5. Migration probabilities are assumed to be a function of house prices for prices below a threshold of 1 million NOK.

Once again, house prices in zone A will to some degree be affected by

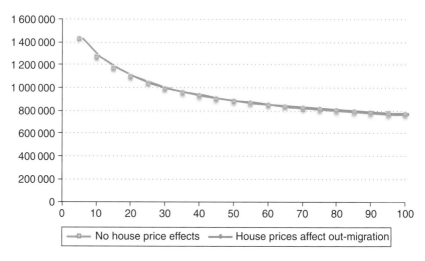

Note: House prices in zone A fall with d_{AB}. This tendency is more or less insensitive to the possibility that the probability to stay in a zone is negatively related to variations in house prices below NOK 1.2 million; $\beta = -0.5$. Population is shown on the vertical axis and the distance d_{AB} on the horizontal axis.

Figure 4.7   Equilibrium population in zone A at various distances from the CBD when housing prices are only marginally affected by out-migration

out-migration from the zone. Since there is a lot more out-migration beyond the bifurcation point, house prices for the corresponding distances should be expected to be affected more than was the case in Figure 4.7. This expectation is confirmed in Figure 4.9. If $70 < d_{AB} < 100$, house prices in zone A are nearly 100 000 NOK lower than the case where out-migration is affected by house prices. Hence, there is a stronger mutual dependency between equilibrium house prices and out-migration in the case with a bifurcation point.

Figure 4.9 demonstrated that a process of total rural depopulation may be prevented if workers are reluctant to sell their households and move when house prices in zone A fall below a specific threshold. In this spatial equilibrium modelling framework we can, however, study the sensitivity of depopulation with respect to the parameters in the relationship between out-migration and house prices. One such parameter is the threshold below which house prices are allowed to affect migration decisions. If house prices exceed this threshold, the migration decisions will be independent of house prices. Figure 4.10 demonstrates how the bifurcation point is reached for higher values of d_{AB} if outmigration is deterred even for relatively high values of house prices. Hence, a high value of the threshold

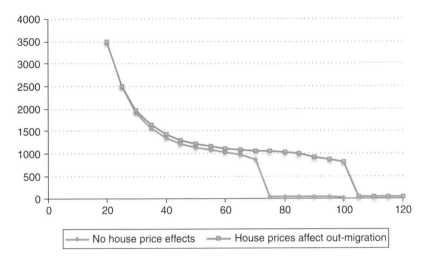

Note: Equilibrium population in zone A in cases with and without the possibility that out-migration is affected by house prices. In the former case, out-migration is affected by house prices lower than NOK 1.0 million, $E_b^A = 200$, $\beta = -1.5$. Population is shown on the vertical axis and the distance d_{AB} on the horizontal axis.

Figure 4.8   *Equilibrium population when accounting for variation in housing prices; the location of the bifurcation point changes*

narrows the prospects for rural depopulation, and contributes to maintaining a decentralized residential location pattern.

4.8   DYNAMIC ASPECTS

So far the analysis has been restricted to comparative static analysis, where the equilibrium solutions for different values of d_{AB} have been compared. While this is interesting, depopulation is a gradual process. It can therefore be interesting to analyse the dynamics of the process. Understanding the timing of the adjustment from one equilibrium to the other can be important for policy-makers. For certain policy interventions, the timing will be crucial. If an intervention occurs too late, then it may fail in reversing a process of depopulation. Fortunately it is possible to gain some information about the dynamic aspects of the process from our modelling framework. This is achieved by recording details of the population and employment distribution for each iteration of the model.

Consider the situation presented in Figure 4.11 where iteration (which

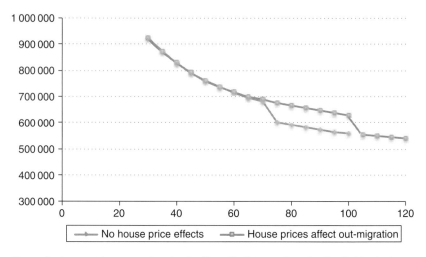

Note: In the case where out-migration is affected by house prices, the threshold value is
assumed to be 1.0 million NOK. E_b^A = 200, β = −1.5.

Figure 4.9   *Housing prices at varying distances from the CBD; the
location of the bifurcation point changes depending on whether
housing prices affect migration or not*

we interpret as time) is shown on the horizontal axis and the population
in zone A is shown on the vertical axis. The situation begins in period 1
where zone A has a population of around 900 with 175 jobs in the basic
sector and β = −1.5. In period 5, a firm closes down reducing the number
of basic sector jobs to 150. This reduction is sufficient to move the zone
to a low-level equilibrium. The speed of the adjustment will depend,
among other things, on the relationship between house prices and out-
migration.

In addition to the employment shock, we consider a policy intervention where the distance (or generalized mobility costs) between zones A
and B is reduced from 75 to 60. We consider three different timings for
this intervention. As can be seen in Figure 4.11, the short- and long-run
consequences of the intervention will depend on the timing. To begin with,
we consider two cases where this intervention takes place both with and
without the house price effect.

The line marked by squares in Figure 4.11 shows the development
without considering the effect of house prices. From the employment
shock in period 5, it takes until around period 17 to reach a low-level equilibrium. A slight inflection can be observed in the curve where the policy
intervention occurred in t = 7. The important point to note here is that

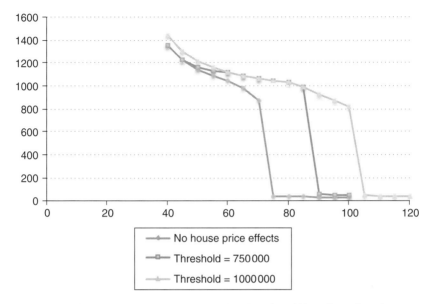

Note: The effect of the choice of threshold on location of the bifurcation point. The population of zone A is shown on the vertical axis, with the distance d_{AB} shown on the horizontal axis. $E_b^A = 200$, $\beta = -1.5$

Figure 4.10 *Sensitivity of out-migration to changes in threshold level of housing prices; the bifurcation point is reached further from the CBD the higher the threshold*

even though the distance is reduced, it is not enough to reverse the depopulation process which began in period 5.

If we include the house price effect (shown in the curve marked with diamonds), which we know acts as a brake on this process, we see that the intervention in $t = 7$ is now sufficient to prevent a complete depopulation. The population declines in response to the employment shock, recovers slightly and then settles at a new equilibrium around ten periods after the shock. While this equilibrium is lower than the starting point, it is much higher than the low-level equilibrium.

The last case considered in Figure 4.11 also considers the effect of house prices, but differs in that the road investment takes place in period 10. This is shown on the line marked with triangles. The inclusion of the house price effect slows the depopulation process compared to what we observed in the first case. The decline is further slowed by the investment in the road. However, neither the house price effect nor the infrastructure investment is enough to prevent a low-level equilibrium being reached.

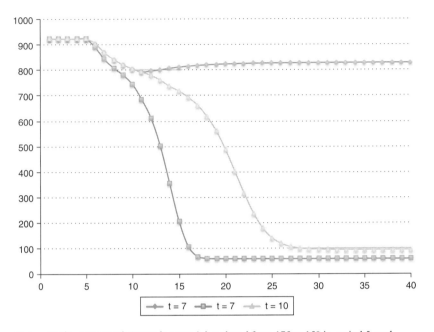

Note: Basic sector employment in zone A is reduced from 175 to 150 in period 5, and investments in road infrastructure at time t lead to a reduction of d_{AB} from 75 to 60. $\beta =$ -1.5. Population is shown on the vertical axis and the distance d_{AB} on the horizontal axis.

Figure 4.11   Changes in population at various points in time (t=7 and t =10) given the occurrence of an employment shock and changes in travel time to the CBD for zone A, without and with house price effect at t=7

Including house price effects here therefore slows the depopulation process, although it does not prevent a depopulated state from being reached. The other small difference is that the depopulated state reached in this case has a slightly higher population than the case with no house price effects.

In Figure 4.12 we consider the sensitivity of the dynamic adjustment to the choice of the threshold parameter, that is, the parameter which determines when the housing market begins to affect out-migration. At the beginning of Figure 4.12, period 5, the population is just at the tipping point where the depopulation process has started. A scenario without housing market effects is considered in addition to one with a threshold of 1 million NOK and one with a threshold of 1.5 million NOK.

As before, when the housing market has an effect on out-migration the

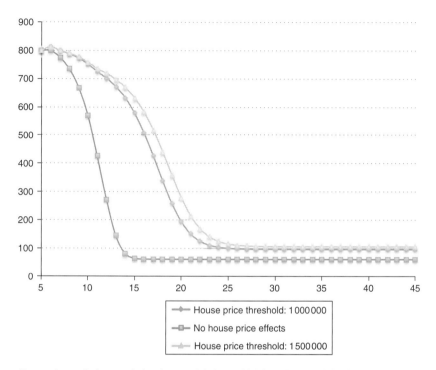

Note: At $t = 5$, the population in zone A is 800, which is so low that it initiates a process of depopulation. The speed of the depopulation depends on the impact of house prices on outmigration. $E_b^A = 150$, $\beta = -1.5$. The population in zone A is shown on the vertical axis and the distance d_{AB} on the horizontal axis

Figure 4.12   Equilibrium number of people in zone A at various distances from the CBD and at various threshold levels for housing price

depopulation proceeds at a slower pace. We can see from Figure 4.12 that changing the threshold from 1 million NOK to 1.5 million NOK acts to further slow the population decline, offsetting the trajectory by a couple of periods. As this parameter is increased, it represents an increased probability of incurring a capital loss when moving to another zone.

In Figure 4.13 we consider the effect of a positive employment shock to zone A. The scenario begins with a stable equilibrium with 825 basic sector jobs in zone A. In period 5, the number of basic sector jobs increases to 3000. The situations with and without housing market effects are presented. In both cases, the positive employment shock causes a rise in population, with the full effect of the shock taking some time to materialize. The magnitude of the effect depends on whether the housing market influences

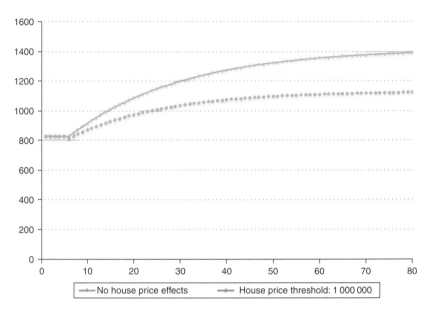

Note: A stable equilibrium with $E_b^A = 825$ is shocked by relocating basic sector jobs at
t = 5. The new distribution of basic sector jobs is given by $E_b^B = 10000$, $E_b^A = E_b^C = E_b^D = E_b^E$
= 3000. The path towards a new equilibrium solution, and the new equilibrium level of
population in zone A, depends on the impact of housing prices on outmigration. β =
−1.5. The population in zone A is shown on the vertical axis with the distance d_{AB} on the
horizontal axis

*Figure 4.13   Housing price variation acts to dampen the effect of a positive
employment shock*

the out-migration probabilities, with the effect being greatest when the
housing market does not affect migration decisions. The reason for the
disparity is that when accessibility increases, so too do house prices. House
prices in this zone were below the threshold to start with (NOK 660 000),
which deterred out-migration. As house prices increase, this deterrence
effect attenuates. This results in increased out-migration from the zone
which dampens the positive effect of the employment shock. House prices
settle at a new equilibrium of NOK 790 000.

4.9   AN EXAMPLE FROM WESTERN NORWAY

In this section we consider an empirical example from the west of
Norway. The purpose of the example is to examine whether the features
predicted by the model can be seen in the real world. This is a first step

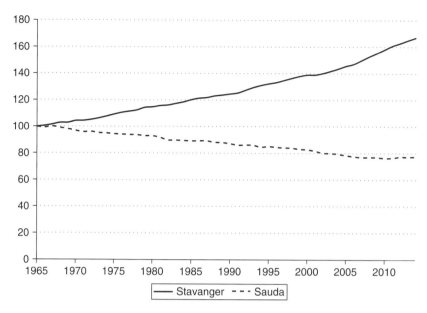

Figure 4.14   Population development in the municipalities of Stavanger and Sauda between 1965 and 2014 (100 = 1965)

towards calibrating the model to a particular case. We leave the full calibration of the model for future research. Figure 4.14 shows the growth in population in two different municipalities of Norway where the population is indexed to 100 in 1965. Both are located in the south-western parts of the country.

Stavanger is one of the largest cities in the country, with the municipality having a population of 130 754 in 2014. It has experienced a large increase in number of inhabitants. From 1965 to 2014 the population has increased by 67 per cent. This growth is relatively far above the national average. The development is due to the fact that Stavanger and the surrounding municipalities host a large proportion of a profitable oil industry. The labour market in Stavanger and the surrounding municipalities is vibrant, highly integrated where inter-municipal commuting is common.

As a contrast to this Sauda, with a population of 4760 in 2014, has experienced a negative growth in population in almost all the preceding years shown. The total reduction from 1965 to 2014 is around 22 per cent. These numbers are according to Statistics Norway.

The municipality of Sauda is relatively isolated due to natural barriers such as mountains and fjords. This increases travelling distance to other important labour market areas. Most importantly, it takes around two hours to travel from Sauda to Stavanger by boat.

Sauda is an industrial municipality with the majority of the working population working in the industry sector. Traditionally the mining and metallurgical industry has dominated, *inter alia* due to the presence of local waterfalls and hence good access to hydroelectrical power. However, in recent years the number of jobs in these basic sector industries has decreased. Given that the possibilities of commuting to nearby labour market areas are few, many inhabitants have responded to this development by migrating to other places in Norway. The number of commuters in and out of Sauda is also low, and the municipality is characterized by net out-commuting. Among those who commute, the majority commute to Stavanger, according to Statistics Norway. See also Vareide (2009). It is worth noting that we do not know if this commuting is daily or less often. This illustrates that the internal labour market is very important in this municipality.

The housing market in Norway is market based and to some extent the development in housing prices mirrors the described development in population. Figure 4.15 shows the growth in housing prices per square metre for single-family houses in the two municipalities. The increase in housing prices in Stavanger is very high. From 1991 to 2013 price per square metre has increased by a factor of eight since 1991. The graph also shows that the development in Sauda is very different. In 1991 on average the difference in housing prices was 26 per cent between these two municipalities. In 2013,

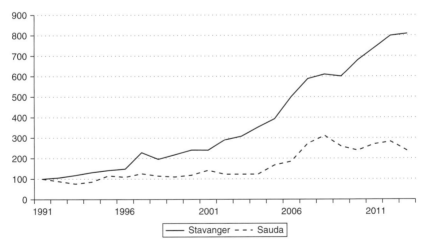

Figure 4.15   House price per square metre in the municipalities of
Stavanger and Sauda between 1991 and 2014 (100 = 1991)

housing prices are on average more than three times higher in Stavanger. Note that prices are not adjusted for inflation, and we do not adjust for any quality differences in the houses sold. The numbers are according to Statistics Norway.

As illustrated in the literature review in the introduction and in the main part of this chapter, housing prices and labour market opportunities represent complex push and pull factors for mobility. For the Stavanger area, an attractive and versatile labour market definitely represents a pull factor for population growth. For many households the development in housing prices, however, represents an important impediment for migrating into the area. The development in housing prices may have served as a balancing mechanism and to some extent reduced the tendency of out-migration from Sauda, given that house prices are far higher in more central, neighbouring labour market areas. The workings of the housing market may, hence, have prevented rural settlements in places like Sauda from not being even more depopulated, at least in the shorter run. This explanation is consistent with the predictions offered by the model.

4.10   CONCLUSIONS

This chapter has expanded the model of rural depopulation presented in McArthur et al. (2014) to account for some of the interactions between migration and house prices. More specifically, the model is expanded by allowing low house prices in rural areas to deter migration from a zone by residents who are unwilling or unable to absorb the capital loss resulting from moving from a low-house-price zone to a more central high-house-price zone. The aim of the chapter has been to explore in different scenarios how such interactions affect a process of depopulation of a peripheral area.

The model results show that when falling house prices influence people's migration decisions, the population level in a zone is less sensitive at more distant locations from the CBD. The aversion to accepting a capital loss associated with moving from a peripheral zone to a central zone maintains a higher population level than would be the case in a model that does not account for housing market interactions. This also generates more employment in the zone's local sector and leads to a higher labour market accessibility. This increased accessibility stops house prices from falling further. When accounting for house price effects, relatively more people choose to live and work in the same zone, as distance to CBD increases.

The experiments in the chapter showed that there is a much stronger mutual dependency between house prices and the population level in cases where there is a bifurcation point. Around these bifurcation points, where a small change in the spatial configuration of the zones or the distribution of employment can lead to dramatically different kinds of equilibria, house prices play a very important role. In the vicinity of such tipping points, the effect of house prices on migration decisions can make the difference between a high- and a low-level equilibrium of population. The higher the probability of incurring a capital loss, represented by a threshold value in our model, the lower the chance of arriving at an equilibrium with a population level.

Important results in terms of policy decisions appear when we account for dynamic aspects in the model. As well as determining the eventual equilibrium, the housing market can also have an effect on the time taken to transition between equilibria. The adjustment after a negative shock was slower when house prices affected migration decisions. This may give more time for policy-makers to take appropriate measures to counteract the depopulation process. Examples of relevant interventions could be investments in transport infrastructure or the establishment of new jobs. The results indicate that if government takes timely action to prevent the effects of, for instance, a negative shock, depopulation may be prevented. If a timely intervention is not undertaken, rural areas can in the longer run be completely depopulated, even when house prices act as a brake on the process. The speed of this process depends, in part, on the sensitivity of migration to house price changes.

We also considered an empirical example from Norway. In contrast to many other countries, successive Norwegian governments have by various means tried to reduce the tendency for centralization and to prevent rural depopulation. Two possible policy responses are improving the transport network and stimulating employment in peripheral areas. Previous applications of our model have shown that such policies can be successful in achieving their aims if they are correctly implemented (McArthur et al. 2014). This chapter has shown that the housing market affects the magnitude and timing of policy interventions needed to avoid depopulation.

REFERENCES

Alonso, A. (1964), *Location and Land Use: Toward a General Theory of Land Rent*, Cambridge, MA: Harvard University Press.

Brunborg, H. (2009), 'Valgaktuelt 2009: Sentraliseringen fortsetter', Statistics

Norway, available at http://www.ssb.no/befolkning/artikler-og-publikasjoner/ sentraliseringen-fortsetter (accessed 17 December 2014).

Dubin, R.A. (1992), 'Spatial autocorrelation and neighborhood quality', *Regional Science and Urban Economics*, **22** (3), 433–452.

Eliasson, K., Lindgren, U. and O. Westerlund (2003), 'Geographical labour mobility: migration or commuting?', *Regional Studies*, **37** (8), 827–837.

Gjestland, A., Thorsen, I. and J. Ubøe (2006), 'Some aspects of the intraregional spatial distribution of local sector activities', *Annals of Regional Science*, **40** (3), 559–582.

Goldner, W. (1971), 'The Lowry model heritage', *Journal of the American Institute of Planners*, **37**, 100–110.

Hämäläinen, K. and P. Böckerman (2004), 'Regional labor market dynamics, housing, and migration', *Journal of Regional Science*, **44** (3), 543–568.

Hansen, W.G. (1959), 'How accessibility shapes land use', *Journal of the American Institute of Planners*, **25** (2), 73–76.

Johnes, G. and T. Hyclak (1999), 'House prices and regional labor markets', *Annals of Regional Science*, **33** (1), 33–49.

Lowry, I.S. (1964), *A Model of Metropolis*, Santa Monica, CA: Rand Corporation.

Lundholm, E. (2010), 'Interregional migration propensity and labour market size in Sweden, 1970–2001', *Regional Studies*, **44** (4), 455–464.

McArthur, D.P., Thorsen, I. and J. Ubøe (2010), 'A micro-simulation approach to modelling spatial unemployment disparities', *Growth and Change*, **41** (3), 374–402.

McArthur, D.P., Thorsen, I. and J. Ubøe (2014), 'Employment, transport infrastructure and rural depopulation: A new spatial equilibrium model', *Environment and Planning A*, **46**, 1652–1665.

McCann, P. (2013), *Modern Urban and Regional Economics*, Oxford: Oxford University Press.

Meen, G. (2001), *Modelling Spatial Housing Markets: Theory, Analysis, and Policy*, Vol. 2, Boston, MA, USA and London, UK: Kluwer Academic Publishers.

Millington, J. (1994), 'Migration, wages, unemployment and the housing market: A literature review', *International Journal of Manpower*, **15** (9), 89–133.

Nivalainen, S. (2003), 'Who move to rural areas? Micro evidence from Finland', Paper presented at the ERSA 2003 conference, Jyväskylä, Finland, available at https://ideas.repec.org/p/wiw/wiwrsa/ersa03p214.html (accessed 17 December 2014).

Osland, L. and I. Thorsen (2008), 'Effects on housing prices of urban attraction and labor-market accessibility', *Environment and Planning A*, **40** (10), 2490–2509.

Partridge, M.D., Ali, K. and M. Olfert (2010), 'Rural-to-urban commuting: Three degrees of integration', *Growth and Change*, **41** (2), 303–335.

Partridge, M.D., Rickman, D.S. and H. Li (2009), 'Who wins from local economic development? A supply decomposition of US county employment growth', *Economic Development Quarterly*, **23** (1), 13–27.

Plantinga, A.J., Detang-Dessendre, C., Hunt, G.L. and V. Piguet (2013), 'Housing prices and inter-urban migration', *Regional Science and Urban Economics*, **43** (2), 296–306.

Potepan, M.J. (1994), 'Intermetropolitan migration and housing prices: Simultaneously determined?', *Journal of Housing Economics*, **3** (2), 77–91.

Rabe, B. and M.P. Taylor (2012), 'Differences in opportunities? Wage, employment and house-price effects on migration', *Oxford Bulletin of Economics and Statistics*, **74** (6), 831–855.

Reitsma, R.F. and D. Vergoossen (1988), 'A causal typology of migration: the role of commuting', *Regional Studies*, **22** (4), 331–340.

Renkow, M. (2007), 'Employment growth and the allocation of new jobs: Spatial spillovers of economic and fiscal impacts', *Applied Economic Perspectives and Policy*, **29** (3), 396–402.

Sandow, E. (2008), 'Commuting behaviour in sparsely populated areas: Evidence from northern Sweden', *Journal of Transport Geography*, **16** (1), 14–27.

Sen, A.K. and T.E. Smith (1995), *Gravity Models of Spatial Interaction Behavior*, Heidelberg: Springer.

Stouffer, S.A. (1940), 'Intervening opportunities: A theory relating mobility and distance', *American Sociological Review*, **5** (6), 845–867.

Van Ham, M. and P. Hooimeijer (2009), 'Regional differences in spatial flexibility: Long commutes and job related migration intentions in the Netherlands', *Applied Spatial Analysis and Policy*, **2** (2), 129–146.

Vareide, K. (2009), 'Regionanalyse Ryfylke: benchmarking av næringsutvikling og attraktivitet', available at https://teora.hit.no/handle/2282/910 (accessed 17 December 2014).

Waddell, P., Berry, B.J. and I. Hoch (1993), 'Residential property values in a multi-nodal urban area: New evidence on the implicit price of location', *Journal of Real Estate Finance and Economics*, **7** (2), 117–141.

PART III

Equity in access to daily activities and services

5. Ensuring accessibility to daily activities for different population segments with respect to sharp increases in mobility costs

Benjamin Büttner, Gebhard Wulfhorst and Jordan Evans

5.1   INTRODUCTION

The share of the household budget being spent on mobility is rising dramatically (Büttner et al. 2013). While residential costs can be estimated both easily and accurately, mobility costs and travel times are often underestimated or even ignored in household location decisions (see Büttner et al. 2012). This disconnect between mobility costs and household location decisions severely impacts upon the budgets of many households in Germany's Munich region.

This chapter aims to analyse how changes in mobility constraints – due to the influence of rising mobility costs on household budgets – can impact upon daily activity schedules, mobility behaviour, and residential and activity locations. By applying prospective shocks to mobility costs, the research seeks to explore and evaluate the resilience of different households to such shocks (that is, the ability of a household to absorb mobility cost stresses without changing its fundamental structure).

The study found that a fuel price shock based on US$200 per barrel would have a limited impact on household activities and only a limited effect on short-term mobility behaviours. The shock tripling of petrol prices, however, would greatly test household resilience. After such a shock, households would be forced to either modify or completely revise their mobility behaviours, scenarios which are difficult to achieve for the most vulnerable households – often lower- to middle-class families relying on a private car and living in suburban areas with poor public transport access.

Communities are only better able to prepare for and adapt to increases in mobility costs once governments recognize the interdependencies between land use and transport. Through discussions with local stakeholders and decision-makers, intervention strategies, policies and recommendations can be formulated to improve public transport infrastructure and to implement more efficient land use and accessibility measures. These measures should aim to place a greater emphasis on dense and mixed-use development patterns that focus on improving the (non-motorized) accessibility of jobs and daily activities.

5.2 BACKGROUND

Despite the dramatic rise of the mobility share in the household budget, mobility costs and travel times are often underestimated or even ignored in household relocation decisions (Büttner et al. 2013; Büttner et al. 2012). Residential costs – a monthly mortgage, for example – remain the focal point for households in deciding where to relocate (Haller et al. 2012).

The Munich region is a prominent example of how migration and especially the growth of work opportunities can cause such a disconnect between residential location decisions and mobility costs. The current housing shortage in Munich is resulting in sharp increases in housing costs (Bulwiengesa 2014), with the most expensive housing market in Germany standing as a barrier between the less skilled and the wealthy. As a consequence, migration to the city of Munich is very costly and in most cases ends in the outer suburbs or even in more remote and correspondingly more affordable locations (Lohr 2013). This lack of proper regional planning, in terms of labour as well as housing, leads to growing distances for both commuting and completing activities as well as fulfilling basic needs.

5.3 RESEARCH CONTEXT AND OBJECTIVE

The majority of the world's population relies on fossil fuels for its everyday mobility, mostly by means of a private car (Kahn Ribeiro et al. 2007). However, the combination of a multitude of factors – including political instability in oil-producing countries, volatility in supply, increasing consumer demand, and peak oil – is leading to sharp and unpredictable increases in mobility costs for households (Wegener 2009). In this context, it is important to research transportation alternatives and strategies so that households can adapt to these increases in mobility costs.

The consequences of sharp increases in mobility costs on accessibility are examined in three stages: scan, explore and prepare (see Figure 5.1). In the first stage a vulnerability assessment is conducted to highlight

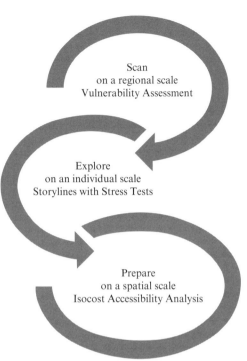

Figure 5.1   Scan–explore–prepare methodology

which regions in Munich are at risk of increasing mobility costs (see Büttner et al. 2013). After having determined the characteristics of each region, the second stage explores individual households' mobility behaviours and develops a range of different storylines which portray real-life responses to mobility price shocks. The third stage gives local stakeholders and decision-makers accessibility recommendations that enable them to prepare better on the spatial scale.

The first stage, described in Büttner et al. (2013) presents the methodological approach of a vulnerability assessment (adapted from Kelly and Adger 2000; Kasperson et al. 2006) based on the Munich region. This assessment was performed with a combination of three key indicators: exposure (fossil fuel consumption), sensitivity (income) and resilience (accessibility to jobs by public transport). Following the assessment, three municipalities representing different settlement structures (urban, suburban and rural) were selected to gain a better understanding and characterize localized differences in vulnerability. Figure 5.2 shows the composite vulnerability index that resulted from the vulnerability assessment.

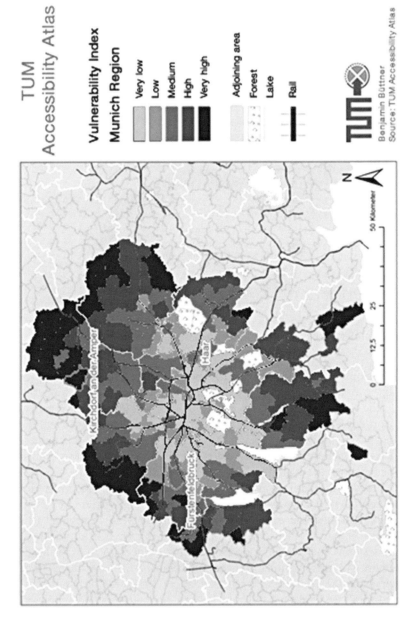

Figure 5.2   Vulnerability related to increases in fuel prices in the Munich region

This chapter describes the second stage of the project: the initial vulnerability assessment through an analysis of how various changes in mobility constraints can impact upon daily activity schedules, mobility behaviour, and residential and activity locations. The chapter evaluates the resilience of three households by applying prospective shocks to mobility costs (that is, severe mobility price increases). In view of indications that the mobility share of the household budget in the Munich region is increasing (Büttner et al. 2013), analysis of how such price shocks influence household mobility is becoming increasingly important. In most cases, vulnerable households are only able to change their mobility behaviour if they are offered more viable transport options (alternatives). Aiding governments in recognizing the interdependencies between land use and transport can help vulnerable communities prepare for and adapt to increases in mobility costs.

Recommendations to public stakeholders and decision-makers have to be based on detailed analyses on a regional level taking into account the development of future residential and mobility costs. In order to foster such sustainable spatial development, policies, intervention strategies and recommendations – which concern dense and mixed-use development patterns alongside the accessibility of jobs and daily activities – should be discussed (Hull et al. 2012). This was emphasized by Geurs et al. (2012), who stated the importance of testing the current accessibility analysis in practice. The implementation of accessibility planning requires a strong collaboration between researchers and planning practitioners.

In this chapter, stress tests are adapted to urban mobility in order to test the effects of potential external shocks on accessibility and mobility. The next section presents the data and methodology developed to implement the stress test approach, with the subsequent section analysing each household's response to these external mobility shocks.

5.4   DATA AND METHODOLOGY

The primary purpose of this research was to analyse the impacts of oil shocks on daily mobility costs and travel behaviour, following a *ceteris paribus* approach. This section establishes the methodology implemented to apply urban mobility stress tests to three fictitious households in Munich, Germany. We used model households representing different demographics and structural data so that we might obtain a range of reactions to fuel price shocks.

5.4.1 Household Identification

Synthetic households and each of their respective mobility behaviours were derived by analysing a range of regional databases. Spatial patterns of movement and their corresponding causes were determined based on a recent migration analysis within the Munich region (Wanderungsmotivuntersuchung II, Landeshauptstadt München 2012). The study 'Mobility in Germany at the level of the region of Munich' (Mobilität in Deutschland (MiDMUC), Landeshauptstadt München 2010) yielded socio-demographic characteristics of the population as well as spatial trip patterns and their corresponding modes of transport. The Bavarian State Office for Statistics and Data Processing provided population data at the municipality level. We made the initial estimation of the community structures with the aid of the GIS-based *TUM Accessibility Atlas* (Büttner et al. 2011), which we subsequently used for the implementation of the data and households. The local communities were asked to review the generated synthetic households (including the individual mobility patterns), and confirmed that they were relevant and reasonable.

5.4.2 Mobility and Activity Behaviour

Housing and activity locations were primarily determined from the activity programmes detailed in the Munich databases, with the origins and destinations being spatially referenced. To calculate the mobility costs and travel times for the synthetic households (based on the individual trip chains and spatially referenced activities), we used the Munich Transport and Tariff Association (MVV) WoMo calculator (see Haller et al. 2012). In cases of relocation, residential costs were also considered. On the basis of the actual address data of the corresponding origin and destination relationships for the calculated activities (work and education, supply, leisure), the GIS-based *TUM Accessibility Atlas* facilitated the initial estimation and visualization of the individual mobility behaviours and spatial trip patterns. As mentioned before, we subsequently used the *TUM Accessibility Atlas* for the implementation of the data and households.

5.4.3 Stress Tests and Assumptions

Many studies (e.g., Institut für Mobilitätsforschung 2010) predict a rise in the crude oil price to US\$200 per barrel. Stress test 1 aimed to demonstrate the effects of such an increase, which would effectively cause the price of fuel at German petrol stations to rise to €2.11/L. The jump from €1.55/L to €2.11/L represents only a moderate shock (a 35 per cent increase). Stress test 2 details the effects of oil prices tripling. This increase, which became a reality in the US between the years of 2007 and 2008, would force German households to spend €4.65/L on fuel.

The stress test scenarios were implemented in line with a simplified economic approach. The research did not focus on the economic theory and variables related to gradual oil price increases, but concentrated on how households would react to drastic oil price hikes, and resulting suddenly increased fuel prices. This would have an immediate effect on the price consumers would pay when refuelling.

With this in mind, the following assumptions were made:

- Shocks on mobility occurred suddenly and consequently were not planned for by households, allowing no rapid structural changes in terms of household size and location.
- Oil price shocks did not have any effect on house prices and rents, meaning that there was no change in the households' housing budgets.
- Shock alternatives depended only on households. Public authorities could not respond to these shocks.
- No public measures such as tax decreases, fuel subsidies or fuel vouchers could be implemented to absorb the shocks even partially.
- The proposed shocks only referred to daily mobility; long-distance travel was not impacted upon by these shocks as it was considered to be outside the scope of a household's everyday needs.
- Public transport costs would rise more moderately and therefore allow people more time to adapt, since public transportation costs are based less on market forces and more on factors of a political nature.

5.5 STRESS TESTS RESPONSES

This chapter investigates three model households, each of which is based on different representative demographics and structural data:

- Household 1: a four-person family who move from the inner city to the city outskirts, characterized by inability to make flexible changes in their mobility behaviour.
- Household 2: a 31-year-old single male who recently moved from another German state to the state of Bavaria to take up a new job in the city of Munich.

- Household 3: a married couple in their seventies, living in the rural periphery of the city and relying on a car for their mobility.

The MOR€CO project report (see Büttner and Wulfhorst 2012) includes additional representative households for a range of different structural settings (for example, age, income and residential location).

5.5.1 Household 1

Current mobility behaviour
A family of four, living in the inner city of Munich, constitutes the first household (see Table 5.1 and Table 5.2). With the father having accepted a new job in the outskirts of the city, the family eventually decide to move from the city centre closer to the father's place of employment.

Work and education
The father initially works full-time for a company of which the offices are located in the city centre (Ottostraße 13). In order to avoid traffic jams during peak hours, he takes advantage of their home's high public transport accessibility to travel to his workplace.

The mother has a part-time job and works near the city centre five days per week (Kapuzinerplatz 1). She is not always able to use public transport because of the high flexibility demanded by her lifestyle, which requires combining daily activities (for example, taking the children to school and then driving to work). As she is more car-dependent than her husband, she uses her own car to go to work twice a week. This allows her to combine

Table 5.1   Members of Household 1

Person	Age	Work/education
Father	40	Full-time
Mother	39	Part-time
Son	9	Elementary school
Daughter	5	Kindergarten

Table 5.2   Household 1 in Au-Haidhausen

Address	Floor space (m²)	Living costs (€/month)	Income (€/month)	Number of rooms	Number of cars
Preysingstraße 67 Au-Haidhausen	89	1332	3750	3	2

several activities easily and flexibly. The children's school (Flurstraße 8) is located close to the family home and can be reached on foot.

Leisure
On Tuesday evenings, the father usually plays soccer with his friends at the Olympic Park (Connollystraße 32). Even though he could go there by public transport, he prefers to use his own car. The mother meets her friends in the city centre once a week (Hohenzollernstraße 25). Most of the time, she goes by public transport; however, she also thinks about potential trip chains that could be conveniently combined if she travelled by car. The central location of the family's home is an advantage, as leisure activities for the children (for example, music and sports) are located within walking distance (Flurstraße 8).

Infrequent trips
Possibilities for daily shopping are available close to the family's home. At weekends, however, the family uses the car to go to a larger shopping centre on the outskirts of Munich while trying to combine these trips with leisure activities such as going bowling or seeing a film (Thomas-Dehler-Straße 12). Once a month, the entire family goes on a day trip outside Munich, for example hiking or visiting friends (Beccostraße 12). For this activity, the family usually take one of their cars.

Other infrequent trips – for example to go to the barber (Innere-Wiener-Straße 48), special occasion dinners or meetings – are made by public transport. On the other hand, the parents use the car to drive their children to other infrequent activities, for example to go to the doctor (Karl-Theodor-Straße 97). Table 5.3 provides an overview of the mobility activities of Household 1.

After the father accepts a new job in Karlsfeld, and considering the commuting time from their place in Au-Haidhausen, the family decide to move to a closer residence in Aubing. From here, Karlsfeld can be reached by car in 14 minutes, via the A99 highway. The drive from the new residence to the mother's work takes 24 minutes, which is acceptable as well. Additionally, the new location is accessible by the S-Bahn suburban train, which provides direct services to the city centre. The station is quite close to the new home (at 1 km). Moving to the outskirts to be closer to the father's new job enables the family to live in a green area where the rents are lower than in the city centre. Table 5.4 summarizes the new living situation of Household 1.

Since the family neither want to lose touch with friends nor change their habits, it continues to carry out exactly the same activities as before. Leisure activities such as playing soccer and meeting with friends

Table 5.3 *Activities of Household 1*

Person	Frequent activities		Leisure (weekly)		Infrequent activities (monthly)	
	Work days					
Father	Full time	Ottostraße 13 (City centre)	Soccer	Connollystraße 32 (Olympic Park)	Barber	Innere Wiener Straße 48 (Au-Haidhausen)
Mother	Part time	Kapuzinerplatz 1 (Isarvorstadt)	Meeting friends / dinner	Hohenzollernstraße 25 (Schwabing)	–	
Son	School	Flurstraße 8 (Au-Haidhausen)	Music academy	Flurstraße 8 (Au-Haidhausen)	Doctor	Karl-Theodor-Straße 97 (Schwabing)
Daughter	Kindergarten	Flurstraße 8 (Au-Haidhausen)			Doctor	Karl-Theodor-Straße 97 (Schwabing)
Together			Shopping / bowling / cinema	Thomas-Dehler-Straße 12 (Neuperlach)	Visiting family / hiking	Beccostraße 12 (Pöcking)

Table 5.4   Household 1 in Aubing

Address	Floor space (m²)	Living costs (€/month)	Income (€/month)	Number of rooms	Number of cars
Industriestraße 61 Aubing	120	1400	3750	4	2

in Munich remain part of the weekly schedule. Overall, Aubing has high public transport accessibility, but the move will still influence the family's monthly transportation expenditure significantly.

Shock scenario: increase to €2.11/L
An increase in fuel prices to €2.11/L (US$200/barrel) would not have a dramatic impact on the family's household budget. Only €77 less would be available per month, compared with the pre-shock scenario. This slight increase in expenditure would most likely not cause a change in the family's mobility behaviour. Nevertheless, some suggestions can be made for potential modifications to regain the level of mobility costs before the price shock.

The mother could use park-and-ride (P+R) four times a week to go to work, instead of solely relying on her car. To remain flexible, she should only take the car to meet with her friends in the city centre. Another simple alternative which would save €30 per month would be to change the weekly route to the music academy. In the pre-shock scenario, the mother drives her child to the school via highway A99 (35 km); however, using a more direct route (22 km) would save some money.

These changes in mobility behaviour have important drawbacks concerning time expenditure. If the mobility patterns are modified as suggested, the household would spend an extra 477 minutes travelling per month. Table 5.5 and Table 5.6 provide an expenditure and budget overview concerning the discussed changes in mobility patterns for Household 1.

Shock scenario: increase to €4.65/L
A jump in fuel prices to €4.65/L (that is, a tripling of current prices) would have a severe impact on the household budget. Each month, the family would spend an extra €429 compared to the current situation, leaving approximately 20 per cent of the budget as discretionary income.

Assuming the family wants to maintain the budget of before the price shock, it aims to become more budget-efficient in relation to its mobility patterns. All family members have to contribute to this aim by using

Table 5.5   Increase to 2.11 €/L: expenditure summary for Household 1 in Aubing

Type of expenditure		Mobility scenario costs		
		€1.55/L	€2.11/L	€2.11L (incl. P+R change)
Living costs per month	Net rent	1100	1100	1100
	Additional living costs	300	300	300
	Total	1400	1400	1400
Mobility costs per month	Car ownership	800	800	800
	Car use	348	426	284
	Public transport	25	25	0
	Commuting allowance savings	91	91	91
	Total	1082	1159	1059
Travel time (minutes/month)		2572	2572	3049

Table 5.6   Increase to €2.11/L: budget summary for Household 1 in Aubing

Income and expenditure	Mobility scenario total costs		
	€1.55/L	€2.11/L	€2.11/L (incl. P+R change)
Net income (€)	3750	3750	3750
Mobility and living costs (€)	2482	2559	2459
Ratio	66%	68%	66%
Discretionary income (€)	1268	1191	1291

public transport for daily activities. The mother experiences a time loss of 20 minutes on her way to work (one-way). She continues to use the car for a trip chain once a week (leisure activities combined with work) as this requires a certain level of flexibility. The son will also use public transport (PuT) to go to music school, losing ten minutes per trip (one way). The father suffers most from this new situation, as he is forced to spend an extra 49 minutes travelling to work.

The father's extra travel time is one major drawback of the chosen residential location, as the public transport connection to his work in Karlsfeld is very inconvenient compared with travelling by car (see Figure 5.3). For all remaining car trips, the shortest route will be chosen in order to minimize fuel consumption. As a result of these changes in everyday mobility,

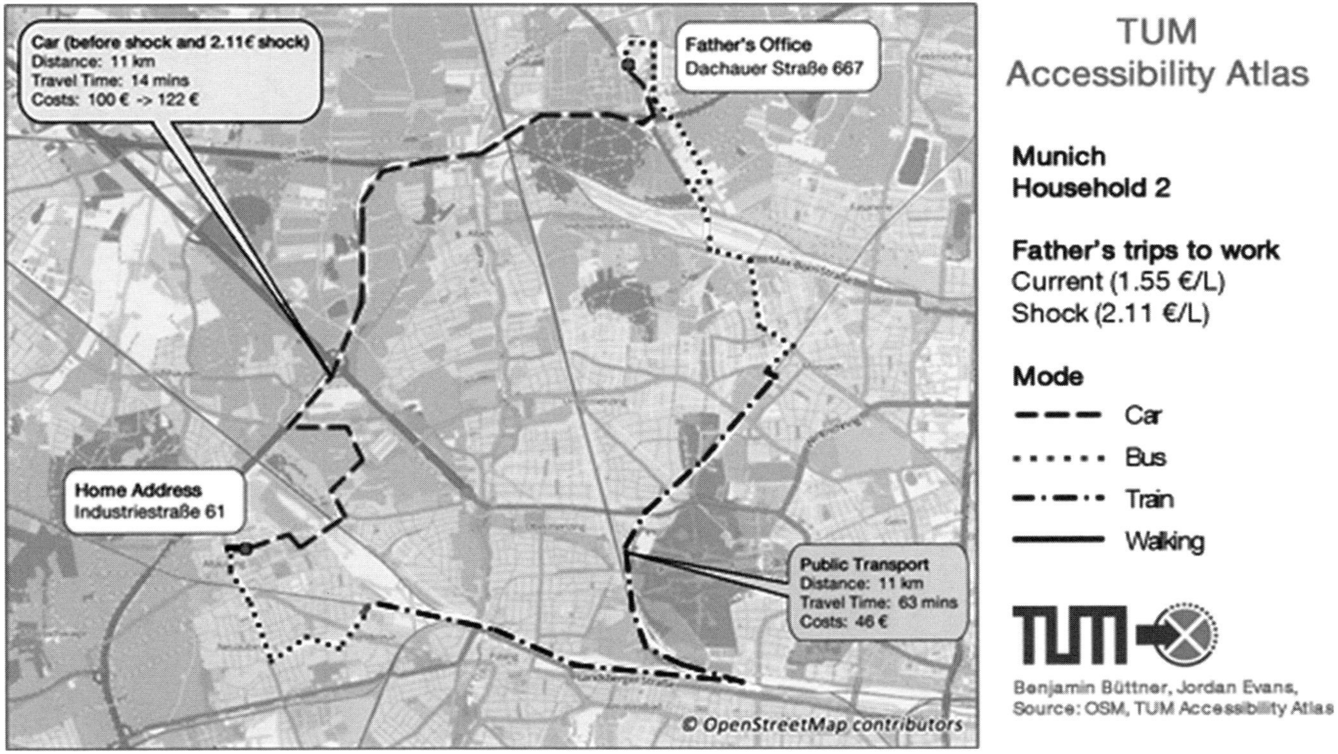

TUM
Accessibility Atlas

Munich
Household 2

Father's trips to work
Current (1.55 €/L)
Shock (2.11 €/L)

Mode
— — — Car
· · · · · · Bus
· — · — Train
——— Walking

Benjamin Büttner, Jordan Evans,
Source: OSM, TUM Accessibility Atlas

Father's Office
Dachauer Straße 667

Public Transport
Distance: 11 km
Travel Time: 63 mins
Costs: 46 €

Car (before shock and 2.11€ shock)
Distance: 11 km
Travel Time: 14 mins
Costs: 100 € -> 122 €

Home Address
Industriestraße 61

© OpenStreetMap contributors

Figure 5.3   Household 1 €2.11/L shock scenario for father's work trip

95

Table 5.7   Increase to €4.65/L: expenditure summary for Household 1 in Aubing

Type of expenditure		Mobility scenario individual costs			
		€1.55/L	€4.65/L	€4.65/L (incl. PuT)	€4.65/L (incl. PuT + selling car)
Living costs per month	Net rent	1100	1100	1100	1100
	Additional living costs	300	300	300	300
	Total	1400	1400	1400	1400
Mobility costs per month	Car ownership	800	800	800	450
	Car use	348	777	164	180
	Public transport	25	25	136	136
	Commuting allowance savings	91	91	91	91
	Total	1082	1511	1008	674
Travel time (minutes/month)		2572	2572	5569	5569

Table 5.8   Increase to €4.65/L: budget summary for Household 1 in Aubing

Income and expenditure	Mobility scenario total costs			
	€1.55/L	€4.65/L	€4.65/L (incl. PuT)	€4.65/L (incl. PuT + selling car)
Net income (€)	3750	3750	3750	3750
Mobility and living costs (€)	2482	2911	2408	2074
Ratio	66%	78%	64%	55%
Discretionary income (€)	1268	839	1342	1676

the family's small car is no longer necessary and can be sold. This saves €350 of fixed car ownership costs per month.

If the mobility patterns are modified as suggested above, the household would spend an additional 2997 minutes or 50 hours travelling per month (see Table 5.7). However, the negative aspects (time losses) can be deemed to be levelled out by the financial gains. Selling one car and adapting the family's trip behaviour will save €408 per month relative to the pre-shock situation (see Table 5.8). Changing the mobility patterns without selling the second car would still free up €74 in the family's budget.

Table 5.9   Members of Household 2

Person	Age	Work/education
Single male	31	Full-time

Table 5.10   Household 2 in Haar

Address	Floor space (m²)	Living costs (€/month)	Income (€/month)	Number of rooms	Number of cars
Ludwig-Thoma-Straße 33 Haar	61	813	2500	2	1

5.5.2 Household 2

Current mobility behaviour
A 31-year-old man residing in Haar forms the second household (see Table 5.9 and Table 5.10). He works full-time and has recently moved to Bavaria after having accepted new employment. As his new place of work is located in Messestadt Ost, he concentrates his apartment searches in this area.

Work and education
The man's place of work is in Hans-Schwindt-Straße, not far from his apartment. He needs only 14 minutes to reach the office by car, whereas it takes him 51 minutes if he uses commuter and underground rail services (see Figure 5.4).

Leisure
By using the car, the man can be rather flexible while trying to combine activities (for example, sport and shopping) with his trip to work. By doing this, he saves both time and money; however, he can clearly save more by either cycling or using public transport. Despite the flexibility they offer, the car-based trip chains are not the most efficient in terms of cost and emissions savings.

As the man's friends live in Munich, he often drives at the weekend, to eat out as well as to go walking and shopping in the pedestrian mall. Although the commuter rail service would provide the optimal connection for these activities, the man prefers to use his car so as to not be dependent on public transport. He is willing to accept the traffic on the road as well as the time to search for a parking spot and the parking fees.

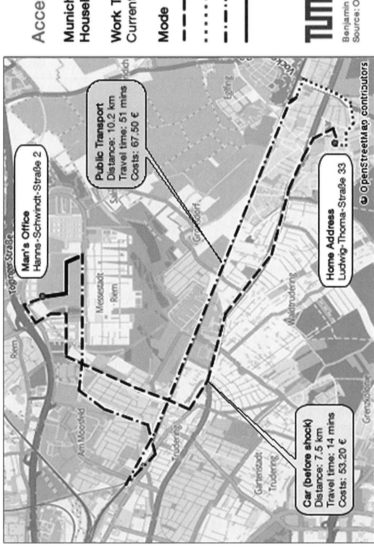

Figure 5.4   Household 2 pre-shock commuting trip

Table 5.11   Activities of Household 2

Person	Frequent activities			Infrequent activities (monthly)	
	Work days	Leisure (weekly)			
Single male	Full-time	Hanns-Schwindt-Straße, Munich	Sport/supermarket Meeting with friends	Münchener Straße, Haar Leopoldstraße 48, Munich	Hiking/Lake	Untere Seefeldstraße 14, Weßling

Infrequent trips

In his spare time, the man drives to the mountains to go hiking or skiing. In addition, he uses his car to drive to the lake to go swimming with friends (Untere Seefeldstraße 14, Weßling). Table 5.11 provides an overview of the mobility activities of Household 2.

Shock scenario: increase to €2.11/L

The man, who is young and lives alone, is only slightly affected by the fuel price increases to €2.11/L. In line with spending half his income on mobility and living expenses, such an increase in fuel prices equates to only an extra €33 in the man's monthly mobility costs.

Just like Household 1, the man's mobility behaviour is unlikely to be affected by this minor increase in mobility expenses. As he is single and has half of his income available for discretionary expenditure, he is flexible and able to absorb such mobility cost stresses without changing the fundamental structure of his mobility behaviour.

Assuming the man is willing to change his mobility behaviour so as to prepare himself for any future fuel price spikes, he could also choose to start using public transport. He could offset the extra €33 in mobility costs by using public transport instead, and maintain approximately the same mobility costs. Table 5.12 and Table 5.13 provide an expenditure and budget overview concerning the discussed changes in mobility patterns for Household 2.

Shock scenario: increase to €4.65/L

In the event of a fuel price increase to €4.65/L, the man would have €183 less discretionary income per month (see Table 5.14). Despite such a large increase in driving costs, he can be deemed not dramatically affected, predominantly owing to his initial less-than-optimal mobility behaviour. For example, the man could save money by using public transport for his commute to work, while relying on park-and-ride services for leisure activities. Such changes in his mobility patterns would take up an extra 50 minutes of time per day (see Table 5.15).

Table 5.12   Increase to €2.11/L: expenditure summary for Household 2 in Haar

Type of expenditure		Mobility scenario individual costs		
		€1.55/L	€2.11/L	€2.11/L (incl. PuT)
Living costs per month	Net rent	641	641	641
	Additional living costs	172	172	172
	Car ownership	350	350	350
	Total	813	813	813
Mobility costs per month	Car use	151	184	118
	Public transport	0	0	68
	Commuting allowance savings	26	26	26
	Total	475	508	510
Travel time (minutes/month)		1538	1538	2708

Table 5.13   Increase to €2.11/L: budget summary for Household 2 in Haar

Income and expenditure	Mobility scenario total costs		
	€1.55/L	€2.11/L	€2.11/L (incl. PuT)
Net income (€)	2500	2500	2500
Mobility and living costs (€)	1288	1321	1323
Ratio	52%	53%	53%
Discretionary income (€)	1212	1179	1177

Table 5.14   Increase to €4.65/L: budget summary for Household 2 in Haar

Income and expenditure	Mobility scenario total costs		
	€1.55/L	€4.65/L	€4.65/L (incl. P+R and PuT)
Net income (€)	2500	2500	2500
Mobility and living costs (€)	1288	1471	1331
Ratio	52%	59%	53%
Discretionary income (€)	1212	1029	1169

If the man were to decide to use public transport more frequently, it would be economical for him to sell his car. This would allow further mobility cost reductions, which could be used to purchase a public transport ticket subscription (see Table 5.15).

Table 5.15   Increase to €4.65/L: expenditure summary for Household 2 in Haar

Type of expenditure		Mobility scenario individual costs		
		€1.55/L	€4.65/L	€4.65/L (incl. P+R and PuT)
Living costs per month	Net rent	641	641	641
	Additional living costs	172	172	172
	Total	813	813	813
Mobility costs per month	Car ownership	350	350	350
	Car use	151	334	126
	Public transport	0	0	68
	Commuting allowance savings	26	26	26
	Total	475	658	518
Travel time (minutes/month)		1538	1538	2843

Table 5.16   Members of Household 3

Person	Age	Work/education
Husband	77	Pensioner
Wife	74	Pensioner

Table 5.17   Household 3 in Kirchdorf

Address	Floor space (m²)	Living costs (€/month)	Income (€/month)	Number of rooms	Number of cars
Frühlingstraße 3 Kirchdorf	95	361	1600	3	1

5.5.3   Household 3

Current mobility behaviour
Having always lived in Kirchdorf, the old married couple still reside in the family home despite all the children having moved out (see Table 5.16 and Table 5.17). The wife relies on her husband for her own mobility, as he is the only one who can drive their car.

Table 5.18   Activities of Household 3

Person	Frequent activities (weekly)					Infrequent activities (monthly)
Husband	Church service	Obere Hauptstraße 6, Kirchdorf	Shopping	Joseph-Fraunhofer-Straße 31, Pfaffenhofen	Football	Werner-Heisenberg-Allee 25, München
Wife			Restaurant	Plantage 2, Freising	Visiting friends	Wolfersdorf

Frequent trips and activities

Every Sunday, the couple attend a service at the local church. Even though the journey on foot takes only ten minutes, the couple choose to use the car. Twice a week, the couple drive almost 20 km to Pfaffenhofen to buy groceries and other items that are not available in Kirchdorf. Despite there being more local shopping options, the couple prefer to go to the larger supermarket in Pfaffenhofen. Every Wednesday, the husband meets with his friends at the local tavern, to which he also travels by car.

Infrequent trips

Once a month, the wife meets with a friend in a neighbouring village (see Table 5.18). As she herself does not drive, her husband takes her there. The husband is a football fan, so he likes attending matches at Munich's Allianz Arena. As public transport to the stadium is generally time-consuming and rather crowded during matches, he drives his car instead.

Shock scenario: increase to €2.11/L

Although the additional costs due to the increased fuel price amount to only €30 a month, the couple would still like to adapt their mobility behaviour to have the same amount of discretionary income as before the fuel price spike. For this reason, the couple decide to use a closer supermarket in Freising for grocery shopping. The husband also decides to drive less frequently (around every six weeks instead of every four) to football matches at the Allianz Arena. By implementing these measures, the €30 in additional costs can be avoided while also achieving some time savings (see Table 5.19 and Table 5.20).

Table 5.19   Increase to €2.11/L: expenditure summary for Household 3 in Kirchdorf

Type of expenditure		Mobility scenario costs		
		€1.55/L	€2.11/L	€2.11/L (less freq. driving)
Living costs per month	Net rent	0	0	0
	Additional living costs	361	361	361
	Total	361	361	361
Mobility costs per month	Car ownership	350	350	350
	Car use	130	159	128
	Public transport	0	0	0
	Commuting allowance savings	0	0	0
	Total	480	509	478
Travel time (minutes/month)		671	671	554

Table 5.20   Increase to €2.11/L: budget summary for Household 3 in Kirchdorf

Income and expenditure	Mobility scenario total costs		
	€1.55/L	€2.11/L	€2.11/L (less freq. driving)
Net income (€)	1600	1600	1600
Mobility and living costs (€)	841	870	839
Ratio	53%	54%	52%
Discretionary income (€)	759	730	761

Shock scenario: increase to €4.65/L

In view of their advanced ages and the high costs of keeping their car on the road, the two decide to dispose of the car. Through eliminating the fixed costs of car ownership, the pair can immediately save €350. The clear downside, however, is that it limits mobility. Previously, the couple drove the short way to church; however, as both wife and husband are still physically fit, they now either walk or cycle to church.

The husband takes Bus 601 to the tavern once a week. From Kirchdorf a.d. Amper, Rathaus he can directly go to Freising Waldsiedlung in less than 15 minutes. Including the walking time to and from the bus stops, one trip takes approximately 30 minutes. For the outward journey, the only reasonably scheduled bus is timetabled at 13:59, with the other four daily

Table 5.21   Increase to €4.65/L: expenditure summary for Household 3 in Kirchdorf

Type of expenditure		Mobility scenario individual costs		
		€1.55/L	€4.65/L	€4.65/L (incl. PuT)
Living costs per month	Net rent	0	0	0
	Additional living costs	361	361	361
	Total	361	361	361
Mobility costs per month	Car ownership	350	350	0
	Car use	130	289	8
	Public transport	0	0	65
	Commuting allowance savings	0	0	0
	Total	480	639	73
Travel time (minutes/month)		671	671	734

journeys either too early in the morning or too late in the evening. The two suitable return journeys are scheduled for 17:01 and 18:05.

The wife also decides to take the bus to her friend's place. With the bus from Kirchdorf a.d. Amper, Rathaus to Wolfersdorf, Siedlung running only at 5:56 and 8:28, the wife must plan her trips rather precisely. The only later option is an on-demand call-a-bus service, while the return journey back to Kirchdorf runs only once, namely at 17:11.

To still be able to go to matches at the Allianz Arena, the husband travels with a friend who owns a car, as the journey by public transport to and from Kirchdorf would be too cumbersome. Owing to the husband being dependent on another person, and match trips having to be coordinated, he does not succeed too often in being able to attend (only once every six weeks).

Now that the couple use public transportation more often, both purchase a year ticket for the outer zone of the public transport tariff area, costing them €65 per month (see Table 5.21). Table 5.21 and Table 5.22 provide an expenditure and budget overview concerning the discussed changes in mobility patterns for Household 3.

Table 5.22　Increase to €4.65/L: budget summary for Household 3 in Kirchdorf

Income and expenditure	Mobility scenario total costs		
	€1.55/L	€4.65/L	€4.65/L (incl. PuT)
Net income (€)	1600	1600	1600
Mobility and living costs (€)	841	1000	434
Ratio	53%	63%	27%
Discretionary income (€)	759	600	1166

5.6　CONCLUSION AND OUTLOOK

This chapter investigates the effects of two different oil shock scenarios on the mobility of three representative households in Munich, Germany. These two scenarios are a fuel price based on an oil price of US$200 a barrel (€2.11/L) and a tripling of fuel prices (€4.65/L).

The results show that a fuel price based on US$200 per barrel has a limited effect on household activities as well as on short-term mobility behaviours. The shock tripling of the price at the fuel station, however, greatly impacts upon household budgets.

In the case of Household 1 and a tripling of oil prices, an extra €429/month in fuel costs would need to be allocated to the mobility budget to maintain the same level of mobility. To offset these costs, the family are forced to travel an additional 50 hours per month by public transport. Clearly, the consequences of such a shock to a household's mobility are severe. For the most vulnerable households – often characterized by lower-class to middle-class demographics, and located in the outer suburban areas with poor public transport access – attempting to overcome such mobility price shocks by switching from private car to public transport may not be an option.

Nevertheless, potential alternatives such as using public transportation, carpooling or changing activities or residential locations can relieve the cost shock imposed on household budgets. Despite increasing fuel prices, households can become less vulnerable to mobility price shocks by employing a number of different strategies:

- Activities like working and shopping can be combined efficiently, while unnecessary trips may be avoided. This is not always possible, as some activity locations cannot be changed so easily. In any case, trip chains can offer an enormous potential in time as well as money savings.

- Choosing a different mode of transportation, when available, can save money and reduce a household's vulnerability to mobility price shocks. This requires attractive public transport services that are easily accessible. It is also possible to bring about a shift towards non-motorized modes by implementing a dense mixed-use settlement structure.
- Commuting by private vehicle can be made more sustainable through sharing rides with other people. Carpooling is an effective strategy to save on the costs of driving alone and can offer faster travel times compared with public transport.
- Park-and-ride (P+R) is another alternative, which combines the advantages of two modes. It offers flexibility and comfort in sparsely populated regions without public transport services. At the same time, congestion and time losses in busy urban centres can be avoided.
- In some instances, teleworking might be another possibility to save on mobility costs.

In most cases, vulnerable households are only able to change their mobility behaviours if they are offered more viable transport alternatives. Recommendations to public stakeholders and decision-makers have to be based on detailed regional analyses, which take into account the future development of residential and mobility costs. To foster more sustainable spatial developments, policies and intervention strategies – which concern dense mixed-use development patterns alongside the (non-motorized) accessibility of jobs and daily activities – need to be discussed among researchers as well as planning practitioners and decision-makers in workshops held in the affected municipalities.

REFERENCES

Bulwiengesa (2014), *Marktstudie 'Neubau-ETW-Projekte in der Innenstadt und innenstadtnahen Stadtteilen in München 2014*, Munich.
Büttner, B., Franz, S., Reutter, U. and G. Wulfhorst (2012), 'MOR€CO – Mobility and Residential Costs: improving the settlement development in the transnational Alpine space region', Paper presented at REAL CORP – International Conference on Urban Planning and Regional Development in the Information Society, Vienna.
Büttner, B., Keller, J. and G. Wulfhorst (2011), *Erreichbarkeitsatlas – Grundlagen für die Zukunft der Mobilität in der Metropolregion München*, Munich: Europäische Metropolregion München e.V.
Büttner, B. and G. Wulfhorst (2012), 'MOR€CO. Untersuchung der künftigen

Wohn- und Mobilitätskosten für private Haushalte in der Region München', Munich.

Büttner, B., Wulfhorst, G., Crozet, Y. and A. Mercier (2013), 'The impact of sharp increases in mobility costs analysed by means of the Vulnerability Assessment, WCTR', Paper presented at the World Conference on Transport Research (WCTR), Rio de Janeiro.

Geurs, K.T., Krizek, K.J. and A. Reggiani (2012), *Accessibility Analysis and Transport Planning: Challenges for Europe and North America*, NECTAR Series on Transportation and Communications Networks Research, Cheltenham, UK and Northampton, MA, USA: Edward Elgar Publishing.

Haller, M., Fink, B., Albrecht, M. and J.M. Gutsche (2012), 'Billiger wohnen im Umland? Mobilitätskosten von Wohnorten. MVV-WoMo – Der Wohn- und Mobilitätsrechner des MVV'. *Nahverkehr*, **1–2**, 46–50.

Hull, A., Silva, C. and L. Bertolini (eds) (2012), *Accessibility Instruments for Planning Practice*, Brussels: COST Office.

Institut für Mobilitätsforschung (ed.) (2010), *Zukunft der Mobilität. Szenarien für das Jahr 2030*, 1st edn, Berlin: Ifmo.

Kahn Ribeiro, S., Kobayashi, S., Beuthe, M., Gasca, J., Greene, D., Lee, D.S., Muromachi, Y., Newton, P.J., Plotkin, S., Sperling, D., Wit, R. and P.J. Zhou (2007), 'Transport and its infrastructure', in B. Metz, O.R. Davidson, P.R. Bosch, R. Dave and L.A. Meyer (eds), *Climate Change 2007: Mitigation. Contribution of Working Group III to the Fourth Assessment Report of the Intergovernmental Panel on Climate Change*, Cambridge, UK and New York, USA: Cambridge University Press.

Kasperson, J.X., Kasperson, R.E., Turner, B.L., Hsieh, W. and A. Schiller (2006), 'Vulnerability to global environmental change', in E. Rosa, A. Diekmann, T. Dietz and C. Jaeger (eds), *The Human Dimension of Global Environmental Change*, Cambridge, MA: MIT Press.

Kelly, P.M. and W.N. Adger (2000), 'Theory and practice in assessing vulnerability to climate change and faciliting adaptation', *Climatic Change*, **47**, 325–352.

Landeshauptstadt München, Referat für Stadtplanung und Bauordnung (eds) (2010), *Mobilität in Deutschland (MiD)*, Alltagsverkehr in München, im Münchner Umland und im MVV-Verbundraum, Munich.

Landeshauptstadt München, Referat für Stadtplanung und Bauordnung (eds) (2012), *Wanderungsmotivuntersuchung II. 2011*, Unter Mitarbeit von Alexander Lang und Hubert Müller, Munich.

Lohr, B. (2013), 'Teure Flucht ins Umland. Viele Menschen unterschätzen die Kosten der Mobilität, die ein Umzug mit sich bringt', *Süddeutsche Zeitung*, **112**, 57.

Wegener, M. (2009), 'Energie, Raum und Verkehr. Auswirkungen hoher Energiepreise auf Stadtentwicklung und Mobilität', *Wissenschaft & Umwelt INTERDISZIPLINÄR*, **12**, 67–75.

6. Efficiency and equity indicators to evaluate different patterns of accessibility to public services: an application to Huambo, Angola

César Pakissi and Tomaz Ponce Dentinho

6.1 INTRODUCTION

The spatial allocation of public services – provided by the state, by non-governmental organizations (NGOs) or by the private sector – is an important issue, very much related to a broad concept of accessibility that involves economic growth, access to work, education and healthcare, and guarantees of sustainability and local planning (Kilby and Smith 2012). The allocation of public services is justified not only by the tension between territorial cohesion and efficient use of public funds, but also by the long-term implications for migration patterns and cumulative effects on urban growth and hierarchies generated by the spatial allocation of public services. This is more so in developing countries in which rural areas are very much characterized by subsistence economies, sometimes dependent on funds transferred from central governments that control the rents of territorial natural resources. The urban hierarchy of the allocation of public services and the related design of infrastructural networks also exert a strong pressure on migration and urbanization, generating slums in major urban areas and desertification in detached rural zones. Although the importance of investment in urban areas in developing countries is recognized, the concentration of public spending in urban areas reinforces migration into those areas, creating spatial disequilibrium; this is because, as stressed by Paul Krugman (1995), the growth of some African cities is promoted by the allocation of public spending which generates cumulative processes of public spending, migration, urban slums and more public spending. In Africa more than 70 per cent of the urban population lives in urban slums, with all the environmental, social and economic structural and cumulative problems that these represent (Baker 2008). According to the 'World Population Prospects' (United Nations 2013) the urban population in Africa will grow from 412 million in 2010 to 566 million in 2020, whereas the rural population will grow from 620 million in 2010 to 704 million in 2020. However, this is not inevitable since, according to Debora Potts (2012), urbanization in Africa is not a uniform process: circular migration trends can be traced in Zimbabwe associated with the spatial evolution of institutional transformations; in Zambia there are instances of counter-urbanization; and Africans often move directly from rural areas to overseas destinations.

People follow more rewarding formal jobs and security wherever those jobs and security are to be found. In which case, it is worthwhile to think about the spatial allocation of public resources based on efficiency, sustainability and equity principles. That was attempted in the spatial allocation of public spending implicit in the Master Plan of Huambo (2012), which highlighted a few questions on the interactions between equity and efficiency that we would like to address in this chapter.

The Huambo Province, also known as the Central Highlands, is located in the Midwestern region of Angola with a land area of 35 771 km², representing 2.6 per cent of the total area of the country. The Municipality of Huambo is one of 11 municipalities of Huambo Province and covers an area of 2720 km², composed of the commune headquarters (551.5 km²) and the communes of Chipipa in the North (813.8 km²) and Calima in the South (1354.6 km²). The city of Huambo corresponds to approximately 7 per cent of the area of Huambo Province but the population represents about 40 per cent of the total population of the province. According to the Master Plan of Huambo (2012) there is a considerable difference between the population densities in rural areas, ranging from 12.5 inhabitants (hab)/km² and 200 hab/km², and the densities in urban areas, which reach 25 000 hab/km² (Figure 6.1).

Without interference the urban population of the provincial capital will grow from 1.2 million in 2010 to 1.5 million in 2020 and the rural population will reduce from 1.2 million to 1.0 million (Master Plan of Huambo 2012). Nevertheless, the Master Plan analysis is that, with adequate public investment and induced private investment in a suitable hierarchical network of secondary and tertiary urban centres, the provincial capital could have a population of 1.4 million in 2020 and the rural areas 1.2 million; allowing the structuration of the slum area in the city and the improvement in the provision of health, education and urban services in the rural areas. This is possible to implement in African countries such as Angola where the main driver of the economy is associated with royalties on oil and mineral exports and related public spending; but the issue is where the money goes: to the capitals, or also to the provinces? To the

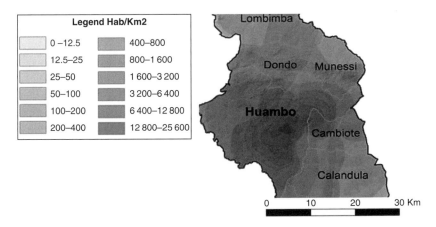

Figure 6.1   Population density in Huambo area

main cities of the provinces, or also to the rural areas? The need is there in terms of accessibility to markets, health and education. But what urban hierarchical network will arise, associated with each perspective of spatial equity? Plans to create new towns and secondary and tertiary urban centres (hereafter, 'centralities') in Europe in the 1950s and 1960s were not very successful (*The Economist* 2013). Will the new secondary and tertiary urban centres of the emerging world fail to provide public services to more remote places, and avoid the rise of urban slums in central areas?

If, in the short and medium term, spatial equity issues are at stake (as is common with the distribution of public services), and, in the long run, new centralities should follow the pattern of old and small ones, then we can use the present spatial distribution of the population centres to assess not only the efficiency implicit in the minimization of the allocation costs for each distance threshold but also the equity associated with the accessibility internal to those thresholds. The aim is to contribute to improve the allocation of public services where their short-term and long-term impacts matter a lot. The context of Africa is interesting not only because this reflection can provide some guidance in terms of effective policy advice, in this case associated with the Master Plan of Huambo, but also because most of the formal economy in remote African areas is, for now, associated with the deployment of public services financed by the royalties linked to oil and minerals extraction.

The chapter proceeds as follows. In section 6.2, we justify the selection of the optimization method of spatial allocation of public services and propose a Gini Index for the patterns of accessibility. In section 6.3, we estimate the location of services for minimum threshold differences for the different levels of public service following a predefined Christaller (1966 [1933]), hierarchical rule and use the proposed Gini index for the patterns of accessibility to assess the equity effects of the optimizing exercise. Finally, in section 6.4, we suggest some conclusions and recommendations to support the design of service allocation policies in developing countries.

6.2 METHODS TO LOCATE SERVICES AND ESTIMATE THEIR EFFECTS ON SPATIAL EQUITY

6.2.1 Location of Services

A large and evolving literature has been developed to address location problems (Stevens 1968; Toregas and ReVelle 1972; Banerji and Fisher 1974; Church and ReVelle 1974; ReVelle and Church 1977; Schuler and Holahan 1977; Thomas 1984; Gerrad and Church 1994; Serra 1996; Owen and Daskin 1998), showing that location issues continue to be one of the pillars of regional science (Isard 1949). Urbanists, geographers, engineers, economists and politicians, all of them have theories and tools for how to allocate services throughout space (Daoqin 2012). Revelle et al. (2008) systematized the various approaches into four main groups: (1) analytical models that, based on uniform density, fix the cost of a service and a cost per distance, and estimate the number of services for different types of spatial metrics; (2) continuous models, like the Weber model that identifies each location with coordinates (x, y) and minimizes the distances weighted by the transport demand of the various origins and destinations; (3) network models that view location as like the design of a tree, composed on optimal nodes; (4) and discrete location models, usually formulated as integer programming problems and divided into weighted demand models, like that of ReVelle and Swain (1970), that assume bigger places deserve more service than smaller ones; and centre and covering problems, that aim to maximize the lowest service standard to any member of the population, like that initially proposed by Toregas et al. (1971). More recent works combine different measures of accessibility to optimize the location of public services (Wang 2012), combine a a global coverage of the area with other objectives for rural areas (Chanta et al. 2014). In this exercise we used distance by road, but Euclidean distances would have been a good proxy; nevertheless we did not have data for time distances that, according to Ho et al. (2014), are not strongly correlated with distances by road, although Phibbs and Luft (2012) find that they are good proxies between each other mainly for longer distances.

Since the preliminary issue is to cover all the villages in the region of Huambo the model adopted follows the Toregas approach. The objective function (6.1) minimizes the number of locations (y_i). Constraints ensure that all nodes can reach any service location below a maximum distance allowed for service (d_{max}). Coefficients (a_{ij}) are equal to 0 if the distance (i,j) is higher than the threshold (d_{max}) and 1 if the distance (i,j) is lower than that limit (6.3):

$$Min \, \Sigma_i \, y_i \tag{6.1}$$

$$\Sigma_i \, a_{ij} y_i \geq 1 \text{ for all } (j) \tag{6.2}$$

$$a_{ij} = 1 \text{ if distance } (i,j) \leq d_{max} \text{ for all } (i,j) \tag{6.3}$$

The exercise allows the determination of the number of service points $(k = \Sigma_i \, y_i)$ for each threshold (d_{max}).

6.2.2   Gini Index for Accessibility Patterns

There are many indicators of accessibility and connectivity (Ribeiro 2009) that have been applied in many theoretical and practical works that compare the degree of accessibility of different regions. Nevertheless, there are not so many applications of equity indexes that compare different spatial structures and patterns; some interesting approaches have been introduced in the work of Talen and Anselin (1998) regarding the access of public playgrounds, and more recently applied to other sorts of services: transit equity (Welch and Mishra 2013), healthcare equity (Khilji et al. 2013) and environmental equity (Wu and Xu 2010).

The Gini index for accessibility patterns proposed in this chapter starts from a Lorenz-type curve (L) (Figure 6.2) that relates the percentage of the population with access to the k points of service (P_n) with the quotient between the real distance of the service provided to the maximum distance of service D_n/D_{max}:

$$D_n/D_{max} = L(P_k) \tag{6.4}$$

The interpretation of the example is as follows. There is 50 per cent of the population below 10 per cent of the maximum distance allowed for the service provided; and there is 70 per cent of the population below 30 per cent of that maximum.

The Gini index for accessibility patterns (G_{ap}) can then be derived as:

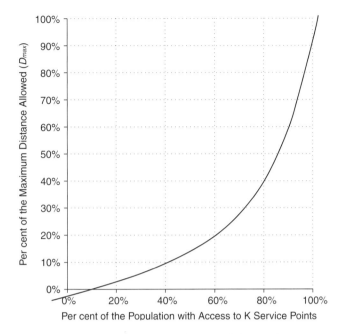

Figure 6.2 *Lorenz curve for patterns of accessibility to N service points for maximum distances of* D_{max}

$$G_{ap} = 1 - [\Sigma_n (D_n/D_{max} + D_{n-1}/D_{max}){\cdot}(P_n - P_{n-1})/2] \qquad (6.5)$$

$G_{ap} = 1$ when there is an equal distance access to services for the whole population; $G_{ap} = 0$ when all the population is located in the border of the service area.

6.3 OPTIMIZING THE LOCATION OF SERVICES IN HUAMBO FOR ADJUSTED DISTANCES

Huambo is one of the major cities in Angola (Figure 6.3), 600 km south-east of Luanda and 300 km from the sea. It has a city centre with urban infrastructures that represents only 10 per cent of the total urban area, which has been steadily increasing in size since the end of the Angolan Civil War in 2002. This slum area is very poorly equipped with public services and that lack of infrastructure and equipment is worse in the neighbouring and far-away villages. The challenge is the structuration of the slum area in the city, and the improvement in the provision of health,

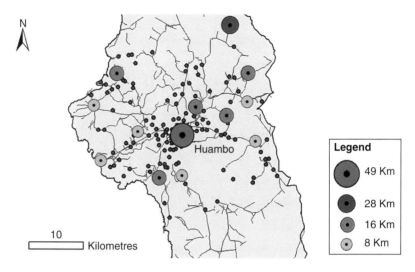

*Figure 6.3   Huambo area with location of population centres and
            hierarchical service centres*

education and urban services in the rural areas. The rationale is to optimize
the location of those services using the model proposed in equations (6.1),
(6.2) and (6.3) for different distance thresholds.

Distances by road were obtained with GIS maps where all villages and
roads were mapped and located. One hundred villages and neighbourhoods to be served were considered by different levels of public services.
The model is first run for the minimum distance (0.4 km), resulting in 100
service locations. Then it is possible to obtain a hierarchy of service centres
for different distance thresholds. And, as proposed in the Christaller
theory, a bottom-up approach was taken for each exercise, meaning that
centres that were not selected for one hierarchical level could not be
selected for any of the upper levels.

As expected, the number of service centres increased as the distance
threshold decreased (Figure 6.4). Nevertheless the hierarchy of centres only
follows the Christaller rules ($K = 3$, $K = 4$ or $K = 7$) – that relate distance
between centres of equal hierarchy with the distance between the different
levels of the urban hierarchical network ($D_n = D_{n-1} \sqrt{k}$) – for lower numbers
of service centres. This can be associated with more homogeneous urban
networks of rural and suburban spatial structures more appropriate to the
African context.

As proposed in section 6.2 it is now possible to estimate the Gini
index for accessibility for each spatial structure of service allocation,

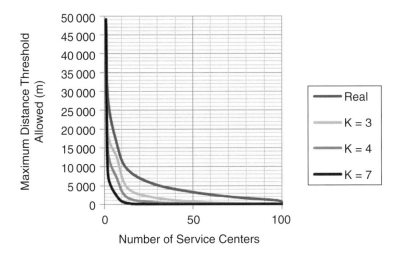

*Figure 6.4   Relation between the number of service centres and maximum
threshold allowed*

characterized by the distance threshold (D_{max}) and the number of centres
(K) that is associated with the minimized cost for the distance threshold.

Figure 6.4 shows the Lorenz curves of each spatial structure of service
allocation and the respective Gini index for accessibility. With a radius of
0.35 km all 100 centres have a service and obviously 100 per cent of the
centres are close to the maximum distance of 0.35 km; and the Gini index
of accessibility is 0. When the threshold is 1.0 km there are 97 centres that
serve themselves and three that are served by others; in this case the Gini
index of accessibility is 0.71. For a maximum radius of 1.8 km the number
of dependent centres is 24 and the Gini index of accessibility is 0.63. The
Gini indexes of accessibility are obtained for thresholds of 3.2 km (G_{ap} =
0.55), 5.5 km (G_{ap} = 0.56) and 9.4 km (G_{ap} = 0.54) that have, respectively,
48, 72 and 87 dependent centres. The Gini indexes of accessibility become
worst for higher-threshold radiuses (16.3 km, 28.3 km, 49.1 km) when just
a few centres are selected (7, 2 and 1). It interesting to notice that although
the Gini index of accessibility refers to the spatial equity of each distribution it does not reveal the profile of the Lorenz curve, which can enrich the
analysis even more. Looking at the best Gini indexes of accessibility, in the
second row of the graphs of Figure 6.5, it is clear that for 13 centres not
only is the Gini index of accessibility slightly better (G_{ap} = 0.54), but also
the slope of the Lorenz curve is more stable, indicating a more homogeneous distribution of centres within each service area.

To complete the exercise we can compare the equity and cost-efficiency

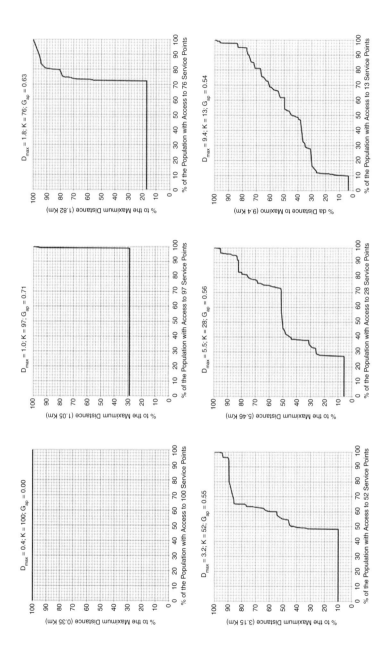

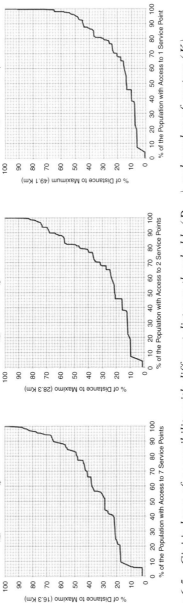

Figure 6.5   Gini indexes of accessibility with different distance thresholds (D_{max}) *and number of centres* (K)

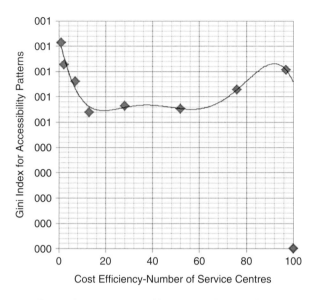

Figure 6.6   Relation between cost-efficiency and spatial equity

indicators, measured by the number of service centres optimized by expressions (6.1), (6.2) and (6.3), for each one of the spatial distribution of services (Figure 6.6). The results shown from this perspective seem to be quite interesting. First, there is not a monotonous trade-off between equity and cost-efficiency for that particular territorial distribution of the population and, we might induce, for many other territorial distributions. Second, if the scenario that serves all the communities is excluded – the one that has 100 service centres and a Gini index of accessibility equal to zero – then the solution with 13 service centres is better not only in terms of cost-efficiency, assessed by the number of service centres associated with each distance threshold, but also in terms of equity, evaluated by the Gini index, being easily recognizable as a dominant solution for these alternatives. Third, the sudden breaks in the trade-offs between cost-efficiency and equity indicators can signal implicit spatial borders of public service, assuming that the equity criteria is very much an implicit condition in a public good.

6.4   CONCLUSIONS

The aim of this chapter was to introduce some reflections on the allocation of public services in Africa. The approach was to compare cost-efficiency and equity indicators in the spatial allocation of public services in the surroundings of Huambo. For that we used an integer linear programming optimization method that minimizes the cost of service centres subject to a distance threshold constraint. We also proposed a Gini index of accessibility to evaluate the spatial equity.

The results seem to be quite interesting, not only because they show the possibility to have consistent efficiency and equity spatial indicators but also because it was possible to identify non-monotonous trade-offs between cost-efficiency of the spatial allocation of public services and spatial equity. The potential of the exercise resides in the opportunity to identify local dominant points between equity and cost-efficiency and a prospective exploitation on the borders of the provision of public goods.

The debate between efficiency and equity, on the one hand, and the multiple indicators of equity, on the other, are not finished. The issues are that, as we try to demonstrate in this chapter, the gap between theoretical, operational and political approaches is becoming thinner. Nevertheless by doing this we highlight the importance of often undiscussed assumptions of theoretical and operational models, and reveal some simplistic mistakes made by planners and politicians. As Wang (2012) questioned: what type of accessibility measures should be used to optimize location? Or, as suggested by Chanta et al. (2014): what are the interconnections between different types of equities? Finally, should border regions have a say in all spatial allocation solutions, since there are border or central situations that can be very sensitive to changes in the threshold distances for services?

ACKNOWLEDGMENTS

Patrícia Leite, Patrícia Goulão, Paulo Silveira and Ana Fuentes helped with the mapping of the villages and neighbourhoods of Huambo.

REFERENCES

Baker, J. (2008), 'Impacts of financial, food and fuel crisis on urban poor', Directions in Urban Development series, December, Washington, DC: Urban Development Unit, World Bank.

Banerji, S. and B. Fisher (1974), 'Hierarchical location analysis for integrated area planning in rural areas', *Papers in Regional Science*, **33** (1), 177–194.

Chanta, S., Mayorga, M.E. and L.A. McLay (2014), 'Improving emergency service in rural areas: A bi-objective covering location model for EMS systems', *Annals of Operational Research*, **221** (1), 133–159.

Christaller, W. (1966 [1933]), *Central Places in Southern Germany*, transl. C.W. Baskin, Englewood Cliffs, NJ: Prentice-Hall.

Church, R. and C. ReVelle (1974), 'The maximal covering location problem', *Papers in Regional Science*, **32**, 101–118.

Daoqin, T. (2012), 'Regional coverage maximization: A new model to account implicitly for complementary coverage', *Geographical Analysis*, **44** (1), 1–14.

The Economist (2013), 'Paradise Lost. Britain's new towns illustrate the value of cheap land and good infrastructure', 3 August.

Gerrad, R.A. and R.L. Church (1994), 'A generalized approach to modelling the hierarchical maximal covering location problem with referral', *Papers in Regional Science*, **73** (4), 425–453.

Isard, W. (1949), 'The general theory of location and space-economy, the Quarterly Owen SH Daskin MS (1998) – Strategic facility location: A review', *Journal of Economics*, **63** (4), 476–506.

Khilji, S.U.S., Rudge, J.W., Drake, T., et al. (2013), 'Distribution of selected healthcare resources for influenza pandemic response in Cambodia', *International Journal for Equity in Health*, **12** (82), http://www.equityhealthj.com/content/12/1/82.

Kilby, K. and N. Smith (2012), 'Accessibility planning policy: Evaluation and future direction', Centre for Research in Social Policy, Epsom: Atkins.

Krugman, P. (1995), 'Urban concentration: The role of increasing returns and transport costs', *Proceedings of the World Bank Annual Conference on Development Economics 1994*, International Bank for Reconstruction and Development / World Bank.

Master Plan of Huambo (2012), *Plano Director do Município do Huambo*, Vol. 1, Mimeo, Huambo: Governo Provincial do Huambo (GPH-Huambo).

Owen, S.H. and M.S. Daskin (1998), 'Strategic facility: A review', *Journal of Economics*, **63** (4), 476–506.

Phibbs, C.S. and H.S. Luft (2012), 'Correlation of travel time on roads versus straight line distance', *Medical Care Research and Review*, **52** (4), 532–542.

Potts, D. (2012), *Whatever Happened to Africa's Rapid Urbanisation?*, London: Edward Paice Africa Research Institute.

ReVelle, C.S. and R. Church (1977), 'A spatial model for the location construct Teitz', *Papers in Regional Science*, **39** (1), 129–135.

ReVelle, C.S., Eiselt, H.A. and M.S. Daskin (2008), 'A bibliography for some fundamental problem categories in discrete location science', *European Journal of Operational Research*, **184**, 817–848.

ReVelle, C.S. and R. Swain (1970), 'Central facilities location', *Geographical Analysis*, **2**, 30–42.

Ribeiro, A. (2009), 'Indicadores de Acessibilidade', in J. Costa, T. Dentinho and P. Nijkamp (eds), *Compêndio de Economia Regional II*, Lisboa: APDR Principia.

Schuler, R.E. and W.L. Holahan (1977), 'The maximum covering location problem revisited', *Papers in Regional Science*, **39** (1), 137–156.

Serra, D. (1996), 'The coherent covering location problem', *Papers in Regional Science*, **75** (1), 79–101.

Stevens, B. (1968), 'Location theory and programming models: The Von Tünen case', **21** (1), 19–34.

Talen, E. and L. Anselin (1998), 'Assessing spatial equity: An evaluation of measures of accessibility to public playgrounds', *Environment and Planning A*, **30** (4), 595–613.

Thomas, I. (1984), 'Towards the simplification of location models for public facilities: The case of the postal service', *Papers in Regional Science*, **55** (1), 47–58.

Toregas, C. and C. Revelle (1972), 'Optimal location under time or distance constraints', *Papers in Regional Science*, **28** (1), 133–144.

Toregas, C., Swain, R., ReVelle, C. and L. Bergman (1971), 'The location of emergency service facilities', *Operations Research*, **19**, 1363–1373.

United Nations (2013), 'World Population Prospects: The 2012 revision, highlights and advance tables', Working Paper No. ESA/P/WP.228, Department of Economic and Social Affairs, Population Division.

Wang, F.H. (2012), 'Measurement, optimization, and impact of health care accessibility: A methodological review', *Annals of the Association of American Geographers*, **102** (5), 1104–1112.

Welch, T.F. and S. Mishra (2013), 'A measure of equity for public transit connectivity', *Journal of Transport Geography*, **33**, 29–41.

Wu, C. and Z. Xu (2010), 'Spatial distribution of the environmental resource consumption in the Heihe River Basin of Northwestern China', *Regional Environmental Change*, **10** (1), 55–63.

PART IV

Efficiency of railroads and train station access

7. Influence of the first and last mile on HSR accessibility levels

Andrés Monzón, Emilio Ortega and Elena López

7.1 INTRODUCTION

Good connectivity to the high-speed rail (HSR) network is a crucial added value in urban agglomerations (Garmendia et al. 2011; Guirao and Campa 2014; Ureña et al. 2009). This applies not only to locations with an HSR station, but also to nearby locations with good access to the HSR network. Extensive research has examined the changes in spatial organization that occur in areas near HSR stations and their surroundings as the land use system seeks to take advantage of the enhanced connectivity to the network (Monzón et al. 2013b; Ureña et al. 2009).

In other words, good access to the network is a critical factor in obtaining the benefit of HSR services (Brons et al. 2009; Givoni 2006). The connection of the HSR station with local transit is a key factor for attracting new riders (Brons et al. 2009), as it guarantees households accessibility and constitutes the last link in a viable and integrated transportation chain.

Accessibility changes resulting from the provision of a new HSR service are mostly measured with formulations based on the reduction in travel time between origin–destination pairs, that is, the travel time savings between HSR stations. These savings have traditionally been included as one of the benefit categories of assessment methodologies, such as cost–benefit analysis (CBA) (Banister and Berechman 2003). Accessibility gains derived from the opening of a new HSR corridor are therefore calculated as justification for the project's funding (Bröcker et al. 2010; López and Monzón 2010; Monzón et al. 2013b).

So far, accessibility research has paid little attention to the quality of both access to the HSR station at the origin of the trip (first mile trip) and from the HSR destination station to the final destination (last mile trip). However, the decision to use an HSR service or a competing mode does not depend solely on travel time between HSR stations. Indeed, some authors have stated (Brons et al. 2009; Givoni and Banister 2012) that the global integrated transportation chain – the door-to-door trip – should be given greater relevance in the study of HSR services.

The importance of the connectivity to the HSR network thus takes on heightened importance (Reggiani 2012), as the demand for HSR services can be assumed to be higher if HSR stations are situated in central locations that are well connected to rail and other transit systems. In HSR, 'most of the travel time (and effort) is spent on getting to and from the HST station, and this constitutes the bulk of the journey travel time' (Givoni and Banister 2012, p. 306). Indeed, the issue of first/last mile trips is one of the current challenges in the provision of HSR services (Johnson 2012; Lane 2012).

This chapter addresses these research gaps by means of an approach that evaluates the importance of first/last mile trips in the calculation of accessibility improvements of HSR extensions. Spatial analysis techniques embedded in a geographical information system (GIS) are used for the accessibility calculations. This chapter is structured as follows. Section 7.2 includes a brief background on the accessibility formulations used in HSR settings. Next, section 7.3 describes the proposed methodology. Section 7.4 includes the application of the methodology to a case study in Spain. Section 7.5 contains the analysis of the corresponding results. Section 7.6 concludes the chapter with a discussion.

7.2   STATE OF THE RESEARCH ON HSR ACCESSIBILITY

7.2.1   The Importance of Connectivity to HSR Networks

What is the best transportation solution for connections to and from HSR stations? Several factors are involved in this decision, including the geographical location of the station, the land use characteristics, and the features of the transportation network in the area under consideration. It has been suggested that new HSR stations should be placed in central, densely populated, highly accessible locations (Brons et al. 2009; Guirao and Campa 2014; Ureña et al. 2009). However, in already developed metropolitan areas, land availability and building restraints make it difficult to establish new HSR stations in central business districts. Indeed, the type of access provided by HSR may pose difficulties in automobile-oriented cities affected by sprawl, which as Lane (2012) warns may be the case in many United States (US) cities.

The impact of improved access to the HSR network is not limited to locations in the immediate vicinity of HSR stations. Travel patterns in cities outside HSR corridors may also change in response to a new HSR service (Garmendia et al. 2012; Garmendia et al. 2011; López et al. 2008; Ureña et al. 2009). For these cities, the nearest HSR station may function as an interchange node to connect to the HSR network, so they too may gain accessibility benefits, whereas cities with their own HSR stations may be transformed into new regional core locations (Monzón et al. 2013a).

Decisions on how best to interconnect HSR stations and local networks have often been made without considering strategic transport planning objectives. The lack of appropriate ranking tools to prioritize new HSR corridors represents an unresolved challenge for research (Barrón et al. 2012; Button 2012; Guirao and Campa 2014). These tools are increasingly needed as key instruments for transport planners and policy-makers, given the high costs of constructing new HSR corridors. Concerns about financing new HSR infrastructure have assumed greater importance given the budgetary constraints faced by governments in the climate of the current global crisis. In addition, the recent interest of the US administration in developing HSR corridors has fuelled the scientific debate surrounding their economic justification (Button 2012; Johnson 2012; Lane 2012).

It has been claimed that frequent network interconnections are the result of somewhat incoherent and complex decision-making (DM) processes (Adamos et al. 2012), involving multiple stakeholders and parties at all the different planning levels. Recent interesting advances have been made in developing integrated DM processes for the efficient interconnection of long-distance and short-distance networks. These frameworks must identify the whole range of actors involved in these processes, which may include European Union (EU) legislative actors, national governments, regional and local authorities, and companies, as well as the end users (see the proposal by Adamos et al. 2012).

7.2.2 HSR Accessibility Analyses

Most HSR trips are one part of a multimodal chain, which combines the use of local and long-distance networks. The HSR station therefore acts as an intermediate – that is, transfer – node, which is not highly attractive in itself, that is, as a final destination where a certain utility is obtained. The importance of the accessibility via the local network to the nearest HSR station lies in its key role as a provider of connectivity to the long-distance network (Givoni and Banister 2012; Reggiani 2012; Tapiador et al. 2009).

The accessibility impacts of HSR extensions have been widely researched within a European context, mostly since the early 1990s (Bröcker et al. 2010; Givoni 2006; Gutiérrez et al. 1996; Gutiérrez and Urbano 1996;

Martín et al. 2007). European transport policy documents from this period promote the development of HSR networks as part of the trans-European transport networks (TEN-Ts) (Bröcker et al. 2010; Gutiérrez and Urbano 1996), intended to foster growth, competitiveness and employment (Bröcker et al. 2010; Vickerman 1995).

The accessibility provided by HSR has been assessed from a wide variety of approaches. The calculation of accessibility indices tends to focus on the travel time between origin and destination HSR stations. Each accessibility formulation provides a complementary approach to the analysis of accessibility (Geurs and Ritsema van Eck 2001; Geurs and van Wee 2004; Reggiani 2012). Selecting the appropriate indicator for each particular case is a complex task. There is generally no single best ideal indicator, but some argue that the analysis is enriched if a set of indicators is computed and the results are analysed from an integrated perspective (Gutiérrez 2001; López et al. 2008; Ortega et al. 2012).

Recent methodological contributions in the accessibility field include procedures to derive synthetic accessibility formulations. This concerns the work by Martín et al. (2007) and Martín et al. (2004), who used principal component analysis (PCA) and data envelopment analysis (DEA) to calculate a synthetic index of global accessibility. Their methodology was tested by its application to three scenarios (1996, 2005 and 2015), calculating global HSR accessibility in major European cities. Other recent contributions use accessibility-based approaches to measure different impacts of HSR developments. Accessibility indicators have been successfully applied to assess the spatial and social equity impacts of HSR (Bröcker et al. 2010; López et al. 2008; Martínez Sanchez-Mateos and Givoni 2012; Ortega et al. 2012; van Wee and Geurs 2011). Spatial spillovers have also recently been measured with accessibility formulations (Gutiérrez et al. 2010; López and Monzón 2009). In addition, scale and zoning issues (related to the modifiable areal unit, MAUP) are gaining importance in the calculation of accessibility indicators (Monzón et al. 2013b; Ortega et al. 2012).

HSR accessibility studies have mostly been carried out in large study areas; accessibility derived from first mile and last mile trips is unevenly and scarcely researched. In other words, accessibility to the HSR network has received less attention than accessibility provided by the HSR network (Givoni and Banister 2012; Johnson 2012). One of the few examples of accessibility formulations dealing with connectivity to the network is the ICON index (MCRIT 1992), which has been used at different planning levels (L'Hostis et al. 2002; Mora and Moreno 2013). Other studies use transport provision measures as indicators of the quality of access to HSR stations. For example, Hagler and Todorovich (2009) – as reviewed by

Guirao and Campa (2014) – selected urban transit connections as one of five main categories of variables ranking the potential of new HSR corridors; the other four being population size, origin–destination distance, economic vitality and congestion. In their model – designed to rank new HSR corridors in the US – this variable is related to the existence of transit services such as commuter rail, heavy rail and light rail in each metropolitan area with an HSR station (Hagler and Todorovich 2009).

Finally, quantifying the contribution of first/last mile trips to HSR accessibility may go some way towards justifying investment in local networks to improve access to and from HSR stations. Recent research (Brons et al. 2009) has identified satisfaction with the level and quality of access to the HSR station as important factors in explaining rail use in the case of Dutch railways. This research applied PCA to customer satisfaction surveys and regression analysis techniques, and its results suggest that improving access to HSR stations may be more cost-efficient as a means of increasing rail use. This issue is related to the problem of interconnections between short-distance and long-distance transport networks (Bröcker et al. 2010; L'Hostis et al. 2002; López et al. 2008; Reggiani 2012).

7.3   METHODOLOGICAL APPROACH

The objective of this chapter is to evaluate to what extent the first/last mile of trips affects the accessibility improvements achieved by HSR extensions. This requires the accessibility values to be split into three parts to determine the contribution of: (1) access to the HSR station (first mile) prior to taking the train; (2) the train trip itself; and (3) the trip from the arrival station to the final destination (last mile). This is not simple, since all three parts are interconnected and comprise three different stages of the same trip. The whole procedure is supported by a GIS to improve the understanding of all the contributions and enable the geographical representation of the results.

7.3.1   Accessibility Calculations

There is a wide spectrum of formulations for measuring the concept of accessibility (see e.g., Reggiani 1998). An economic potential accessibility (PA) formulation (equation 7.1) was selected as the most suitable formulation because of its proven consistency and applicability in transport planning studies at strategic levels (Gutierrez et al. 2011; López et al. 2008; Martin et al. 2004; Ortega et al. 2012; Ortega et al. 2014a):

$$Potential\ Accessibility\ =\ PA_i\ =\ \sum_j \frac{P_j}{I_{ij}}, \qquad (7.1)$$

where PA_i is the accessibility of trips from each origin i to all j destinations. P_j represents the population at the destination j and I_{ij} the travel impedance (usually measured as travel time or generalized travel cost) between each origin–destination pair.

Given the large scale of HSR accessibility studies, travel time is usually considered the variable that measures the impedance between origin–destination pairs (López et al. 2008; Ortega et al. 2012, 2014a). Generalized travel cost calculations are more frequently used for smaller scales.

7.3.2   Evaluation of the Importance of First/Last Mile Trips

To evaluate the impact of the first/last mile on total accessibility, the generalized travel cost must be disaggregated into three parts of the trip. As Figure 7.1 shows, each trip can be divided into three stages: the connecting trip from the origin to the nearest HSR station (entry station), the trip on the HSR service, and the final trip from the arrival train station to the end destination. Both the first mile and last mile parts are calculated by using a minimum-path algorithm along the road network in the area. This calculation is a commonly accepted methodology across HSR accessibility studies (see e.g., López et al. 2008; Ortega et al. 2012, 2014a). Each link in the road network has some attributes in the GIS, including distances and average speed. The GIS system then determines the path of minimum time between Oi and SA_i, and SB_j and Dj, respectively.

Therefore, equation (7.1) can be formulated as follows, where total trip time is split into the three parts:

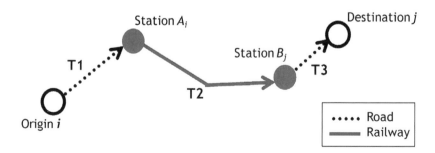

Figure 7.1   Travel stages including access, rail service and connection to destination

$$PA_i = \sum_j \frac{P_j}{I_{ij}} = \sum_j \frac{P_j}{T_{ij}} = \sum_j \frac{P_j}{(T1_i + T2_{i,j} + T3_{i,j})}, \qquad (7.2)$$

where $T1_i$ is the time from the origin i to its nearest HSR station SA_i. $T2_{i,j}$ is the rail travel time from station SA_i to station SB_j, corresponding to the $i - j$ relation. $T3_{i,j}$ is the travel time from HSR station SB_j to destination j.

It is important to note that $T1_i + T2_{i,j} + T3_{i,j}$ may be greater than the travel time from origin i to destination j by road, as occurs when the distance to the destination is rather short, or the connecting rail service requires a long waiting time. Cases in which the road alternative is faster than the HSR option are not considered in the calculation. The method only considers trips for which the use of HSR services is the quickest option for travelling from origin to destination.

As the objective of this study is to distinguish which part of the accessibility values corresponds to the rail service and which to the road connections, equation (7.2) is converted into equation (7.3), in which each part of the trip is considered independently in the PA_i value:

$$PA_i = \sum_j \frac{P_j}{(T1_i + T2_{i,j} + T3_{i,j})} = \sum_j \frac{P_j \cdot T1_i}{(T1_i + T2_{i,j} + T3_{i,j})^2}$$

$$+ \sum_j \frac{P_j \cdot T2_{i,j}}{(T1_i + T2_{i,j} + T3_{i,j})^2} + \sum_j \frac{P_j \cdot T3_{i,j}}{(T1_i + T2_{i,j} + T3_{i,j})^2} \qquad (7.3)$$

Here, $PA_{i,1} = \sum_j \frac{P_j \cdot T1_i}{(T1_i + T2_{i,j} + T3_{i,j})^2} \approx$ corresponds to the first mile, $PA_{i,2} = \sum_j \frac{P_j \cdot T2_{i,j}}{(T1_i + T2_{i,j} + T3_{i,j})^2} \approx$ corresponds to the rail trip, and $PA_{i,3} = \sum_j \frac{P_j \cdot T3_{i,j}}{(T1_i + T2_{i,j} + T3_{i,j})^2} \approx$ corresponds to the last mile.

Once these three results are known, their importance in the accessibility value can be calculated as percentage of the total accessibility value (PA_i). According to the formula, low PA_i values mean high accessibility, whereas high PA_i values correspond to municipalities with poor accessibility levels. The findings can be analysed from different perspectives; we can consider the results of the first mile, the last mile, and of the first plus last mile, which represents the contribution of the connecting road trips to the global accessibility value.

7.4   CASE STUDY: THE MADRID–LEVANTE HSR CORRIDOR

This section contains an example of the application of this methodology. The HSR infrastructure under consideration is the Madrid–Levante HSR corridor (Figure 7.2). This corridor started operating in December 2010. Demand increased from 703 000 passengers in 2010 to 1 836 000 in 2011. It has two branches with a total length of 770 km and a commercial speed of 220 km/h. The corridor is characterized by the short travel time of 1 hour 40 minutes for the service between Madrid and Valencia. It connects Madrid – the capital of Spain – with major cities on the Mediterranean coast such as Valencia and Alicante, and others such as Albacete, Requena and Cuenca. It attracts both business and holiday trips as it links two of Spain's main economic centres (Madrid and Valencia) and also because Valencia and Alicante are popular tourist and holiday destinations.

7.4.1   Population Distribution and Access to HSR Stations

The population distribution is not homogeneous along the corridor. The main urban agglomerations are at both ends, with Madrid in the centre of the country, Valencia and Alicante on the coast, and less densely populated

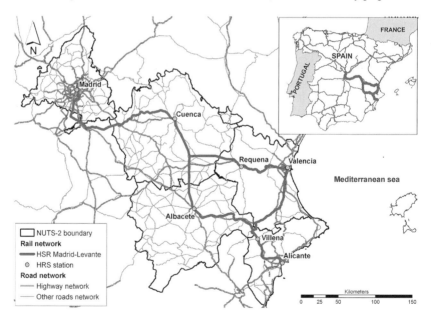

Figure 7.2   Madrid–Levante HSR corridor

Table 7.1 Population in the Madrid–Levante corridor

	Province (NUTS 3)	Main city
Madrid	6 414 709	3 200 000
Valencia	2 578 719	810 000
Alicante	1 945 642	335 000
Albacete	402 837	172 700
Cuenca	211 899	56 100

areas in between. There are numerous towns in the vicinity of Madrid, Valencia and Alicante. By contrast, the provinces of Cuenca and Albacete are much less populated. Table 7.1 shows the population values of the five provinces that are intersected by the corridor.

The corridor contains 907 municipalities, but only 15 per cent have more than 10 000 inhabitants, and 50 per cent have fewer than 1000. Figure 7.3 shows the population distribution in the corridor.

The HSR stations are distributed along the corridor, providing new options for long-distance trips. Figure 7.4 shows the isochrones[1] for access from each municipality to the nearest HSR station, by driving along the minimum time path in the road network. By comparing

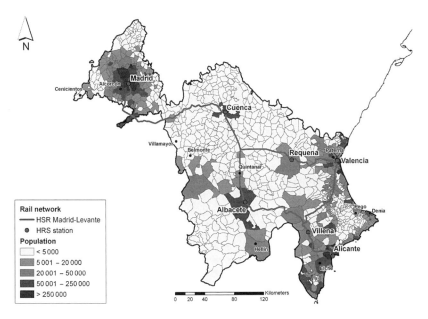

Figure 7.3 Population distribution in the Madrid–Levante corridor

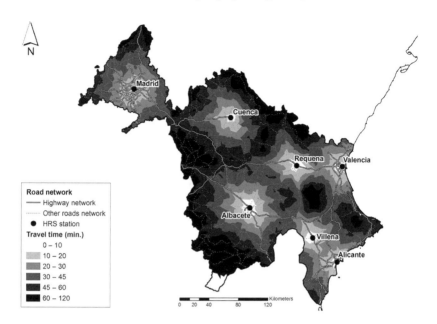

Figure 7.4   Road travel time to HSR stations

Figures 7.3 and 7.4, we can identify the stations that serve highly populated areas, and others with very few potential users in the vicinity.

7.4.2   Disaggregated Accessibility Calculations

Accessibility calculations firstly require selecting a particular zoning
system configuration, that is, the definition of how the study area will be
structured and modelled. In this case, as explained below, the scale or planning level corresponds to the corridor level as defined by NUTS 3[2] regions,
and the units of analysis correspond to the municipality level (NUTS 5).
The selection of this particular zoning configuration has implications on
the accessibility results, as they are affected by the MAUP (modifiable
areal unit problem) (Fotheringham and Wong 1991). It is beyond the scope
of this chapter to elaborate on these MAUP-related issues; empirical evidence and literature on the topic can be found in publications by Ortega
et al. (2012, 2014a).

In our case, once the corridor was clearly defined, the potential accessibility indicator was calculated for each of the 907 municipalities within the
study area. The study was focused on the municipality level, delimited by
the borders of the five NUTS 3 regions interconnected by the HSR project.

Figure 7.2 shows the HSR corridor and the location of the HSR stations. It also includes the main road networks in the study area.

The GIS database contained road and HSR networks, which were considered independently. The length and travel time were recorded for each arc (according to the typology), as in previous similar studies (López et al. 2008; Ortega et al. 2012, 2014a). The information on the location of the municipality centroids – which serve as the starting and destination points – and stations is also independent. The population values were included in the municipality GIS database.

The integration of the networks with population centres and stations occurred as follows. The municipality centroids are displaced to the nearest road, using a snapping GIS tool. The stations are also displaced to the nearest road. The railway lines subsequently need to be displaced to coincide with the stations. Finally, the road network, the conventional railway network and the HSR network are linked together to create the network nodes. The change in transport modes occurs at the railway stations. The GIS process calculation was explained in detail by Ortega et al. (2011).

In each case, travel time is equal to the sum of the travel times of the arcs of each itinerary, along the minimum time path, according to Dijkstra's algorithm (1959). The total travel time is calculated as the sum of three partial times: (1) time by road from the origin (municipality centroid) to the nearest station; (2) rail travel time; and (3) time from the final station to the destination. Displacement along the railway network is subject to a series of penalties caused by transfer from road to rail and the frequency of services. López (2007) gives a detailed description of the generalized travel time calculation.

The potential accessibility value (PA_i) of each municipality i was computed according to equation (7.3). Accessibility was calculated using two GIS network accessibility toolboxes: TITIM-GIS tool (Ortega et al. 2014b) and AccesstUls,[3] which operate in ArcInfo Workstation. Only alternatives in which the rail option is quicker than the road-only trip were considered. The mean value of destinations for which the rail option is quicker for each origin is 382. This means that 42 per cent of the 823 000 relations (trips) would be made by rail. The maximum value corresponds to the city of Cuenca, with 633 destinations, and the lowest value is only 2.

7.5   ANALYSIS OF RESULTS

The disaggregated methodology reveals the contribution of each of the three stages of the trip to the PA_i, and of the access and egress part of the trip to and from the HSR stations to the total PA_i values. The global

Table 7.2   Global potential accessibility values for the corridor

		PA-1 (access)	PA-2 (rail)	PA-3 (egress)	Total PA
PA (equation 7.3)	Accessibility values	8643	23934	3263	35840
	%	24.12	66.78	9.10	100.00

results for the whole corridor are shown in Table 7.2, and correspond to the mean value of the 907 municipalities considered. The $PA_{i,1}$, $PA_{i,2}$ and $PA_{i,3}$ values are calculated by applying the calculations of equation (7.3), which consider the quality of the multimodal O–D connexion, weighted by the population at the destination. The differences between stage 1 and 3 indicate that the HSR stations are located near the larger cities that are most important for the accessibility values. Table 7.2 displays these results. The contributions of the two-tier connecting trips are quite different; the first mile represents 24.1 per cent and the last mile 9.1 per cent. This reveals that the accessibility levels are 33.2 per cent lower, on average, because of the time dedicated to these connecting trips.

For the first mile part, the calculation of the accessibility from each origin is based on the road time ($T1$), which is the same for all destinations; its influence on the PA_i value of the first plus last mile is therefore rather high. The PA value of the first mile ($PA_{i,1}$) depends on the quality of the access road to the HSR station and the global accessibility value of the municipality (origin). By contrast, in the case of the last mile, the road time differs for each destination. In general, the destinations with the greatest influence on the accessibility value of an origin are the ones that are best connected by road to the HSR stations. As a consequence, when calculating PA, the municipalities with the worst connections to the HSR network have a lower accessibility level for the last mile part.

Figure 7.5 shows similar results, namely the contribution of the first plus last mile to the accessibility value of each municipality. The lower accessibility values are concentrated in the surroundings of the HSR stations (good PA); the values increase with distance from the HSR stations (poor PA). Madrid, Valencia and Alicante have lower values than Albacete and Cuenca because the latter have better road connections with their regional municipalities than the three more central HSR stations. This is especially significant in Cuenca, where the contribution of the first plus last mile to the accessibility is more than 40 per cent in most municipalities.

The white areas in Figure 7.5 denote municipalities that are well connected to HSR stations that form key nodes on the connecting road

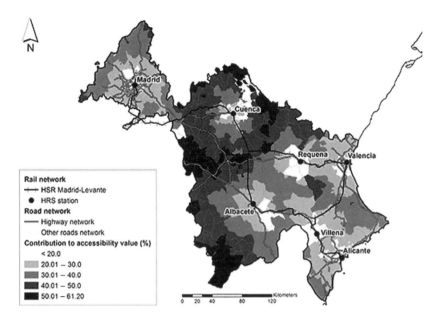

Figure 7.5   Contribution of the first plus last mile to PA values

networks. In 6 per cent of the municipalities, $PA_{i,1}$ and $PA_{i,3}$ contribute less than 20 per cent to the accessibility value. This is normally the case with major cities or metropolitan areas, which tend to be very well connected with rail nodes. Darkest areas correspond to scattered populations with poor-quality roads located far from the main rail nodes. In 25 per cent of the municipalities, $PA_{i,1}$ and $PA_{i,3}$ contribute more than 40 per cent to the accessibility value.

To analyse this difference in detail, Table 7.3 includes the *PA* values for a number of selected municipalities. The upper section lists seven cities with HSR stations. They share some features: the $PA_{i,1}$ is clearly lower than the $PA_{i,3}$ as the stations are very near to their inhabitants. The connecting trips account for 15 per cent of the total accessibility. The lowest accessibility values correspond to the most populated areas, but this is because they are located at both ends of the corridor. Madrid has an even lower PA_i, as this station is quite far from any of the others, while Valencia and Alicante are closer to each other and to Albacete and Requena. In all cases, most of the connections with the other municipalities are better served by HSR than by car trips, except in the case of Requena.

The middle part of Table 7.3 corresponds to cities that have an HSR station at a distance of less than 30 minutes travel time. In these cases,

Table 7.3   Accessibility values in selected municipalities

City	Population (000)	No. of destinations	PAi	$PA_{i,1}$	$PA_{i,2}$	$PA_{i,3}$	$(PA_{i,1} + PA_{i,3})/ PA_i$ (%)
Cities with HSR station							
Madrid	3342.6	607	28453	1036	24083	3333	15.36
Valencia	833.2	495	58759	1534	49960	7264	14.97
Alicante	353.0	592	54306	2833	46582	4890	14.22
Albacete	172.8	519	78307	7069	61802	9435	21.08
Cuenca	55.2	633	105462	925	88798	15738	15.80
Requena	21.2	347	72328	2108	62648	7572	13.38
Villena	36.3	538	63856	1069	56203	6582	11.98
Cities near HSR station (< 30 min.)							
Alcorcon	177.5	592	26190	2883	20448	2857	21.92
Elche	235.1	515	46763	7058	36094	3610	22.81
Paterna	61.0	405	54462	3570	44673	6218	17.97
Hellin	33.0	401	51025	14997	32137	3890	37.20
Quintanar	8.4	158	40441	9727	26709	4004	33.96
Cities far from HSR station (> 60 min.)							
Cenicientos	2.0	589	19917	6338	11856	1723	40.47
Pego	11.2	299	29326	9311	18005	2009	38.60
Denia	51.0	313	26626	7502	17448	1676	34.47
Villamayor	2.8	209	16845	7477	7948	1418	52.81
Belmonte	2.1	121	14603	6437	6683	1482	54.23

the values are different and depend on the relative location of the nearest station. It is worth pointing out that although they are quite far from the stations, half the municipalities in the corridor are better connected by HSR than by car, except in the case of Quintanar. Finally, the lower section of Table 7.3 includes municipalities that are far from any HSR station. Their rail connections are not very competitive for most of the destinations; this leads to a loss of almost half of their *PA* values.

Thus first/last mile connecting trips can be seen to be very relevant in achieving good accessibility values. It is also worth noting that HSR services can be very competitive with car trips, even in cities that are not near stations if they have good connections. In other words, the territorial impact of rail services is enhanced by good connecting networks.

7.6   CONCLUSIONS AND POLICY RECOMMENDATIONS

The results highlight the importance of considering the access/egress part of rail trips. The benefits of improving rail services could be cancelled out by the absence of good-enough connections to and from the stations. Road-based trips are usually the connecting mode for rail services. If the connectivity of the road network is low, all the benefits of major investments in improving rail lines could vanish. This implies that factors like congestion, quality of road surfaces and number of crossings are of pivotal importance in increasing rail use, as stated in key European transport policy documents such as the *White Paper 2011. Roadmap to a Single European Transport Area* (European Union 2011). In other words, co-modality and good connections between road and rail networks are crucial factors in encouraging the use of more sustainable transport modes such as rail.

The results in the case of the Madrid–Levante corridor in Spain show that the contribution of the connecting trips can be as high as 35 per cent of the total accessibility of rail trips, on average. The distance to the station accounts for a difference in accessibility of around 10 per cent in cities near the station and more than 50 per cent when the station is very far away. These findings agree with recent research on the key role played by first/last mile trips, as opposed to the rail trip per se (see e.g., Brons et al. 2009; Givoni and Banister 2012).

A further key issue is the relative location of the station. This location must be central both for the city where it is located and for its metropolitan conurbation (Garmendia et al. 2012; Monzón et al. 2013a). The first point implies that urban public transport should have good connectivity with the rail stations; seamless connections should be planned in order to improve citizens' rail accessibility levels (Brons et al. 2009), otherwise road trips will be more efficient. The second point is the connectivity of the rail station from cities in suburban areas. Congestion problems in accessing the city centre hinder the competitiveness of rail services. Efficient transport interchange stations play a pivotal role in providing good connectivity between public transport services (Monzón et al. 2013a). Again, good suburban rail services, well integrated in the HSR stations, appear to be significant elements for successful rail improvements.

The methodology developed in this chapter is able to analyse the locations and type of trips in which road connections fail to contribute to the attractiveness of rail services. It could also be used for correctly analysing equity levels. The development of a quality secondary road network to improve accessibility to the rail network would therefore improve territorial equity/cohesion objectives, and minimize the risks of HSR inducing negative equity/cohesion impacts (Ortega et al. 2012, 2014a; van Wee and Geurs 2011).

Finally, this methodology is also useful for identifying which stations are suitable candidates for stops along HSR services, based on the improved accessibility levels they provide for a number of locations. Other stations that are less well connected should therefore not be assigned high priorities when planning quality rail services. These connectivity issues should be included in decision-making processes for new HSR developments (Adamos et al. 2012). Enhanced assessment methodologies for the construction of new HSR corridors and stations are therefore needed as an aid in strategic policy-making processes (Guirao and Campa 2014; López and Monzón 2010).

In conclusion, the first/last mile of HSR trips is a key element for creating attractive services that compete with other modes such as car or plane. Our findings support the idea that increased policy efforts should be devoted to improving accessibility to the rail network. Car access to the station should be considered in great detail when planning rail services, because connecting trips by road or public transport could be as important as the rail connection constituting the longest part of the trip.

NOTES

1. Isochrone: a line drawn on a map connecting points at which something occurs or arrives at the same value.
2. NUTS 3: the NUTS classification is a hierarchical system for dividing up the economic territory of the EU for the collection, development and harmonization of EU regional statistics. NUTS 3 corresponds to the third level (provinces, in the case of Spain).
3. AccesstUls.aml (Network Accessibility Analysis Toolbox), developed by Santiago Mancebo in 2007. Not published.

REFERENCES

Adamos, G., Nathanail, E. and E. Zacharaki (2012), 'Developing a decision-making framework for collaborative practices in long-short distance transport interconnection', *Procedia-Social and Behavioral Sciences*, **48**, 2849–2858.

Banister, D. and J. Berechman (2003), 'The economic development effects of transport investments', in A. Pearman, P. Mackie and J. Nellthorp (ed.), *Transport Projects, Programmes, and Policies: Evaluation Needs and Capabilities*, Aldershot: Ashgate.

Barrón, I., Campos, J., Gagnepain, P., Nash, C., Vickerman, R. and A. Ulied (2012), 'Economic analysis of high speed rail in Europe', in G. de Rus (ed.), *Economic Analysis of High Speed Rail in Europe*, Bilbao: Fundación BBVA.

Bröcker, J., Korzhenevych, A. and C. Schürmann (2010), 'Assessing spatial equity and efficiency impacts of transport infrastructure projects', *Transportation Research Part B: Methodological*, **44** (7), 795–811.

Brons, M., Givoni, M. and P. Rietveld (2009), 'Access to railway stations and its potential in increasing rail use', *Transportation Research Part A: Policy and Practice*, **43**, 136–149.

Button, K. (2012), 'Is there any economic justification for high-speed railways in the United States?', *Journal of Transport Geography*, **22**, 300–302.

Dijkstra, E.W. (1959), 'A note on two problems in connexion with graphs', *Numeriske Mathematik*, **1**, 269–271.

European Union (2011), *White Paper 2011. Roadmap to a Single European Transport Area – Towards a Competitive and Resource Efficient Transport System*, COM/2011/0144.

Fotheringham, A.S. and D.W.S. Wong (1991), 'The modifiable areal unit problem in multivariate analysis', *Environment and Planning A*, **23**, 1025–1044.

Garmendia, M., Ribalaygua, C. and J. Ureña (2012), 'High speed rail: implications for cities', *Cities*, **29**, 26–31.

Garmendia, M., Ureña, J. and J. Coronado (2011), 'Long-distance trips in a sparsely populated region: The impact of high-speed infrastructures', *Journal of Transport Geography*, **19** (4), 537–551.

Geurs, K.T. and J. Ritsema van Eck (2001), *Accessibility Measures: Review and Applications. Evaluation of Accessibility Impacts of Land-Use Transportation Scenarios, and Related Social and Economic Impact*, Bilthoven: RIVM, National Institute of Public Health and the Environment.

Geurs, K.T. and B. van Wee (2004), 'Accessibility evaluation of land-use and transport strategies: Review and research directions', *Journal of Transport Geography*, **12**, 127–140.

Givoni, M. (2006), 'Development and impact of the modern high-speed train: A review', *Transport Reviews*, **26** (5), 593–611.

Givoni, M. and D. Banister (2012), 'Speed: The less important element of the high-speed train', *Journal of Transport Geography*, **22**, 306–307.

Guirao, B. and J. Campa (2014), 'The construction of a HSR network using a ranking methodology to prioritise corridors', *Land Use Policy*, **38**, 290–299.

Gutiérrez, J. (2001), 'Location, economic potential and daily accessibility: An analysis of the accessibility impact of the high-speed line Madrid–Barcelona–French border', *Journal of Transport Geography*, **9**, 229–242.

Gutiérrez, J., Condeço-Melhorado, A., López, E. and A. Monzón (2011), 'Evaluating the European added value of TEN-T projects: A methodological proposal based on spatial spillovers, accessibility and GIS', *Journal of Transport Geography*, **19** (4), 840–850.

Gutiérrez, J., Condeço-Melhorado, A. and J. Martín (2010), 'Using accessibility indicators and GIS to assess spatial spillovers of transport infrastructure investment', *Journal of Transport Geography*, **18** (1), 141–152.

Gutiérrez, J., González, R. and G. Gómez (1996), 'The European high-speed train network: Predicted effects on accessibility patterns', *Journal of Transport Geography*, **4**, 227–238.

Gutiérrez, J. and P. Urbano (1996), 'Accessibility in the European Union: The impact of the trans-European road network', *Journal of Transport Geography*, **4**, 15–25.

Hagler, Y. and P. Todorovich (2009), *America 2050: Where High-Speed Rail Works Best*, New York: Regional Planning Association.

Johnson, B. (2012), 'American intercity passenger rail must be truly high-speed and transit-oriented', *Journal of Transport Geography*, **22**, 282–284.

L'Hostis, A., Mathis, P., Reynaud, C., Spiekermann, K., Ulied, A. and M. Wegener (2002), *Research Project ESPON 1.2. 1. On Transport Services and Networks*.

Territorial Trends and Basic Supply of Infrastructure, Luxembourg: ESPON Coordination Unit.

Lane, B. (2012), 'On the utility and challenges of high-speed rail in the United States', *Journal of Transport Geography*, **22**, 282–284.

López, E. (2007), 'Assessment of transport infrastructure plans: A strategic approach integrating efficiency, cohesion and environmental aspects', PhD dissertation, Universidad Politécnica de Madrid, Madrid, available at http://www.ad.upm.es.

López, E., Gutiérrez, J. and G. Gómez (2008), 'Measuring regional cohesion effects of large-scale transport infrastructure investments: An accessibility approach', *European Planning Studies*, **16** (2), 277–301.

López, E. and A. Monzón (2009), 'Assessment of cross-border spillover effects of national transport infrastructure plans: An accessibility approach', *Transport Reviews*, **29** (4), 515–536.

López, E. and A. Monzón (2010), 'Integration of sustainability issues in strategic transportation planning: A multi-criteria model for the assessment of transport infrastructure plans', *Computer Aided Civil and Infrastructure Engineering*, **25** (6), 440–451.

Martín, J.C., Gutiérrez, J. and C. Román (2004), 'Data envelopment analysis (DEA) index to measure the accessibility impacts of new infrastructure investments: The case of the high-speed train corridor Madrid', *Regional Studies*, **38** (6), 697–712.

Martín, J.C., Reggiani, A. and J. Martin (2007), 'Recent methodological developments to measure spatial interaction: Synthetic accessibility indices applied to high-speed train investments', *Transport Reviews*, **27**, 551–571.

Martínez Sanchez-Mateos, H.S. and M. Givoni (2012), 'The accessibility impact of a new high-speed rail line in the UK – a preliminary analysis of winners and losers', *Journal of Transport Geography*, **25**, 105–114.

MCRIT (1992), *Estudio de accesibilidad a la red de infraestructuras para el PDI*, Madrid: MCRIT.

Monzón, A., Alonso, A. and M.E. López-Lambas (2013a), 'Key factors affecting the efficiency of transport interchanges', 13th World Conference on Transport Research, 15–18 June, Río de Janeiro.

Monzón, A., Ortega, E. and E. López (2013b), 'Efficiency and spatial equity impacts of high-speed rail extensions in urban areas', *Cities*, **30**, 18–30.

Mora, T. and R. Moreno (2013), 'The role of network access on regional specialization in manufacturing across Europe', *Regional Studies*, **47** (6), 951–962.

Ortega, E., López, E. and A. Monzón (2012), 'Territorial cohesion impacts of high-speed rail at different planning levels', *Journal of Transport Geography*, **24**, 130–141.

Ortega, E., López, E. and A. Monzón (2014a), 'Territorial cohesion impacts of high-speed rail under different zoning systems', *Journal of Transport Geography*, **34**, 16–24.

Ortega, E., Mancebo, S. and I. Otero (2011), 'Road and railway accessibility atlas of Spain', *Journal of Maps*, **2011**, 31–41.

Ortega, E., Otero, I. and S. Mancebo (2014b), 'TITIM GIS-tool: A GIS-based decision support system for measuring the territorial impact of transport infrastructures', *Expert Systems with Applications*, **41**, 7641–7652.

Reggiani, A. (1998), *Accessibility, Trade and Location Behaviour*, Aldershot: Ashgate.

Reggiani, A. (2012), 'Accessibility, connectivity and resilience in complex networks', in K. Geurs, K. Krizek and A. Reggiani (eds), *Accessibility and Transport Planning*, Cheltenham, UK and Northampton, MA, USA: Edward Elgar Publishing.

Tapiador, F., Burckhart, K. and J. Martí-Henneberg (2009), 'Characterizing European high speed train stations using intermodal time and entropy metrics', *Transportation Research Part A: Policy and Practice*, **43** (2), 197–208.

Ureña, J., Menerault, P. and M. Garmendia (2009), 'The high-speed rail challenge for big intermediate cities: A national, regional and local perspective', *Cities*, **26** (5), 266–279.

Van Wee, B. and K. Geurs (2011), 'Discussing equity and social exclusion in accessibility evaluations', *European Journal of Transport and Infrastructure Research*, **11** (4), 350–367.

Vickerman, R. (1995), 'Location, accessibility and regional development: the appraisal of trans-European networks', *Transport Policy*, **2** (4), 225–234.

8. Train station access and train use: a joint stated and revealed preference choice modelling study

Lissy La Paix and Karst T. Geurs

8.1 INTRODUCTION

Public transport accessibility depends not only on the places and opportunities that can be reached by transit, but also on accessibility to public transport. The characteristics of access and egress modes influence accessibility patterns but also ridership levels of public transport modes. In particular, public transport companies and city planners in Northern Europe have increasingly recognized the key role that bicycling plays as a feeder and distributor service for public transport (Pucher and Buehler 2008). However, the literature is still limited on how characteristics of access and egress modes influence the choice of the main mode of travel. In this chapter, we examine the key factors that influence access and egress mode choice and their influence on train use in the wider metropolitan area of The Hague–Rotterdam, in the Netherlands.

In this chapter, we estimate mode choice models based on a joint estimation of revealed preference (RP) and stated preference (SP) data to overcome the constraints of each of these two types of data sets (Bradley and Daly 1997). Most of the studies in the literature on feeder modes are based on RP data. In general, RP methods allow the construction of a picture of real situations and patterns, but often do not provide enough information to draw important inferences. As a result, most of the studies in the literature on feeder mode choice did not test the effect of improved service of feeder modes to access the train station. Moreover, variables such as cost and time are often correlated in the RP surveys (Cherchi and Ortúzar 2002). Therefore, one of the major benefits of SP methods is the ability to capture the response to diverse attribute combinations which are not otherwise observed in the market (Hensher 1994). Only a few studies have collected stated preference (SP) data about access mode choice. For example, Hensher and Rose (2007) analysed main mode choice, but included only car, walking and bus as feeder modes. One of the main limitations of SP experiments in this context is the restricted applicability. The hypothetical scenarios presented in SP experiments can be unrealistic or inconsistent, or the sample can be biased due to self-selection of respondents (Krizek et al. 2007).

In the literature, joint estimations of RP–SP data are advocated in order to overcome these issues. It is argued that RP data can act as a reference point for pivoting the levels of the attributes in the stated choice experiment. The mixing of sources (SP and RP) means the opportunity to position an SP data set relative to an RP data set within the one empirical analysis on the common choice problem. It enables the modeller to extend and infill the relationship between variations in choice response and levels of the attributes of alternatives in a choice set, and hence increase the explanatory power of the RP choice model, as stated in Hensher (1994). The statistical methods to jointly estimate RP–SP can be divided in two main procedures: the nested logit specification and mixed model specification with non-linear effects. The non-linear specification appears to be more suitable as not only does it obtain better model results in other published studies, but also the real distribution of the error terms was revealed (Cherchi and Ortúzar 2002). The nested logit approach is not capable of dealing with the effect of repeating observations, as demonstrated in Hensher et al. (2008).

In this study we use a mixed logit model with a non-linear specification to model mode choice, based on joint RP–SP data. The joint RP–SP estimation allows us to develop more reliable conclusions about access and egress generalized costs to train stations. We develop a set of policy scenarios and estimate the change in probabilities to use train according to the variations of time, cost and quality attributes, and estimate value of travel time savings (VTTS) and willingness to pay (WTP) for changes in attributes in both access and egress modes. To the authors' knowledge, this study is the first attempt to develop mode-specific VTTS and WTP for access and egress modes to train stations. The results of this chapter are interesting for both researchers and planners. We examine the effect of different model structures and the use of different data types, and examine the effectiveness of different types of measures (for example, bicycle pricing, 'liveliness' of railway stations) to influence train use.

The chapter is structured as follows. We first give a brief overview of the available literature on station access and egress (section 8.2). We discuss the case study and survey design (section 8.3), followed by a description of the econometric framework developed for this research (section 8.4). The results of the joint RP–SP model estimations (section 8.5), VTTS estimations (section 8.6), and the effects of policy measures on market shares are described (section 8.7). Finally, the conclusions from the research are presented (section 8.8).

8.2   LITERATURE ON STATION ACCESS AND EGRESS

The number of studies on station access or egress modes is fairly limited. A number of studies have examined the importance of feeder modes in railway use (Ben-Akiva and Morikawa 1990; O'Sullivan and Morrall 1996; Pucher and Buehler 2009). Specifically in the Netherlands, the bicycle as feeder mode has motivated many studies (Brons et al. 2009; Debrezion et al. 2009; Givoni and Rietveld 2007; Keijer and Rietveld 2000; Martens 2007; Rietveld 2000) based on revealed preference data.

The inclusion of realistic attributes in the SP experiment is important for the interpretation of the hypothetical scenarios. Moreover, when new alternatives are being evaluated, making the attribute levels believable (and deliverable) becomes a primary consideration (Hensher 1994). For example, relevant attributes to consider in the mode choice of station access or egress are: cost, time and mode facilities (Martens 2004), transfer and waiting time (Hensher and Rose 2007), and station environment. Different elements of station environment have received attention in the past decade: Cozens et al. (2003) discussed passengers' perceptions of crime and nuisance at the station and immediate routes. Lee and Lam (2003) investigated the level of service of stairways in mass rapid transit stations. Ampofo et al. (2004) found a correlation between passengers who are dissatisfied due to thermal conditions within the underground railway system. More recently, Cascetta and Cartenì (2014) found that train users are more willing to walk nine more minutes to reach a high-aesthetic-quality station. They quantified the 'value of station's quality' as €0.35–€0.50/trip, by train. They suggested that further research could extend the scope to include the specification of mode choice models with specific aesthetic quality parameters. However, the effect of those elements in modes of access and egress has never been analysed, to the authors' knowledge.

As stated in the introduction, only a small number of studies have analysed access and egress mode choice based on stated preferences. Therefore, WTP for the implementation of specific transport policies has received little attention. At the same time, the effect of the value of travel time savings in the station access or egress journey has rarely been studied. Hensher and Rose (2007) estimated VTTS for both access and egress modes. However, the VTTS relate to all public transport modes, rather than specific public transport modes, such as bus and train. Similarly, since the choice set was composed of main modes (that is, new light rail, new bus way, bus, existing and new train, and so on), cost and time attributes were not disentangled by access modes (that is, walking, cycling, bus/tram/metro, car). However, they did demonstrate clear differences between VTTS of access and egress time

(AU$6–AU$10/hour and AU$4–AU$7/hour, respectively). Similarly, there is no specific and published value of time for access and egress modes to train stations. Finally, the effect of various policy scenarios has rarely been tested over SP data. No scenario has been described combining both quality of station and level of service of feeder modes.

Continuing from the review of research presented above, the objective of this chapter is twofold: (1) to develop a joint RP–SP estimation of access and egress mode, which allows us to estimate more reliable VTTS and WTP for new transport measures; and (2) based on the SP data, to calculate the influence of various policy scenarios on train ridership, and to draw specific conclusions about both access and egress modes in different journey purposes.

8.3 CASE STUDY AREA, DATA COLLECTION AND SURVEY DESIGN

Our case study area is the wider metropolitan area of The Hague–Rotterdam in the Netherlands (see Figure 8.1). The metropolitan region of The Hague–Rotterdam and surroundings comprises 3 million residents and is one of the most urbanized areas in the Netherlands. This area is also known as Randstad South in Dutch policy and planning documents. We conducted an online survey among paid members of an online commercial panel, in the mid-summer and early autumn of 2013. This study involved a total of 1524 respondents. The survey had a response rate of 84 per cent.

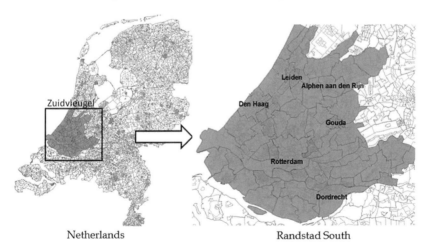

Netherlands   Randstad South

Figure 8.1   Case study area: the wider metropolitan area of The Hague–Rotterdam

The recruitment was based on the following three criteria:

- Residential location. We only recruited inhabitants living within a 5 km catchment area of one of the 38 railway stations in the case study area.
- Frequency of travelling by train for both work and non-work purposes. Three types of passenger were established: 'frequent' (a person who travels once per week or more), 'infrequent' (a person who travels once per year up to three times per month), and 'never' (a person who travels less than once per year). The objective was a balanced distribution of user type, but the non-users were very reluctant to complete the survey. As a result, 44 per cent of the respondents who completed the survey belong to the frequent traveller category, 40 per cent are infrequent travellers, and only 16 per cent expressed that they never travel by train.
- Type of departure station. We distinguished between large (intercity) railway stations (for example, Rotterdam Central Station, The Hague Central Station), medium-sized (intercity) stations (for example, Leiden Central Station) and small (local) railway stations.

The questionnaire comprised two parts: revealed preference and stated preference experiment. The RP part included questions related to the most recent trip in the study area (travel time, purpose, origin, destination, and so on). Table 8.1 shows the variables in the RP context. In the SP part, each respondent completed 12 cards, six for each access and egress mode choice. The cards included five alternatives, differing between access and egress modes. In the access cards, the respondents chose from: bus/tram/metro (BTM), car, walk, bicycle, other mode and non-choice. The non-choice has two sub-options: 'I would not travel by train' and 'I would find another way to go to the station'. In the egress part, the respondents chose among: BTM, own bicycle, public transport bicycle (PT-bicycle; in Dutch: *OV-fiets*), walk and the non-choice option as in the access experiment. The PT-bicycle is a popular members-only rental scheme in the Netherlands, primarily used at the activity end of a train trip. Users pay a small yearly fee to subscribe (€10, 2013 price) and a rental fee (€2.85 for 24 hrs, 2013 price). The subscription can be linked to the national smart card system (*OV-chipkaart*) to allow for fast identification and easy payment. The PT-bicycles are parked at regular guarded parking facilities or in special bicycle lockers, within easy access of the train platforms, at every railway station in the Netherlands.

Each alternative was assigned with a time attribute. Car, BTM and bicycle were additionally provided with a cost attribute. Car and bicycle

Figure 8.2   Example of card in the stated choice experiment

parking represent the cost attribute of car and bicycle, respectively. BTM cost belongs to the price of the trip. For both cycling and walking specific statements about route quality were included. An example of choice card is shown in Figure 8.2 (in Dutch). Table 8.2 presents the variables and attributes included in both RP and SP contexts.

It is important to highlight that for both access and egress time is adaptive from the revealed preference part. Travel time was adapted from the RP survey by adding 0, 5 and 10 minutes to the access time indicated in the survey. Similarly, in the SP experiment, bicycle access cost includes three levels: free, €1.25/day and €2.50/day. Both 'free' and '€1.25/day' belong to the current situation. More information about the design of the SP experiment can be found in La Paix and Geurs (2014).

8.4   MODEL SPECIFICATION

8.4.1   Mixed Logit (ML) and Nested Mixed Logit (NML)

This section discusses the econometric structure of the mixed logit model, which is used in the estimations with both joint RP–SP and the SP-only data. The ML is a highly flexible model that can approximate any random

Table 8.1   Variables in the RP context

Name	Description	Notation
Socio-economic characteristics (SE)		
Age	Continuous variable. Alternative specific for BTM and non-train user.	β_{age-i}
Gender	Equal to 1 if male. Alternative specific for BTM	$\beta_{gender-i}$
Frequency of trip	1 if equal to four times per week, zero if otherwise. Alternative specific for BTM and car	$\beta_{frequency-i}$ X_6
Work	Dummy variable, equal to 1 if trip purpose is 'work', zero if otherwise. Alternative specific for car and bicycle.	β_{work-i} X_3
Level of service (LOS)		
Access time BTM	Dummy variable. Equal to 1 if travel time is equal to 5−10 minutes	$\beta_{access\ time-btm}$
Access time car	Dummy variable. Equal to 1 if travel time is equal to 10−15 minutes	$\beta_{access\ time-car}$
Access time bicycle	Dummy variable. Equal to 1 if travel time is equal to 10−15 minutes	$\beta_{access\ time-bicycle}$
Access time walk	Dummy variable. Equal to 1 if travel time is equal to 5−10 minutes	$\beta_{access\ time-walk}$
Cost BTM and Bicycle	Continuous variable	$\beta_{costBTMRP}$ $\beta_{costbicycleRP}$

utility model (McFadden and Train 1996), which has been widely applied for many years in the field of transport econometrics (see e.g., Brownstone and Train 1998; Train 2003). The ML probabilities are the integral of standard logit probabilities over a density of parameters, expressed in the following form, as in Train (2003):

$$P_{nj} = \int L_{ni}(\beta)f(\beta)\,d\beta, \qquad (8.1)$$

where $L_{ni}(\beta)$ is the logit probability evaluated at parameters β, $f(\beta)$ is the density function:

$$L_{ni}(\beta) = \frac{e^{V_{ni}(\beta)}}{\sum_{j=1} e^{V_{nj}(\beta)}}. \qquad (8.2)$$

Table 8.2   Variables, attributes and levels in RP and SP context

Attribute	Levels	Description	Notation
Alternatives, access mode	5	Car driver/passenger, BTM, Bicycle (own), Walking, No choice (other mode, non-train use)	
Alternatives, egress mode	5	BTM, bicycle (own), PT-bicycle, walking, no choice (other mode, non-train use)	
Travel time access/egress: adaptive RP	3	+ 0, 5, 10 minutes	
Cost bus	2	Cost per journey €3.6/return journey €2.2/return journey	
Cost car	2	Cost of parking per day €8/day	
Cost bicycle parking	3	Free €1.25/day €2.5/day	
Cost PT-bicycle	2	2.85 €/day 0.5 €/day	
Cyclist infrastructure: delays			
No delays	0	Equal to 1 if quality attribute is 0; and 0 if otherwise	C_{sp}
Addition of 5 minutes in the route by bicycle due to number of interruptions, cyclist	1	Equal to 1 if quality attribute is 1; and 0 if otherwise	C_{sp1}
Addition of 2 minutes in walking from bicycle parking to platform	2	Equal to 1 if quality attribute is equal to 2; and 0 if otherwise	C_{sp2}
Addition of 5 minutes in walking from bicycle parking to platform	3	Reference category	
Pedestrian infrastructure: delays			
2 minutes waiting time for pedestrians at traffic lights on the route to the station	0	Equal to 1 if quality attribute is 0; and zero if otherwise	P_{sp}
5 minutes waiting time for pedestrians at the traffic lights on the route to the station	1	Equal to 1 if quality attribute is 1; and 0 if otherwise	P_{sp1}
Improvement of current station environment for train passengers	2	Equal to 1 if quality attribute is 2; and 0 if otherwise	P_{sp2}
No improvement of current station environment	3	Reference category	P_{sp3}

$V_{ni}(\beta) = \beta x_{ni}$ is the deterministic part of the utility function. The density of β can be specified with mean b and covariance W. Substituting $L_{ni}(\beta)$ and V_{ni} in equation (8.2), the choice probability under this density becomes:

$$P_{ni} = \int \frac{e^{\beta x_{ni}}}{\sum_j e^{\beta x_{nj}}} f(\beta|b,W) d\beta. \tag{8.3}$$

Simulation is normally used to estimate the ML. Given the values that describe the population parameter of the individual parameters, R values of β are drawn from its distribution and the probability in equation (8.3) is calculated conditional on each realization. The simulated probability (*SP*) is the average of the conditional probabilities over the R draws:

$$SP_n = \frac{1}{R} \sum_{r=1,\dots,R} P_{ni}(\beta^r). \tag{8.4}$$

8.4.2 The Joint Estimation RP–SP

As stated in the introduction, in the joint RP–SP estimation, a scale parameter is estimated. The RP parameters are considered the true parameters which scale the SP parameters. The structure is similar to a nested logit model in which we have two nests: RP and SP alternatives. Therefore, given two sources of data, RP and SP, the random utility functions associated with alternative i can be specified as follows:

$$U_i^{RP} = \beta X_i^{RP} + \alpha Y_i^{RP} + \varepsilon_i^{RP} \text{ and } U_i^{SP} = \beta X_i^{SP} + \gamma Z_i^{SP} + \varepsilon_i^{SP}, \tag{8.5}$$

where α, β, γ are vectors of parameters to be estimated, X_i^{RP} and Y_i^{SP} vectors of attributes common on both data sets, that is, socio-economic characteristics, Y_i^{RP} and Z_i^{SP} are vectors of attributes to each type of data, that is, alternative specific constants (ASCs) and level of service (LOS) parameters. ε_i^{RP} and ε_i^{SP} are the error terms, which take into account multiple responses of the generic individual i. An efficient estimation with two different data sources is to scale one data set to achieve the same variance in both sets (Cherchi and Ortúzar 2006a). Then:

$$\tilde{U}_i^{RP} = \theta U_i^{SP}. \tag{8.6}$$

This means that the standard deviations in RP are equal to the standard deviations in SP multiplied by a parameter (θ_{SP}^{RP}). The θ_{SP}^{RP} parameter is actually the ratio between the scale parameters in the RP and SP, written as:

$$\theta \frac{RP}{SP} = \frac{\lambda_{RP}}{\lambda_{SP}}. \tag{8.7}$$

Therefore the likelihood function is L implicitly estimated as the product of the RP and the SP probabilities, which is written as:

$$L = \prod_{RP} \frac{e^{U_i^{\lambda_{RP}RP}}}{\sum_{i \in J^{RP}} e^{U^{RP}_i}} * \prod_{SP} \frac{e^{U_i^{\lambda_{SP}SP}}}{\sum_{i \in J^{SP}} e^{U^{SP}_i}} \tag{8.8}$$

Additionally, in the SP models, the equations (8.5) and (8.6) are scaled by a nested parameter ϑ_m, where we have two nests:

- Train users. Given the inherent correlation across the modes of access to the station because all of them can be selected by the train users, the nested structure keeps in the same nest the alternatives related to train use. Those alternatives are the access or egress to the station: car, BTM, bicycle/PT-bicycle, walk and other mode.
- Non-users. The option 'I would not travel by train' is more associated with non-train use than with access/egress modes and is placed in a 'non-users' nest.

The parameter ϑ_m takes the value 1 if the alternative belongs to the 'non-users' nest, and takes the value θ_m if the alternative belongs to the 'train-users' nest. θ_m is an estimated parameter in the model. This structure is called mixed nested logit, and it allows the estimation of the more realistic market shares of train users, and it is applied in the scenarios of section 8.6.

8.4.3 Model Structure

In a joint RP–SP estimation, the model structure deserves special attention. In this particular case, the alternatives are not exactly the same in the SP as in the RP data. Moreover, the LOS information about the alternatives (cost, time) is not available in both data sets, or is not measured on the same scale (that is, travel time is either a categorical or continuous variable). This generates additional drawbacks in the joint estimation. Some authors have used only the LOS information available in the SP data and estimate ASC specifically for RP and RP, for example Bhat and Sardesai (2006). Other authors argue that if RP and SP alternatives are not exactly the same, then the ASC should be adjusted to match the market shares of the base year (Cherchi and Ortúzar 2006b). Additionally, they consider specific LOS parameters for RP and SP, and additionally estimated two different models with specific and generic ASCs. However, the specification of generic or specific ASCs did not have any effect on results. This was certainly an important issue in the estimation because the two data sets are complementary and there is no relation between the mean of the error terms (Cherchi and Ortúzar 2006b). The common parameters will be the socio-economic parameters. In this way, we are allowing each data source to capture those aspects of the choice process for which it is superior, as explained in Cherchi and Ortúzar (2006a).

The utilities for the RP context are specified as:

$$Car\ passenger: V1_{RP} = ASC_{1RP} + \sum \beta^i_{SE} X_{SE} + \sum \beta_{LOS} X_{LOS} + \zeta_{CAR}$$

$$Car\ driver: V2_{RP} = ASC_{2RP} + \sum \beta^i_{SE} X_{SE} + \sum \beta_{LOS} X_{LOS} + \zeta_{CAR}$$

$$BTM: V3_{RP} = ASC_{3RP} + \sum \beta^i_{SE} X_{SE} + \sum \beta_{LOS} X_{LOS} + \zeta_{BTM}$$

$$Bicycle: V4_{RP} = ASC_{4RP} + \sum \beta^i_{SE} X_{SE} + \sum \beta_{LOS} X_{LOS} + \zeta_{BIKE}$$

$$Walk: V5_{RP} = ASC_{4RP} + \sum \beta^i_{SE} X_{SE} + \sum \beta_{LOS} X_{LOS} + \zeta_{WALK}$$

$$Others: V6_{RP} = ASC_{6RP}$$
$$Non\text{-}train: V7_{RP} = ASC_{7RP} + \zeta_{NONTRAINRP.} \tag{8.9}$$

Similarly, the utility equations for SP context are specified as:

$$BTM: V0_{SP} = ASC_{0_{SP}} + \sum \beta^i_{SE} X_{SE} + \sum \beta_{LOS} X_{LOS} + \zeta_{BTM}$$

$$Car\ passenger: V1_{SP} = ASC_{1_{SP}} + \sum \beta^i_{SE} X_{SE} + \sum \beta_{LOS} X_{LOS} + \zeta_{CAR}$$

$$Bicycle: V2_{SP} = ASC_{2_{SP}} + \sum \beta^i_{SE} X_{SE} + \sum \beta_{LOS} X_{LOS} + \zeta_{BIKE}$$

$$Walk: V3_{SP} = ASC_{3_{SP}} + \sum \beta^i_{SE} X_{SE} + \sum \beta_{LOS} X_{LOS} + \zeta_{WALK}$$

$$Others: V4_{SP} = ASC_{4_{SP}} + \beta_{bike_{cost4}} X_{bike_{cost}}$$

$$Non\text{-}train: V5_{SP} = ASC_{5_{SP}} + \beta_{bike_{time5}} X_{time_{bike}} + \zeta_{NONTRAIN,} \tag{8.10}$$

swhere β^i_{SE} indicates a vector of alternative specific parameters of socio-economic characteristics, common for both SP and RP contexts. β_{LOS} is a vector of level of service characteristics (cost and time). Equations (8.9) and (8.10) show that the error components (ζ_i) are also shared by both SP and RP, and these are alternative specific.

8.5   RESULTS OF JOINT RP–SP ESTIMATIONS

This section contains the results of the joint estimation of RP and SP surveys. The alternatives included in the RP context are: car driver, car passenger, BTM, walking, others and non-train use. The alternatives included in the SP context have been already described in section 8.3.

The parameters are either specific or unique for each database. Two parameters of socio-economic (SE) characteristics (gender and age) were estimated common to both RP and SP contexts. In the RP context, Table 8.3 shows six parameters related to travel characteristics, among which three are estimated for frequency of the journey and two parameters for trip purpose. Six parameters of level of service were estimated as dummy variables, among which four parameters belong to access time (BTM, walking, car and bus), and two parameters belong to cost (BTM and bicycle). Car cost was not collected in the survey to reduce the complexity of the questionnaire. Similarly, Table 8.3 shows the estimated parameters in the SP context: three cost parameters (BTM, car and bicycle), four parameters of time (BTM, car, bicycle and walking) and three parameters of cyclist infrastructure.

To obtain an advanced joint RP–SP estimation, the SE characteristics were estimated as generic parameters between RP and SP. LOS parameters are specific to RP and SP because: (1) the scale of travel time variables was categorical in the RP survey, whilst it was continuous in the SP experiment; (2) the information about cost was calculated via geographical information systems (GIS), since the BTM cost was not asked for the RP survey. The standard deviations in the RP survey were not significant, which is reasonable because one person chooses only one RP alternative. By contrast, the standard deviations in the SP data were all relevant. If the value is positive, this indicates that the individuals tend to choose the same alternative across different SP cards. Furthermore, the non-linear specification allows the distribution of the error terms according to possible correlation between modes. As can be observed in the standard deviation of BTM (σ_{BTM}) and bicycle ($\sigma_{Bicycle}$), those modes seem to be either correlated or competing. Consistent with the introductory discussion, the non-linear specification is more suitable for analysing SP data, and also reveals the real distribution of the error terms (Cherchi and Ortúzar 2002).

As can be seen in Table 8.3, the parameter λ_{RP} is statistically significant, which means that alternatives in the RP part are correlated among

Table 8.3 Results for SP and joint estimation RP–SP

Name	SP estimation value	Robust t-test	Joint RP–SP value	Robust t-test	Affected utility
$ASC\_2\_$			0.930	2.940	Car driver
ASC_0_SP			7.730	11.160	BTM SP
ASC_1RP			0.960	2.760	Car passenger RP
ASC_1_SP	−1.36	−3.83	6.110	12.480	Car passenger SP
ASC_2_SP	−0.428	−1.37	6.930	13.960	Bicycle SP
ASC_4RP			1.630	9.500	Bicycle RP
ASC_3RP					BTM-RP
ASC_3_SP	2.02	5.90	1.360	7.930	Walk-SP
ASC_5RP			9.660	18.980	Walk-RP
ASC_4_SP	−4.11	−9.35	2.090	10.850	Other mode-SP
ASC_6RP					Other mode-RP
ASC_5_SP	−3.54	−8.65	4.110	7.570	Non-train SP
ASC_7RP			0.988	8.700	Non-train RP
SE	SP unique		RP–SP generic		
$\beta_{age.BTM}$	0.00412	2.92	0.001	0.440	BTM
$\beta_{age-car}$	0.00274	1.81	−0.002	−1.710	Car
$\beta_{age-non-train}$	0.00474	4.82			Non-train
$\beta_{gender-car}$	−0.371	−1.55	−0.481	−3.400	Car
$\beta_{gender-bicycle}$	−0.2	−0.79			Bicycle
Travel related			RP-unique		
$\beta_{frequency_{CAR}}$			−0.62	−2.11	Car
$\beta_{frequency_{BTM}}$			−0.753	−4.38	BTM
$\beta_{work_{CAR}}$			−0.66	−2.83	Car
$\beta_{work_{bicycle}}$			0.327	2.81	Bicycle
LOS			RP-specific		
$\beta_{accesstime-btm}$			−1.000	−7.100	BTM
$\beta_{accesstime-walk}$			−2.230	−5.800	Walk
$\beta_{accesstime-car}$			−2.190	−8.680	Car
$\beta_{accesstime-bicycle}$			−1.870	−6.790	Bicycle
$\beta_{costBTMRP}$			0.104	2.650	BTM
$\beta_{costbicycle.RP}$			2.000	8.070	Bicycle

LOS	(SP-specific)				
$\beta_{time_{BTM}}$	−0.114	−6.14	−0.123	−5.050	BTM
β_{cost_BTM}	−0.179	−4.12	−0.193	−10.910	BTM
$\beta_{time_{walk}}$	−0.199	−11.03	−0.275	−4.750	Walk
$\beta_{time_{car}}$	−0.077	−3.27	−0.089	−4.280	Car
$\beta_{time_{bicycle}}$	−0.13	−4.81	−0.134	−4.990	Bicycle
$\beta_{cost_{bicycle}}$	−0.412	−10.69	−0.357	−10.230	Bicycle
$\beta_{cost_{bicycle}}$	0.0327	0.54	1.250	22.910	Other mode
$\beta_{cost_{bicycle}}$	−0.0802	−3.13			Non-train

Quality of cyclist and pedestrian infrastructure (SP-unique)

	(SP-specific)				
$\beta_{C_{sp}}$	0.266	3.18	0.245	3.09	Bicycle
$\beta_{C_{sp1}}$	0.548	3.21	0.613	3.67	Bicycle
$\beta_{C_{sp2}}$	0.589	4.96	0.531	4.65	Bicycle
$\beta_{P_{sp}}$	0.0439	0.60	0.0495	0.74	Walk
$\beta_{P_{sp1}}$	−0.214	−1.85	−0.103	−0.98	Walk
$\beta_{P_{sp4}}$	−0.366	−2.36			Other mode
$\beta_{P_{sp1}}$	−0.833	−3.69			Other mode
$\beta_{P_{sp0}}$	−0.372	−4.34			Non-train
$\beta_{P_{sp2}}$	−0.368	−2.74			Non-train
$\beta_{P_{sp1}}$	−0.401	−2.40			Non-train

Standard deviations (error components for panel effects)

	(SP-specific)				
σ_{WALK}	−1.14	−2.12	−0.101	−0.030	Walk SP
σ_{BTM}	−1.52	−3.20	2.330	4.670	BTM SP
σ_{CAR}	0.983	2.08	−1.440	−3.850	Car SP
σ_{BIKE}	2.29	13.53	−2.010	−11.890	Bicycle SP
$\sigma_{nontrain}$	−2.63	−6.84	1.750	4.690	Non-train SP
σ_{WALKRP}			−0.035	−0.710	Walk RP
σ_{BTMRP}			−0.008	−0.070	BTM RP
$\sigma_{NOTRAINRP}$			0.007	0.120	Non-train RP
σ_{BIKERP}			0.018	0.350	Bicycle RP
$\lambda_{SP/RP}$			1.610	4.410	All alternatives

themselves and, at the same time, those alternatives are independent of the alternatives in the SP part. It also means that the choice behaviour on the SP situations can be scaled to the RP data by a factor λ_{RP}. The heterogeneity in taste from the combined RP and SP data can be elicited only with the SP data if this is scaled by λ_{RP}.

The travel-related variables are RP-specific. It means that those variables were only included in the utility function of RP alternatives. As can be seen in Table 8.3, two travel-related variables are included in the specification: frequency and type of journey. Frequency of the trip is included as alternative specific parameter in both car and BTM access modes. Journey frequency is a dummy variable which is set as 1 if the person travels more than four times per week, and otherwise 0. In both cases, users are more likely to choose modes other than the car or BTM for frequent journeys. This is confirmed by the working trips parameter affecting the utility of bicycle (RP). The sign and t-test of this parameter indicates that workers (who are at the same time frequent travellers) tend to choose bicycle as their access mode to the train station.

The LOS parameters are RP and SP specific. Regarding the RP coefficients, the parameters of access time are negative, as expected. However, the parameter of BTM cost is positive, which is not consistent with the expectations. This is associated to the nature of this variable. The BTM cost was calculated based on a kilometre rate. The trip distance was calculated via GIS analysis from the home postcode provided by the respondent, to the departure station. The distance travelled in a journey by BTM tends to be longer than those by non-motorized modes, that is, bicycle. Then the average cost for BTM users is higher than for other modes. Consistently, the sign of the BTM parameter is positive.

The parameters of LOS, pedestrian and cyclist infrastructure keep similar magnitudes in both SP and joint RP–SP estimations. This means that the joint estimation is now improved but the SP estimation is unbiased. The parameter $\beta_{P_{sp2}}$ (improvement of current station environment for train passengers) is acting in the utility function of non-train use. As can be seen, this is a significant attribute for choosing train as main mode, as shown by the t-test of the estimated parameter $\beta_{P_{sp2}}$ (improvement of current station environment). Consistent with Cascetta and Cartenì (2014), the results show that enhancing the 'liveliness' at the train station (that is, the existence of cafés, restaurants and places to sit and talk) increases the likelihood of using the station. Additionally, regarding the selection of other access modes, the results show that a better quality of station environment encourages both bicycle and public transport use. The parameters $\beta_{P_{sp0}}$ and $\beta_{P_{sp1}}$ are negative, indicating that interruptions along the route deter train users from walking to the station.

8.6   VTTS BY TRIP PURPOSE AND MODEL STRUCTURE

Table 8.4 shows the VTTS for access and egress journeys for BTM and bicycle by trip purpose. Models labelled as ML (mixed logit) assume non-nested alternatives, as explained in section 8.4. θ_m is equal to one; while models labelled as NML (nested mixed logit) estimate a correlation parameter across alternatives in the same nest (θ_m). The correlation parameter is kept in the model structure only if it is statistically significant.

As can be seen, the VTTS in the egress journey by bicycle is higher than the VTTS in the access journey. This is consistent with previous (unpublished) studies by the NS (Netherlands Railways). Furthermore, the VTTS by bicycle is higher than the VTTS by BTM in both working and non-working journeys. This means that travel costs are higher for cyclists, therefore bicycle use is less attractive than BTM as an access mode. Additionally, this result is associated with the asymmetry between bicycle use for access and egress journeys. Bicycle use is substantially more difficult in the egress journey than in the access journey, given the bicycle availability at the train station.

It is interesting to analyse the VTTS of PT-bicycle users. The average price per hour is €6, while the VTTS of own bicycle use is €24 per hour. This result represents the amount of effort that cyclists need to make in using their own bicycle to leave the train station. At the same time, the VTTS of BTM users is €5 per hour, which means that the PT-bicycle is seen as a public transport mode that competes with BTM in the egress journey.

Moreover, the difference between VTTS by journey purposes is large in the egress part, where the VTTS –BTM increases substantially for non-working trips with respect to working journeys. At the same time, the VTTS for access is in general lower than the VTTS for egress, consistent with Hensher and Rose (2007), who found that VTTS by public transport is higher in the access than in the egress journey of working trips. To the authors' knowledge, this is the first published result on mode specific VTTS in access and egress journeys to the station in the Dutch context.

For the present research, in the case of bicycle access, VTTS-egress is higher than VTTS-access; while in the case of BTM, VTTS-egress is lower than VTTS-access. Table 8.4 also shows the WTPs for better cyclist infrastructure. As can be see, the WTP for a better infrastructure is higher in the egress journey than in the access journey. The values of WTP for avoiding five minutes of delay in the egress journey double the size of WTP in the access. By contrast, the WTP for a two-minute reduction from bicycle parking to platform is similar for both access and egress journeys.

Table 8.4 VTTS and WTP for access and egress journeys

	Model 1	Model 2	Model 3	Model 4	Model 5	Model 6	Model 7	Model 8
Type of model	ML	ML	ML	NML	NML	ML	NL	NL
Journey purpose	All	Working	Non-working	All	Working	All	Working	Non-working
Stage of journey	Access	Access	Access	Access	Access	Egress	Egress	Egress
Number of estimated parameters	37	29	28	38	30	28	28	28
Sample size	9144	3864	5508	9144	3636	9144	3636	5508
Rho squared	0.385	0.385	0.322	0.385	0.366	0.348	0.522	0.499
VTTS BTM (€/hour)	9.84	18.15	22.61	10.05	15.95	5.14	8.46	4.38
VTTS bicycle (€/hour)	15.87	23.15	19.36	15.96	22.18	24.66	24.60	25.11
VTTS PT-bicycle (€/hour)						6.07	4.79	9.10
WTP: no delays (C0) (€)	−0.80	−0.85	−1.11	−0.80	−0.79	−0.25	−0.02	−0.48
WTP: avoid delays 5 mins intersection (C1) (€)	0.85	−0.46	−2.46	−1.98	−1.97	−2.95	−2.49	−3.33
WTP: avoid delays 2 mins from platform (C2) (€)	−1.70	−1.68	−2.03	−1.72	−1.75	−1.88	−1.65	−2.17
ASC/bicycle (€)	−3.37	−0.46	0.919	−3.59	−4.49	−4.39	−6.48	−6.39
ASC/PT-bicycle cost (€)						0.92	−0.37	2.617

Of particular significance here is the high VTTS of non-working trips, for both access and egress journeys. This result is in line with Wardman (2004), who claimed that early walking to public transport is seen as a 'distressing' activity. According to this notion, the access to a railway station before work is more relaxing than during a non-working journey. Also, Wardman (2004) found substantially larger values of VTTS in leisure journeys than business travel by public transport. Particularly, the large VTTS of egress by bicycle in non-working journeys is related to the unavailability of bicycles at arrival stations.

Finally, the results in Table 8.4 highlight the differences in VTTS by model structures, which are the NML and ML. This indicates that omitting important correlations across access mode alternatives leads to overestimation of time valuation by train users. Methodologically, it means that selecting a proper model structure is very important for the accurate economic appraisal of transport measures.

8.7   SCENARIOS AND MARKET SHARES OF TRAIN RIDERSHIP

Using the parameters of Model 4 (access) and Model 6 (egress), we forecast scenarios according to hypothetical improvements in the LOS (cost and time) and station level. We select this model because it is the most generic approach. The scenarios are described as follows:

- Scenario 1: in this scenario, it is assumed that (guarded and unguarded) bicycle parking is free for all the choice situations.
- Scenario 2: improved station environment, only for medium-sized and small stations (less than 10 000 passengers per day), which means more restaurants and cafés that increases the 'liveliness'.
- Scenario 3: in this scenario, in addition to the implementation of free bicycle parking, the access time by BTM is reduced by 15 per cent.
- Scenario 1-egress: in this scenario, free (guarded and unguarded) bicycle parking is provided in the egress part of the SP experiment. It means that free bicycle parking is provided at arrival station.

Figure 8.3 shows the change in both bicycle and non-train user share. The differences are calculated in respect to a baseline scenario. The baseline scenario represents the stated choice experiment as it was conducted. We first compare the results of the baseline scenario with the current scenario. For example, the market share of non-users is 12 per cent, which represents the population that never use the train. The baseline is consistent with

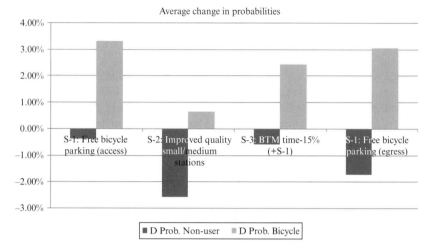

Figure 8.3 *Changes in probabilities of train and bicycle use for access and egress scenarios*

the Customer Satisfaction Survey (KTO, acronym in Dutch) analysed by Givoni and Rietveld (2007) and Brons et al. (2009).

The differences between scenario 1 and the baseline shows that assuming that free bicycle parking in the access journey is provided, the probability of bicycle use increases by 3.4 per cent on average, while the probability of non-users would be reduced by 0.4 per cent.

The difference between scenario 2 and the baseline shows that by enhancing the 'liveliness' of medium-sized and small stations, the number of train passengers would increase by 2.5 per cent. It means that train ridership is influenced by both bicycle parking cost and station quality. Moreover, the 'liveliness' of station environment plays a role almost as important as the bicycle parking cost in the decision to travel by train or not.

Scenario 3 assesses the importance of improving public transport accessibility to the station. Reducing the travel time by BTM by 15 per cent would increase the train ridership by 0.5 per cent, equivalent to 3100 passengers/day among the 38 stations sampled. The results indicate that investments in public transport connection to the rail station would increase rail use, by making the journey a smoother chain of public transport modes. Consistent with Brons et al. (2009), the results show the effects of a smoother chain of modes in the whole train journey.

Table 8.5 shows the average changes in market shares of access modes by station type. The last column on the right shows the average number of passengers per day depending on the station size. The total increase

Table 8.5 Average change in market shares of access modes by station type

Row labels	Average of S1 Δ BIKE (%)	Average of S2 Δ BIKE (%)	Average of S2 Δ BTM (%)	Average of S1Δ NON- USER (%)	Average of S2 Δ NON- USER (%)	Δ S1 Total # of passengers	Av. passengers/ day
1	3.30	−0.74	1.72	−0.35	−0.21	71	10 000
2	3.31	−0.77	1.79	−0.36	−0.22	1404	65 000
3	3.31	−0.70	1.60	−0.32	−0.18	258	20 000
4	3.27	−0.63	1.44	−0.30	−0.16	127	6000
5	3.27	−0.61	1.40	−0.30	−0.16	121	2500
6	3.24	−0.70	1.61	−0.32	−0.20	19	2000
Total	3.29	−0.71	1.64	−0.34	−0.20	1999	

Note: N = 38 stations.

in passengers is calculated by multiplying the change in non-users by the number of respondents by station type in the sampled network. For scenario 1, a total of 2000 passengers would be added to the 38 stations analysed in the survey.

8.8   CONCLUSIONS

This chapter estimates both joint RP–SP and SP choice models of station access and egress mode in the wider metropolitan area of The Hague–Rotterdam, in the Netherlands. The joint RP–SP estimation allows the verification of unbiased results in the SP models. Moreover, this chapter analyses mode specific VTTS and measures specific WTP. Finally, by developing different attribute combinations, a sensitivity analysis of train ridership is calculated.

The results show that train ridership strongly depends on access time by the different access modes. At the same time, train passengers are attracted by both free bicycle parking costs and low bus, tram or metro fares. The positive effect of free bicycle parking on train ridership is consistent for both access and egress journeys. In addition, improving the 'liveliness' of stations also increases the probability of train use in the small and medium-sized stations.

From a methodological perspective, the results show that the model structure is relevant for the estimation of accurate market shares in modes of access and egress. The estimation of both ML and NML shows that omitting the correlation across alternatives tends to overestimate the market shares, and also the VTTS and WTP.

In future research, the calculation of VTTS by car for access and egress would complete the mode specific research. In this study, that was not possible because the cost of car access/egress was not available in the SP experiment. In addition, we did not include network effects which are likely to occur when the quality of access and egress transport changes. Changes in station accessibility, however, affect the catchment area of railway stations and are likely to result in network effects. Bicyclists might, for example, choose a larger railway station farther away as a departure station when bicycle parking is improved, instead of choosing the closest local train station. This can be included by incorporating the VTTS and WTP values in a regional or national transport demand model which would also allow a comparison between market shares from discrete-choice models and simulation models to be possible.

ACKNOWLEDGEMENTS

This work has been funded by the NWO (Netherlands Organisation for Scientific Research) programme Sustainable Accessibility of the Randstad. The authors want to thank Dr Elisabetta Cherchi for her feedback on the joint estimation process. However any errors made during the process or invalid conclusions are the responsibility of the authors.

REFERENCES

Ampofo, F., Maidment, G. and J. Missenden (2004), 'Underground railway environment in the UK Part 1: Review of thermal comfort', *Applied Thermal Engineering*, **24** (5–6), 611–631.

Ben-Akiva, M. and T. Morikawa (1990), 'Estimation of switching models from revealed preferences and stated intentions', *Transportation Research Part A: General*, **24** (6), 485–495.

Bhat, C.R. and R. Sardesai (2006), 'The impact of stop-making and travel time reliability on commute mode choice', *Transportation Research Part B: Methodological*, **40** (9), 709–730.

Bradley, M.A. and A.J. Daly (1997), 'Estimation of logit choice models using mixed stated-preference and revealed-preference information', in P. Stopher and M. Lee-Gosselin (eds), *Understanding Travel Behaviour in an Era of Change*, Bingley: Emerald Group Publishing.

Brons, M., Givoni, M. and P. Rietveld (2009), 'Access to railway stations and its potential in increasing rail use', *Transportation Research Part A: Policy and Practice*, **43** (2), 136–149, DOI: 10.1016/j.tra.2008.08.002.

Brownstone, D. and K. Train (1998), 'Forecasting new product penetration with flexible substitution patterns', *Journal of Econometrics*, **89** (1–2), 109–129.

Cascetta, E. and A. Cartenì (2014), 'The hedonic value of railways terminals: A quantitative analysis of the impact of stations quality on travellers behaviour', *Transportation Research Part A: Policy and Practice*, **61**, 41–52.

Cherchi, E. and J. Ortúzar (2002), 'Mixed RP/SP models incorporating interaction effects', *Transportation*, **29** (4), 371–395.

Cherchi, E. and J. Ortúzar (2006a), 'Use of mixed revealed-preference and stated-preference models with nonlinear effects in forecasting', *Transportation Research Record: Journal of the Transportation Research Board*, **1977** (1), 27–34.

Cherchi, E. and J. de D. Ortúzar (2006b), 'On fitting mode specific constants in the presence of new options in RP/SP models', *Transportation Research Part A: Policy and Practice*, **40** (1), 1–18.

Cozens, P., Neale, R., Whitaker, J. and D. Hillier (2003), 'Managing crime and the fear of crime at railway stations – a case study in South Wales (UK)', *International Journal of Transport Management*, **1** (3), 121–132.

Debrezion, G., Pels, E. and P. Rietveld (2009), 'Modelling the joint access mode and railway station choice', *Transportation Research Part E: Logistics and Transportation Review*, **45** (1), 270–283, DOI: 10.1016/j.tre.2008.07.001.

Givoni, M. and P. Rietveld (2007), 'The access journey to the railway station and its role in passengers' satisfaction with rail travel', *Transport Policy*, **14** (5), 357–365.

Hensher, D.A. (1994), 'Stated preference analysis of travel choices: the state of practice', *Transportation*, **21** (2), 107–133.

Hensher, D.A. and J.M. Rose (2007), 'Development of commuter and non-commuter mode choice models for the assessment of new public transport infrastructure projects: A case study', *Transportation Research Part A: Policy and Practice*, **41** (5), 428–443.

Hensher, D.A., Rose, J.M. and W.H. Greene (2008), 'Combining RP and SP data: biases in using the nested logit 'trick' – contrasts with flexible mixed logit incorporating panel and scale effects', *Journal of Transport Geography*, **16** (2), 126–133.

Keijer, M.J.N. and P. Rietveld (2000), 'How do people get to the railway station? The Dutch experience', *Transportation Planning and Technology*, **23** (3), 215–235.

Krizek, K., El-Geneidy, A. and K. Thompson (2007), 'A detailed analysis of how an urban trail system affects cyclists' travel', *Transportation*, **34** (5), 611–624.

La Paix, L. and K. Geurs (2014), 'Adaptive stated choice experiment for access and egress mode choice to train stations', Paper presented at the World Symposium of Land-Use and Research, Delft, the Netherlands.

Lee, J. and W. Lam (2003), 'Levels of service for stairway in Hong Kong underground stations', *Journal of Transportation Engineering*, **129** (2), 196–202.

Martens, K. (2004), 'The bicycle as a feedering mode: Experiences from three European countries', *Transportation Research Part D: Transport and Environment*, **9** (4), 281–294.

Martens, K. (2007), 'Promoting bike-and-ride: The Dutch experience', *Transportation Research Part A: Policy and Practice*, **41** (4), 326–338.

McFadden, D. and K. Train (1996), 'Consumers' evaluation of new products: Learning from self and others', *Journal of Political Economy*, **104**, 683–703.

O'Sullivan, S. and J. Morrall (1996), 'Walking distances to and from light-rail transit stations', *Transportation Research Record: Journal of the Transportation Research Board*, **1538** (1), 19–26.

Pucher, J. and R. Buehler (2008), 'Making cycling irresistible: Lessons from the Netherlands, Denmark and Germany', *Transport Reviews: A Transnational Transdisciplinary Journal*, **28** (4), 495–528.

Pucher, J. and R. Buehler (2009), 'Integrating bicycling and public transport in North America', *Journal of Public Transportation*, **12** (3), 79–104.

Rietveld, P. (2000), 'The accessibility of railway stations: The role of the bicycle in The Netherlands', *Transportation Research Part D*, **5** (1), 71–75.

Train, K. (2003), *Discrete Choice Methods with Simulation*, New York: Cambridge University Press.

Wardman, M. (2004), 'Public transport values of time', *TransportPolicy*, **11** (4), 363–377.

9. Industrial accessibility and the efficiency of the US freight railroads

Kenneth Button, Zhenhua Chen and Rui Neiva

9.1 INTRODUCTION

The majority of the analyses of accessibility have involved the implicit underlying assumption that government action, often involving subsidies or public investment, could improve accessibility. Furthermore, the emphases of these analyses have seen a focus on personal travel, often concerning notions of social equity.[1] Here we make no judgment about the underlying ethos of this way of approaching accessibility, or whether it has resulted in significant social welfare gains. Our interest is in freight transportation and the ways in which institutional changes have improved access of producers to markets and of suppliers of inputs to the production process. Accessibility in this context is seen as relating to the efficiency of provision and not just to the existence of transportation capacity. Inadequate or over-costly freight transportation, and with it lower levels of access, can stymie production, and thus limit social welfare.

The analysis is limited to the United States (US) railroad system, and to considering the impact that regulatory changes over 40 years have had on its efficiency and its ability to provide industry and consumers with access to the inputs and goods that they are seeking. It is not concerned with developing some hypothetical accessibility index, or making any external, normative judgment concerning the merits of particular patterns of accessibility, but rather describing what has happened regarding the accessibility offered when an important transportation mode is largely left to market-driven suppliers.

The Staggers Rail Act of 1980 is a US federal law that fundamentally deregulated the American railroad industry, representing the last major Act of a decade of change that replaced the regulatory structure that had existed since the 1887 Interstate Commerce Act.[2] The outcomes of the reforms have been extensively studied as the freight railroad system has gradually transformed itself; changes that are often seen as one of the major successes of the 'Age of Regulatory Reform' spanning the late 1970s to the 1990s.[3]

Efficiency in supplying transportation services reduces costs to users, and by releasing resources allows for higher levels of consumption across the economy. Put another way, increased efficiency in freight transportation provides those that use it with cheaper access to an important input to their production processes and, for consumers of the goods transported, *de facto* increases in their real incomes. Here we are not concerned with hypothetical levels of railroad efficiency as a proxy for industrial accessibility, but with the revealed preference for accessibility disclosed through actual changes in railroad efficiency and in its use.[4] Basically, a free market in rail services allows customers to select those routes and services that provide them with their desired level of accessibility. Although not completely positive in its approach, it moves away from many of the normative judgments found in much of the work on personal accessibility that in general focuses on the availability of access irrespective of whether individuals wish to make use of it, and of the opportunity costs of its provision.

This chapter is also not concerned with adding additional empirical evidence to the work on US freight railroad efficiency, but rather concentrates on what has already been done and the extent to which findings from the US may be useful elsewhere.[5] The importance of this is not just in offering a review of the US situation more than 30 years after reform, but also to glean some insights into the relevance of the changes in the US for Europe, at a time when it is seen that 'the creation of an internal rail market, in particular with regard to freight transport, is an essential factor in making progress towards sustainable mobility' (European Commission 2010).[6]

9.2 CHANGING RAILROAD DEREGULATION AND CONSUMER ACCESSIBILITY

The plethora of both *de facto* and *de jure* changes in the approach to the economic regulation of transportation in the late 1970s and early 1980s, as the US sought under initially President Carter, and subsequently President Reagan, to combat the country's decline into stagflation, are almost classic 'Big Bang' approaches to reform. The temporal concentration of changes involving the airlines, railroads, trucking and intercity buses were not only close together, but each involved almost instantaneous reforms within the individual industries spanning just a few years.[7] This is in contrast to the transportation reforms that have been seen in Europe where, for largely institutional reasons emanating from the international nature of the European Union (EU) market, reforms have been gradual and often very haphazard, often allowing those with vested interests to stymie reforming trends.[8] The US railroad reforms fall both within the overall shift in policy in the US under Carter and Reagan, and within the Big Bang framework.

The US rail industry has been operated by the private sector since its inception, but the monopoly power of railroads in several regions, combined with their strategic importance, means that the industry has traditionally been the subject of economic regulation. The Interstate Commerce Commission (ICC) was established in 1887 to control freight rates, oversee mergers and acquisitions, and regulate competition between the modes by limiting cross-ownership. The advent of competition from road transport subsequently adversely affected the role of railroads; a situation exacerbated by regulation stymying the railroads' abilities to react, especially with the ICC setting rates low for farm products[9] and higher for general freight, which was the most susceptible to truck competition. At the same time the railroad companies had little incentive to modernize because the ICC had to rule on major changes, leading to difficulties in closing unprofitable tracks and services. The result was that while in 1920 railroads accounted for 75 percent of intercity freight movements, by 1975 their share had declined by 35 percent.

By the mid-1970s, with a third of the US rail industry bankrupt or close to it, and with the system's physical infrastructure in a state of serious deterioration (track conditions got so bad that there were 'standing derailments', with stationary freight cars falling off the rails due to rotten cross-ties), reforms began; see Table 9.1. The passenger activities of the railroads were consolidated and given over to Amtrak, although most of the infrastructure remained with the traditional railroads. The Railroad Revitalization and Regulatory Reform Act (the '4Rs' Act) initiated the creation of ConRail by the federal government in an effort to save Penn Central and other bankrupt eastern railroads. However, it was losing $1 million a day.

The 1980 Staggers Act produced a major regulatory restructuring. Change could have taken several forms, but the approach adopted was in part influenced by evidence that the regulatory boards had been 'captured' by the industry itself, with members being drawn largely from the rail companies. While the 4Rs Act had initiated some measures to lighten freight rate regulation, the ICC had initially not put much effect into its new legislative mandates. But as further, more specific regulatory change began to appear between 1976 and 1979, including the phasing in of the loss of collective rate-making authority, most of the major railroads shifted away from their efforts to maintain the historic regulatory system,

Table 9.1   Major pieces of US legislation impacting on freight railroads

Year	Legislation	Main economic implications
1887	Interstate Commerce Act	The federal government empowered to regulate railways; including, requirements that fares are 'reasonable and just', and that fare discrimination between long- and short-haul services is not permitted. The Interstate Commerce Commission (ICC) enforced the Act.
1893	Railroad Safety Appliance Act	Requires air brakes and automatic couplers on all trains.
1926	Railway Labor Act	Settle disputes and avoid strikes.
1966	Department of Transportation Act	Created the Federal Railroad Administration to promulgate and enforce rail safety regulations, administer assistance programs, conduct research and development to improve safety and national rail transportation policy, rehabilitate Northeast Corridor rail passenger service, and consolidate government support of railroad activities.
1970	Rail Passenger Service Act	Created Amtrak, a federal-owned passenger railroad that allowed participating suppliers to discontinue passenger service. Of 26 railroads eligible, 20 became exclusively freight railroads, with the remainder continuing to provide passenger service; by 1989 all had stopped doing so.
1973	Regional Rail Reorganization Act	Provided interim funding to bankrupt railroads and authorized creation of the Consolidated Rail Corporation (Conrail) to take over the assets previously owned by railroads in the North-East.
1976	Railroad Revitalization and Regulatory Reform Act	Provided funds for ConRail and offered leeway to the ICC to exempt some categories of traffic from economic regulation. It changed the definition of what constitutes 'reasonable and just' fares.
1980	Staggers Rail Act	Replaced the Interstate Commerce Act by deregulating most of the freight railroads' activities, except in cases where they had monopoly power.
1995	Interstate Commerce Commission Termination Act of 1995	Interstate Commerce Commission replaced by the Surface Transportation Board.

and came to support greater freedom for economic rate setting, both at higher and lower rate levels. Major railroad shippers also continued to be of the view that they would be better served by more flexibility to arrive at tailored arrangements mutually beneficial to a particular shipper, and to the carrier serving a particular shipper. These judgments supported a second round of legislation, hence the Staggers Act (Gallamore and Meyer 2014).

Whereas the ICC had been created in 1887 to equalize rail rates, irrespective of the size of the customer, with the objective of blunting the power of the owners of what were seen as spatial monopoly railroad networks, after 1980 the railroads could negotiate confidential contracts with customers and charge what the traffic would bear. In simple economics, price discrimination was allowed, and with this came the ability of the railroads, with their decreasing cost structures, to recover their full costs and to invest in improved infrastructure. This also facilitated their meeting the competition of barge and truck freight modes. In terms of accessibility, this allowed those needing rail transportation for their commercial business more choice of services and of the rates to be paid.

The Staggers Act also came at a time when there were major technological changes that were advantageous to freight railroads, and when demand conditions were moving in favor of the attributes of the mode. Containerization had existed since the mid-1960s, but for it to be commercially viable for railroads there had to be scale economies and new ways of providing services. The growth in the economy in the 1980s, and in particular in international trade, accompanied by larger ships that deposited thousands of containers at a time at seaports, and in manufacturing, provided that demand. In turn this demand made it viable to lengthen trains, and to invest in consolidation facilities and the infrastructure needed for double stacking. New information technology allowed railroads to keep track of containers and manage their operations.

Of the major regulatory changes embodied in the Staggers Act, the most significant reforms were:

- A rail carrier could establish any rate for a rail service unless the ICC determined that there was no effective competition for it.
- Rail shippers and carriers would be allowed to establish contracts without effective ICC review, unless the Commission were to determine that the contract service would interfere with the rail carrier's ability to meet common carrier obligations.
- The scope of authority to control rates to prevent 'discrimination' among shippers was substantially curtailed.
- Across-the-board industry-wide rate increases were phased out.

- Dismantling of the collective rate-making machinery among railroads begun in 1976 was reaffirmed, with railroads neither permitted to agree as to the rates they could perform on their own systems, nor allowed to participate in the determination of rates on traffic in which they did not participate.

The Act also had provisions allowing the Commission to require access by one railroad to another railroad's facilities where one railroad had in effect 'bottleneck' control of traffic; technically this involved 'reciprocal switching' and 'trackage rights'.

9.3   THE BROAD OUTCOME

The initial economic outcomes of the Staggers Act came relatively fast. The railroads, having divested themselves of their unprofitable passenger business, had from 1976 begun to concentrate on their core freight activities, and especially bulk freight, coal, grain and ores, and to move towards more market rate setting.[10] Although general freight produced greater revenues per ton it was subject to more competition from trucking, and therefore initially received less attention. Given the high cost of maintaining unprofitable routes, the immediate post-Staggers Act period also saw the railroads abandoning tracks; more than 160 000 km were abandoned as the focus moved to strategic, long-distance corridors linking major gateways and inland markets.[11] These emerged as the types of service that meet the particular attributes of accessibility that industry seeks, rather than those that policy-makers think they need or, for some reason, should have. There was a growth in short-line railroads that largely provided services in rural areas, and by 2010 these amounted to 31 percent of the national freight rail network.[12] There were pronounced developments of hub-and-spoke systems by the Class I companies as they shed their short-line business; for example, 37 500 rail cars passing through Chicago, the largest hub, daily.

Operating costs were reduced significantly by staff reductions and other labor concessions, such as hours of work and in the daily distances crews are allowed to operate. Freight train crews, for example, were cut to two or three from four or five, and cabooses were replaced by electronic gear at the end of trains. On the revenue side, the railroads began charging market rates and, being allowed to enter into confidential contracts, had greater flexibility in negotiating with large-volume shippers. Added to this, the relaxation of controls over entry and exit produced a significant number of mergers[13] and takeovers that reduced the 56 Class I railroads in 1975 to seven in 2013 (excluding Amtrak), two of which are Canadian.[14] This has generally helped the industry achieve economies of scale, scope and density as well as strengthening its revenue flows. These gains have been reinforced by the relaxation of restrictions on intermodal ownership and operations that has led to a significant growth in the general freight business as the result of alliances with trucking companies ceding to rail parts of their long-distance cargo; by 2003 intermodal traffic accounted for the majority of rail revenues. The much higher overall levels of performance has also seen significant declines in most freight rates, with the railroad industry making a small profit since deregulation.[15]

On the pricing side, the reforms led to greater price discrimination, both to generate more revenue and to allocate traffic more efficiently. These included multi-car services, contracts between shippers and carriers, and priority pricing programs. The effects on efficiency of allowing for larger trains also transmitted through the consolidation of shipments (MacDonald and Cavalluzzo 1996).

Some indication of the patterns of operation that have emerged in North American Class 1 railroads can be seen in the network that is serviced by the second-largest, BNSF (formerly Burlington Northern and Santa Fe Railway); Figure 9.1. The various line shadings show the track BNSF owns or has access rights to, the regional linkages it enjoys, and its intermodal arrangements. The railroad carries a wide variety of commodities, from bulk to containers, and has a number of hubs that tie in with

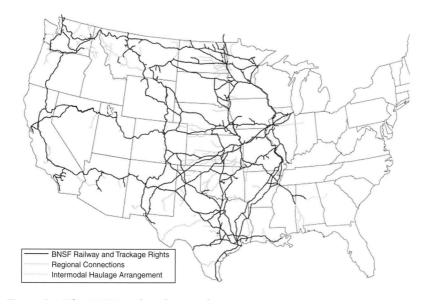

Figure 9.1 The BNSF railroad network

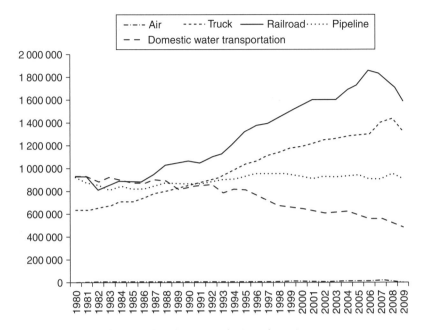

Figure 9.2   Freight modal spilt (ton-miles) in the USA

particular types of traffic flows, including 33 intermodal centers and nine
hump yards, with a centralized operations center for train dispatching and
network operations monitoring in Fort Worth.

In aggregate terms, since the enactment of the Staggers Act, US
railroads have become the dominant physical form of domestic freight
movement (Figure 9.2). There are 153 000 kilometers of Class 1 railroads
in the US, and another 67 000 of regional and local freight railroads,
with the former operating 397 730 freight cars and 23 893 locomotives.
They carried 1.33 trillion tonne kilometers in 1975, which doubled to
2.65 trillion in 2001, reaching 2.47 trillion tonne kilometers in 2011,
after a peak of almost 3.18 trillion in 2008.[16] Railroads employed about
229 000 people in 2011, compared to 1 million in 1990. Across studies,
while there are variations (a fact we return to in more detail later), the
general view seems to follow Wilson (1997) that variable costs in the
industry fell by between 41 and 44 percent by 1989 following the enactment of the Staggers Act.[17] In terms of fuel consumption, railroads are
three times as efficient as trucks. In 2011 the US Class I railroads carried
1 tonne of freight 219.79 km on a liter of fuel. In financial terms they
are all privately owned, with very small subsidies, generally for specific

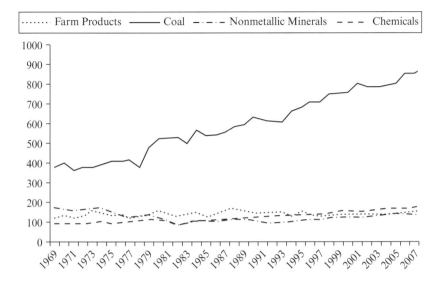

Figure 9.3   Bulk tons originated by freight type (thousand tons)

non-commercial projects, and by law have to allow Amtrak priority on their right of way and are only permitted to charge the marginal track maintenance cost for this. Since they were paying, the railroad customers were presumably getting the level of accessibility that was required for them to be economically efficient.

The types of goods carried have also changed quite considerably since 1980; the increased movement of coal being particularly pronounced (Figure 9.3). Some of the changes have been due to structural shifts in the economy, agricultural output having stabilized for example, but clean air legislation passed in 1990 increased demand for transporting low-sulfur coal from Wyoming's Powder River Basin to power plants across much of the US. The recent oil and gas boom has generated new traffic involving the hauling of crude oil from remote locations in places such as North Dakota not served by pipelines. Nevertheless, there is evidence of increased use of rail for bulk commodities prior to these events as rates fell (Wilson and Wilson 2001).

By way of comparison, the reforms in Western Europe have been much slower to take place, largely because of legacy effects leading to more focus on the integration of systems through open access, and the international nature of the reforms. The formation of the European Coal and Steel Community in 1951 led to efforts to reduce national preferences in the carriage of raw material in terms of removing explicit subsidies, but also reducing both split rates when the commodities crossed borders and domestic rate tapers that favored domestic production of coal and steel over international trade.[18] The move towards an integrated European freight rail system, with the aim of allowing wider access to the network, began in 1991 when EU Directive 91/440 made it a legal requirement for independent companies to be able to apply for non-discriminatory track access on any EU country's track. The measure was aimed at enhancing efficiency and thus opening access by reducing user costs, by creating greater competition, with member states being required to ensure that organizations operating rail infrastructure and services are separate and run on a commercial basis. Additionally railway companies from all member states are allowed to run services on any other member states' rail infrastructure, for both passenger transport and goods.

This approach clearly differs from that in the US where competition is seen to be between integrated rail company networks and alternative modes, rather than competition between operators on a common track and with other modes. Additionally, unlike the Big Bang approach favored in the US, the reforms have been gradual and piecemeal. For example, further directives were issued in 2001 as the First Railway Package, to clarify the details of the situation and initially allow cross-border freight operations on the whole European network, with the need for safety and operating standards to be set out clearly and administered by an organization that did not run commercial services, and for the separate accounting of freight and passenger service revenues and costs. A framework was set out for the development of bodies to regulate the allocation of line possessions to companies and charges for the use of track, and railway licenses granted in one member state became generally valid in all other member states. In a Second Package of 2004 it was directed that by 2007 any licensed EU rail freight operator would have access to the European rail network.

The speed at which member states implemented the legislation varied. By 2004, for example, the UK had gone far beyond the original remit by privatizing its entire railway system, whereas Finland and France had created separate infrastructure and railway companies from their state-run enterprises. Others such as Germany had created separate subsidiaries for different service providers, and subsidiaries for infrastructure and track, and yet others had only separated accounting between organizational sections. By 2009 most countries in the EU still had a state-owned infrastructure company, but many had privatized part or all of their service providers, or were working towards it. In June 2010 the European Commission instigated legal proceedings through the European Court of Justice against 13 states that had not fully implemented the First

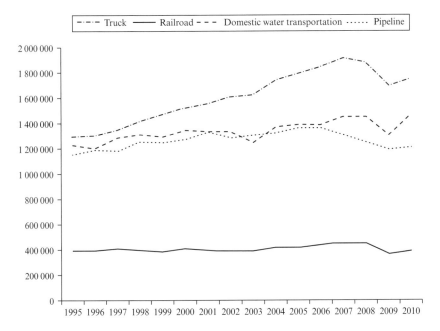

Figure 9.4   Freight modal spilt (ton-miles) in the EU-27

Package, but in 2012 the actions against Germany and Austria were rejected because their infrastructure and operating companies were sufficiently separated. Legal action for non-implementation against Bulgaria was passed to the Court in 2012, and in February 2013 the Court ruled that Hungary and Spain's infrastructure management was not sufficiently separated from train operations. Ireland derogated its obligation to implement the legislation; until 2012 its train operations and infrastructure businesses remained undivided, a similar situation to Northern Ireland.

The impacts of rail freight reform have been much less pronounced in Europe than in North America (Figure 9.4). In the 1950s the US and Europe moved roughly the same percentage of freight by rail, but by 2007 the share of US tonne-kilometers of freight moved by rail was 40 percent, although in terms of value it is less than 4 percent; whereas in contrast only 18 percent of freight traveled by rail in the 27-nation EU.[19] In 2006, while US Class I railroads moved 2587 billion ton-kilometers of freight, the 25-nation EU moved only 396 billion tonne-kilometers.

9.4 FACTORS AFFECTING THE RAILROADS' PERFORMANCE

There are manifest physical differences in the markets that the North American and the European freight railroads serve, and these inevitably affect the traffic in each region. The US has traditionally been a single geographical market, and there have been strong ties between it and the markets on its northern and southern borders, that have been further strengthened by the signing of the North American Free Trade Agreement. The Agreement opens a large geographical market in the north and south for US railroads, either through their own activities or through alliances. The EU in contrast is a set of independent states that have developed their own rail networks and have a tradition of planning and operating to meet national objectives, with borders an institutional barrier to international movements.

In any analysis of these institutional issues, the pure physical differences between the US and the EU need to be considered, especially regarding demand features. The US has major coastlines on both the east and the west with considerable flows of freight into and out of its seaports on both sides, a large amount of which goes by rail. The human geography of the US, with major inland centers as well as those on the coast lead to natural traffic from the international gateways to inland hubs. Figure 9.1 demonstrates this for BNSF, but it applies to the other Class I freight carriers. While the population of the EU is larger than that of the US, and its gross domestic product is about the same, a significant proportion of its population and of economic activity is concentrated in a discontinuous corridor of urbanization in Western Europe, with a population of around 110 million stretching from North West England in the north to Milan – the 'Blue Banana'. This pattern of activity leads to longer freight movements in the US, the average freight rail haul being about 1500 km, compared to Europe where rail hauls are somewhat over 250 km. The hub-and-spoke nature of the US market, coupled with the distances involved, allow for economies of scale; this is reflected in the increased traffic using a significantly smaller network.[20]

In terms of the supply side, there is also less competition in the US for longer-haul bulk transportation. The main inland water alternatives run north–south (for example, the Mississippi navigation) whereas much of the freight traffic moves between east to west. In contrast, European freight rail has to compete with inland water transportation that takes traffic from seaports into the main inland markets (for example, the Rhine navigation). This fact is picked up in the relative shares of inland water movements in the two markets seen in Figures 9.1 and 9.2.[21]

There are also issues of the use of track and of the priorities of the railway companies. US freight railroads own and maintain their track, although Amtrak has access, and unless otherwise stipulated as exclusions must allow each other access to their systems at an economic rate. They invest heavily in these networks. Over recent years the average has been about $12 billion annually on tracks, signals and other infrastructure, and another $9 billion on locomotives, freight cars and other equipment. The system is essentially geared for the commercial movement of freight. This contrasts with the European system, much of which is more metropolitan in its orientation and decidedly more focused on passenger transportation (it achieved some 397.8 billion passenger-kilometers in 2011, compared to 17.2 billion in the US), although the introduction of high-speed dedicated infrastructure in some corridors has freed capacity for freight movements.

9.5   THE ECONOMICS OF THE US SYSTEM

9.5.1   Demand Elasticities

The efficiency of any freight transportation mode depends to some extent on demand: with larger volumes of traffic, economies of scale, scope and density come into play. But equally, demand elasticities can be seen as indicators of the attributes of accessibility that shippers value. The previous figures have given some indication of the growth in traffic, which in part has been stimulated by lower rates, and in turn reinforced by outward shifts in the demand function as income and other factors have led to increased consumption. The isolation of these factors is not easy.

Freight transportation involves the movement of a vast array of goods in a diversity of contexts, and assessing, say, the elasticity of demand for bulk coal movement to a power station involves very different considerations to hauling containers of high-value electronics. Also while freight costs may only be a small part of the overall costs of transportation in the US – some 8–10 percent of the total – they vary a lot by industry and location, and can be large in relation to profit margins. The markets for rail freight are clearly different in Europe than the US; the tonne-kilometers of coal moved in the US by rail, for example, exceed the total rail freight in the EU.[22] Most demand elasticities for freight rail services are thus based on the commodity being carried.

So what do we know about any changes in elasticities after 1980? Early work after the Staggers Act, for example that of Levin (1978) and Babcock and German (1983), found greater elasticity in the demand for the movement of manufactures than for bulk commodities, which was hardly surprising given that the competition from truck freight in the former markets was partly dented by the flexibility that the railroads could now enjoy. This ability to compete, and with it to enjoy the economies of larger-scale activities, would seem to have inevitably allowed railroads to benefit from economies of scale.

9.5.2   Productivity Measures

There are major challenges in measuring efficiency for any capital-intensive industry, offering a non-durable product with numerous complementarities in the allocation of costs to traffic (not least of which is the return-load situation), and facing a multi-product demand function. The US freight railroads are also run by profit-maximizing, private companies that protect their commercial confidentiality. Set against this, from the analytical perspective, the Staggers reforms occurred at a time when new approaches to modeling and new econometric and programming estimation techniques were coming on line, allowing more complete analysis of cost and production functions. In particular, this has involved the development of data envelopment analysis (DEA) and various forms of flexible cost functions (for example, the transcendental logistic) with associated estimation techniques. These analytical methodologies have been applied to the rail sector, along with more traditional modeling frameworks and estimation procedures. The periods studied have also varied considerably, influenced by the particular issue being examined and the date of the analysis.[23] As a result of these variations in method and data, quite a wide range of results have emerged regarding efficiency, and *ipso facto* accessibility.

As with all activities, the efficiency of supply depends in part on the internal management of the business, the external physical conditions under which supplies are produced, and the institutional structure that determines the legal parameters under which production may take place. In the context of freight railroads there are considerable variations in terms of the last two factors, both between markets and over time. Summarizing the results is far from easy; the lack of consistency in reporting poses particular problem.[24] Also many of the studies, particularly those that focus on elasticities, do not provide aggregate figures but disaggregate by commodity to reflect the numerous sub-markets that the US railroads serve.

To get a better assessment of the findings of the studies that have looked at the efficiency of US freight railroads, a meta-analysis is conducted. There are challenges in using meta-analysis.[25] The selection of studies adopted is perhaps the most obvious. This can often be flawed by issues of omission, and in particular studies that have appeared in the 'gray' literature (basically reports and working papers), and issues of inclusion, and in particular when the meta-work embraces analysis with flawed results. There are problems in defining a viable common target variable (with authors using a variety of measures for their outputs), and in identifying and quantifying the important moderator variables, the factors that make each study unique. Added to this is the need for the studies included in the synthesis to be independent. There is a tendency, however, for the number of individuals who normally work in a detailed area of analysis to be small, with extensive cross-fertilization of thinking. There are also issues regarding the appropriate methodology to use in assessing the importance of the moderator effects.

The approach used here is meta-regression analysis making use of the generalized framework set out by Stanley and Jarrell (1989):

$$b_j = \beta + \sum_{K=1}^{K} \alpha_k Z_{jk} + e_j, \ \ j = 1, 2, \ldots L, \tag{9.1}$$

where b_j is the reported estimate of $\hat{a}$ in the jth study in the literature that is made up of L studies; $\hat{a}$ is the 'true' value of the parameter of interest; Z_{jk} includes various independent variables that measure the relevant characteristics of an empirical study and explain the variations from studies; α_k is the coefficient that reflects the biasing effect of particular study characteristics; and e_j is the error term.

We take the various estimates of output elasticities as the variable of interest (and as a proxy for accessibility) and regress these on a set of moderators to seek explanations for their variations. These on the right-hand side are divided between those that reflect the data used, the estimation methodology adopted, the policies assessed, and economic changes over the study periods, namely:

- *Deregulation* equals 1 if the study explicitly considers deregulation.
- *Merge* equals 1 if the study considers merge as a variable.
- *Before/After Staggers* equals 1 if the data period covers 1980.
- *Pre-Staggers* equals 1 if the data period only covers years prior to 1980.
- *Post-Staggers* equals 1 if the data only covers years after 1980.
- *Total Productivity Function* equals 1 when the study adopts this technique.
- *Data Envelopment Analysis* equals 1 if the study uses this technique.
- *Translog* equals 1 if the study adopts this function.
- *Endogeneity*: equals 1 if the study considers endogeneity.
- *Fixed Effects* equals 1 if the study controls for the fixed effects of the panel data.

The meta-data set includes some purely pre-Staggers Act estimates to see whether the legislation caused a shift in the elasticity, as well as those that specifically focused on the impact of Staggers. The vast majority of studies included were conducted prior to 2003. One reason for this is simply that the main interest in railroad efficiency was just prior to the Staggers Act, when efforts were being made to model the industry to seek out the factors causing its clear inefficiency, often with the intent of initiating more modest regulator reforms than Staggers produced; and after the Staggers Act, when the implications of liberalization were of interest. By the early 2000s the industry was generally seen as having stabilized. Added to this, the US economy, and in particular its international trade, began to change significantly after about 2003 with the rise in the Chinese economy, and this required somewhat different patterns and forms of railroad services.

One caveat with the data is that it has no aggregate output measure included. This variable is seldom reported in the studies. If the objective was to produce forecasts then this may be a serious omission because the left-side variable is an elasticity and thus is a composite of the slope of the cost/output curve and the location of that curve in cost and output space. Because we are primarily concerned with description of the past and the impact of institutional change, the fixed effects approach acts partially as a way of circumventing the absence of any output level effects.

The data embrace 26 observations, but some of these are from the same study.[26] To allow for this, weighted least squares is adopted: essentially, if there are three different results from a study because, say, a variety of sub-time periods were used, each observations is given a weight of a third. In terms of the number of studies included this is very much in line with other meta-analysis in the social sciences where academic studies are brought together. It is larger than the number often found in medical work, where statistical studies of outbreaks of rare diseases are, by definition, small; but smaller than that found in some meta studies that involved bringing together a large number of individual studies in which a systematical analytical technique has been used, often to meet legal requirements (Button et al. 1999). The results for the unweighted (Model 1) and weighted (Model 2) regressions are shown in Table 9.2.

Overall the models provide a reasonable level of overall statistical fit in each case, but few parameters are significant.[27] What we do see is that the explicit importance of deregulation in both cases is positive, although insignificant in the weighted regression case. But we also find that the studies that only cover the post-Staggers period are both positive and exhibit a reasonable degree of significance, indicating an upward move in the elasticity post-1980.[28] Thus while the meta-analysis is far from conclusive, it is indicative of enhanced efficiency after the regulatory reform.

Table 9.2   Results of meta-analysis of output elasticities

Variable	Model 1	Model 2
Constant	−4.08	−0.02
Deregulation	3.05*	1.53
Merger	1.57	−0.11
Before/After Staggers	5.91**	0.62
Pre-Staggers	3.52	2.12
Post-Staggers	5.60**	3.72*
Total Productivity Function	3.24	1.71
Data Envelopment Analysis	6.26*	5.23*
Translog	−0.52	−1.44
Endogeneity	−3.46	−2.23
Fixed Effects	0.29	−0.25
R^2	0.589	0.622

Notes: * Significant at 1%; ** significant at 5%; significant at 10%.

The method of estimation and model form seems to have exerted little influence on the results of the cases examined.[29]

9.6   CONCLUSIONS

Access to markets and to inputs is important to business, and in particular in enhancing business efficiency. While we can try to develop models of optimal levels of freight transportation accessibility, modeling has to date not proved very successful, largely because of the complexity and dynamism of modern industry (Button 2005). The liberalization of the US railroad system led to considerable increases in its economic performance, reduced its rates, and allowed more firms – in particular those needing long-distance transportation – access to its services. It moved away from the idea of uniformity, and the waste that can accompany providing excessive accessibility to those that cannot or do not make full use of it, and towards more diversity in the matching of accessibility to the needs of transportation users.

North America, however, is a particular market and the extent to which one can transfer experiences may be questioned. Certainly its freight railroads have performed very much better than their counterparts in Europe that suffer from significantly more government interference and thus an inability to provide the accessibility that industry needs. What is clear, therefore, is that whatever the particulars of the underlying geographical and economic conditions of the US market, the efficiency of its rail freight system has increased considerably, whereas that in Europe, where regulatory reforms have been much less pronounced, has not.

What we have focused on here is consideration of just how much the institutional structure in the US has influenced railroad efficiency and the access it provides for industry, including agriculture. There are plenty of studies highlighting the general positive impacts of the Staggers Act, but few assessing why there are differences in the efficiency estimates that have emerged. Our meta-analysis provides indications that the methods of estimation play little part in explaining the range of results that have been produced. These variations are likely due to the exact details of the normalizing variables included in the econometric and programming models, and to the types of traffic that were considered. Thus, while there is considerable evidence that industry in the US has much greater access to the rail services it needs to be more efficient, the exact extent of the new levels of accessibility is still foggy. But it is clear from the choices made by users that the level of accessibility has grown considerably since the US government imposed rules governing who could provide services and at what prices.

ACKNOWLEDGEMENTS

Rui Neiva was supported by a PhD scholarship from the Fundação para a Ciência e Tecnologia (SFRH/BD/64730/2009), funded under the POPH (Programa Operacional Potencial Humano) and QREN (Quadro de Referência Estratégica Nacional) Portugal programs. Zhenhua Chen acknowledges financial support from the Center for Transportation Public–Private Partnership Policy at George Mason University, USA. Data support from the Association of American Railroads is highly appreciated.

NOTES

1. Geurs and van Wee (2004) provide a survey of this approach and variants of it.
2. The US term 'railroad' is used throughout rather than 'railway', which is the more common terminology in Europe.
3. For a wider perspective of what occurred at that time, see papers in Button and Swann (1989).
4. For an examination of the theoretical accessibility offered by intermodal freight transportation in the US see, Lim and Thill (2008). What this does not do is relate the supply of facilities to what may be seen as useful by potential freight movers.
5. There are other, more extensive studies that have at various times focused on providing more general surveys of work on US rail productivity, for example Oum et al. (1999).

The measurement of freight accessibility in the US is hampered not only by the usual issues of definition and the difficulty of developing an appropriate matrix (simply defining it as the degree of spatial separation between a location and an opportunity is far too vague), but also by a lack of solid data (Transportation Research Board 2003), but there is no doubt that variation in accessibility does exist (Vachal et al. 2007) just as there are variations in all other factor prices.

6. The analytical analysis of European freight rail transportation is relatively limited; Weigmans and Donders (2007) and Himola (2007) are exceptions. The notion of mobility is somewhat different to that of accessibility, and entails a general notion of enhancing the ability to move around a system, as opposed to having the ability to reach specific types of destination. We assume here that individuals and businesses have a better appreciation of accessibility than mobility.

7. This should not be taken to infer that there were no general difficulties with this approach, for example regarding such things as stranded costs and short-term issues of disequilibria as actors in both the supply and demand side adjustments (Meyer and Tye 1985).

8. For an assessment of the general pros and cons of the 'Big Bang' versus gradualist approaches, see Button and Johnson (1998).

9. The idea being that this would allow farmers better accessibility to a wider range of markets.

10. Amtrak operates more than 300 trains each day on 34 111 km of track connecting more than 500 destinations in 46 states and three Canadian provinces. In fiscal year 2012, it served 31.2 million passengers, although this is just 0.007 percent of daily commuter trips and 0.4 percent of intercity trips; and had $2.02 billion in revenue while employing more than 20 000 people. It has received more than $13 billion of federal subsidies since 1972, with an average subsidy per passenger of $100. The subsidy in 2012 was $1.42 billion.

11. Grimm and Harris (1988) discuss some of the network implications of this.

12. See Grimm and Sapienza (1993) for a discussion of short-line railroads.

13. While mergers began in the mid-1970s there were more after the Staggers Act. The impact of these mergers is considered in Bitzan and Wilson (2007), Chapin and Schmidt (1999), Grimm (1984), Grimm and Harris (1983, 1985) and Winston et al. (2011).

14. Railroad companies in the US are now generally separated into three categories based on their annual revenues: Class I for freight railroads with operating revenues above $398.7 million (2010 dollars), Class II for freight railroads with revenues between $31.9 million and $398.7 million, and Class III for all other freight revenues. The distinction largely relates to labor laws that differ for Class II and III railroads, although the designations are now rarely used outside industry. The more widely used distinctions are those of the Association of American Railroads that typically divides non-Class I companies into regional railroads operating at least 560 km or that make at least $40 million per year; local railroads, non-regional railroads that engage in line-haul service; and switching and terminal railroads that mainly switch cars between other railroads or provide service from other lines to a common terminal. The focus here is almost exclusively on Class I railroads.

15. With this consolidation has come some concerns about monopoly power; see US Government Accountability Office (2006).

16. In terms of value, rail freight is less dominant, carrying only $574 billion in 2007, compared to $12 193 billion by truck and $357 billion by air. Some $1917 billion were moved by multiple modes, and some of this would embrace rail.

17. Other rail cost studies include Barbera et al. (1987), Bitzan (2003), Bitzan and Wilson (2007), Boyer (1987) and Wilson (1997).

18. The situation was somewhat different in the Communist bloc of Eastern Europe where the planned rail freight network was essentially designed to move goods from satellite states to Russia. This posed problems after the geopolitical changes in 1989 (Button 1993).

19. In terms of value, less than 4 percent of freight was moved by rail.
20. Unlike the airlines, economies of scope have been less significant than density effects, especially in the movement of bulk commodities that are essentially point-to-point activities. The US railroads already had significant hubbing activities prior to the Staggers Act, often involving joint ownership of hubs. What the reforms did was to allow concentration of resources on the routes where demand is greatest. There had been little to prevent this prior to 1980.
21. The EU also has significant bulk movement of freight by coastal shipping, whereas this is much less important in North America, partly because of geography but also because institutionally, the 1920s Jones Act limits most traffic to US carriers and American-built ships.
22. One reason for this is that only 19 percent of energy used in the US is nuclear, compared to 75 percent in France, 51 percent in Belgium and 46 percent in Hungary.
23. As examples, the output elasticity ranges from 12.34 (Bereskin 1996), 3.5 (Caves et al. 1981) and 3.34 (Gordon 1991), to 0.91 (Bitzan and Wilson 2007), 0.05 (Davis and Wilson 2003) and 0.77 (Bitzan 2003).
24. Martland (2006, 2012) provides an overview of trends in productivity.
25. Meta-analysis is only one of several ways of synthesizing the findings of a series of independent studies; see Button (1998). For a critical assessment of the use of meta-analysis in microeconomics work, see Button et al. (1999).
26. The studies included are, with the number of estimates from each given in squared parentheses: Bereskin (1996) [5]; Bitzan (2003) [1]; Bitzan and Keeler (2003) [1]; Bitzan and Wilson (2007) [1]; Caves et al. (1980) [2]; Caves et al. (1981) [2]; Chapin and Schmidt (1999) [1]; Davis and Wilson (2003) [1]; Duke et al. (1992) [1]; Fishlow (1966) [1]; Gollop and Jorgenson (1980) [1]; Gordon (1991) [1]; Interstate Commerce Commission (1997) [1]; Ivaldi and McCullough (2001) [1]; Kendrick (1973) [1]; Kendrick and Grossman (1980) [2]; Meyer and Morton (1975) [1]; and Wilson (1997) [1]. The output elasticities found in the studies range from −1.8 to 12.34.
27. Inspection of the correlation matrix suggests that there may be some concerns about multicollinerity, but these are not major.
28. The pre-Staggers parameters are also positive, although insignificant and in both cases smaller than the post-Staggers coefficient, but this should be taken in the context of the negative constant.
29. This finding is not inconsistent with the meta-work of Pels and Rietveld (2003), although they combined US/Canadian and European data that really embrace two entirely different types of network: one freight-dominated and the other passenger-dominated. Dummy variables are used to isolate these.

REFERENCES

Babcock, M.W. and W. German (1983), '1985 forecast: Rail share of intercity manufactures freight markets', *Transportation Research Forum*, **24**, 614–620.

Barbera, A., Grimm, C., Phillips, K. and L. Selzer (1987), 'Railroad cost structure – revisited', *Journal of the Transportation Research Forum*, **28**, 237–244.

Bereskin, C.G. (1996), 'Econometric estimation of the effects of deregulation on railway productivity growth', *Transportation Journal*, **35**, 34–43.

Bitzan, J.D. (2003), 'Railroad costs and competition: The implications of introducing competition to railroad networks', *Journal of Transport Economics and Policy*, **37**, 201–225.

Bitzan, J.D. and T.E. Keeler (2003), 'Productivity growth and some of its determinants in the deregulated US railroad industry', *Southern Economic Journal*, **70**, 232–253.

Bitzan, J.D. and W. Wilson (2007), 'Industry costs and consolidation: Efficiency gains and mergers in the US railroad industry', *Review of Industrial Organization*, **30**, 81–105.

Boyer, K.D. (1987), 'The costs of price regulation: Lessons from railroad deregulation', *RAND Journal of Economics*, **18**, 408–416.

Button, K.J. (1993), 'The development of East–West transport in Europe', in D. Banister and J. Berechman (eds), *Transportation in Unified Europe: Policies and Challenges*, Amsterdam: Elsevier.

Button, K.J. (1998), 'The three faces of synthesis: Bringing together quantitative findings in the field of transport and environmental policy', *Environment and Planning C*, **16**, 516–528.

Button, K.J. (2005), 'Can freight transport models be transferred across the Atlantic?' in A. Regiani and L. Schintler (eds), *Methods and Models in Transport and Telecommunications: Across Atlantic Perspectives*, Berlin: Springer-Verlag.

Button, K.J. and K. Johnson (1998), 'Incremental versus trend-break change in airline regulation', *Transportation Journal*, **37**, 25–34.

Button, K.J., Jongma, S.M. and J. Kerr (1999), 'Meta-analysis approaches and applied microeconomics', *International Journal of Development Planning Literature*, **14**, 75–102.

Button, K.J. and D. Swann (eds) (1989), *The Age of Regulatory Reform*, Oxford: Oxford University Press.

Caves, D.W., Christensen, L.R. and J.A. Swanson (1980), 'Productivity in US railroads, 1951–1974', *Bell Journal of Economics*, **11**, 166–181.

Caves, D.W., Christensen, L.R. and J.A. Swanson (1981), 'Economic performance in regulated and unregulated environments: A comparison of US and Canadian railroads', *Quarterly Journal of Economics*, **96**, 559–581.

Chapin, A. and S. Schmidt (1999), 'Do mergers improve efficiency? Evidence from deregulated rail freight', *Journal of Transport Economics and Policy*, **33**, 147–162.

Davis, D.E. and W.W. Wilson (2003), 'Wages in rail markets: Deregulation, mergers, and changing network characteristics', *Southern Economic Journal*, **69**, 865–885.

Duke, J., Litz, D. and L. Usher (1992), 'Multifactor productivity in railroad transportation', *Monthly Labor Review*, August, 49–58.

European Commission (2010), 'Regulation (EU) No 913/2010 of the European Parliament and of the Council of 22 September 2010 Concerning a European Rail Network for Competitive Freight; Text with EEA relevance', *Official Journal* L 276, 20/10/2010 P. 0022–0032.

Fishlow, A. (1966), 'Productivity and technical change in the railroad sector, 1840–1910', *Studies in Income and Wealth*, **30**, 583–646.

Gallamore, R.E. and J.R. Meyer (2014), *American Railroad: Decline and Renaissance in the Twentieth Century*, Cambridge, MA: Harvard University Press.

Geurs, K.T. and B. van Wee (2004), 'Accessibility evaluation of land-use and transport strategies: review and research directions', *Journal of Transport Geography*, **12**, 127–140.

Gollop, F. and D. Dale Jorgenson (1980), 'US productivity growth by industry, 1947–73', in J.W. Kendrick and B.N. Vaccara (eds), *New Developments in Productivity Measurement*, New York: National Bureau of Economic Research.

Gordon, R.J. (1991), 'Productivity in the transportation sector', NBER Working Paper No. 3815, Cambridge, MA: National Bureau of Economic Research.

Grimm, C. (1984), 'An evaluation of economic issues in the UP–MP–WP railroad merger', *Logistics and Transportation Review*, **20** (3), 239–259.

Grimm, C. and R.G. Harris (1983), 'Structural economics of the US rail freight industry: Concepts, evidence, and merger policy implications', *Transportation Research A*, **17**, 271–281.

Grimm, C. and R.G. Harris (1985), 'The effects of railroad mergers on industry performance and productivity', *Transportation Research Record*, **1029**, 9–17.

Grimm, C. and R.G. Harris (1988), 'A qualitative choice analysis of rail routings: Implications for vertical foreclosure and competition policy', *Logistics and Transportation Review*, **24**, 49–67.

Grimm, C. and H. Sapienza (1993), 'Determinants of short-line railroad performance', *Transportation Journal*, **32**, 5–13.

Himola, O-P. (2007), 'European railway freight transportation and adaptation to demand decline: Efficiency and partial productivity analysis for period of 1980–2003', *International Journal of Productivity and Performance Management*, **56**, 205–225.

Interstate Commerce Commission (1997), 'Railroad cost recovery procedures and productivity adjustments', Decision STB Ex Parte 290 (Sub-No. 4), Washington, DC.

Ivaldi, M. and G. McCullough (2001), 'Density and integration effects on Class I US freight railroads', *Journal of Regulatory Economics*, **19**, 161–182.

Kendrick, J.W. (1973), *Post-war Productivity Trends in the United States, 1948–1966*, New York: National Bureau of Economic Research.

Kendrick, J.W. and E.S. Grossman (1980), *Productivity in the United States: Trends and Cycles*, Baltimore, MD: Johns Hopkins University Press.

Levin, R.C. (1978), 'Allocation in surface freight transportation: Does rate regulation matter?', *Bell Journal of Economics*, **9**, 18–45.

Lim, H. and J.C. Thill (2008), 'Intermodal freight transportation and regional accessibility in the United States', *Environment and Planning A*, **40**, 2006–2025.

MacDonald, J.M. and L.C. Cavalluzzo (1996), 'Railroad deregulation: Pricing reforms, shipper responses, and the effects on labor', *Industrial and Labour Relations Review*, **50**, 80–91.

Martland, C.D. (2006), 'Productivity, pricing and profitability in the US rail freight industry 1995–2004', *Journal of the Transportation Research Forum*, **45**, 93–108.

Martland, C.D. (2012), 'Productivity improvements in the US rail freight industry 1980–2010', Paper presented to the Transportation Research Forum Annual Forum, Tampa.

Meyer, J.R. and A.I. Morton (1975), 'The US railroad industry in the post-World War II period: A profile', *Explorations in Economic Research*, **2**, 449–501.

Meyer, J.R. and W.B. Tye (1985), 'The regulatory transition', *American Economic Review, Papers and Proceedings*, **75**, 46–51.

Oum, T.H., Waters, W.G. and C. Yu (1999), 'A survey of productivity and efficiency measurement in rail transport', *Journal of Transport Economics and Policy*, **33**, 9–42.

Pels, E. and P. Rietveld (2003), 'Rail cost functions and scale elasticities: A meta-analysis', Research Memorandum (2003–03), Faculteit der Economische Wetenschappen en Econometrie, Free University, Amsterdam.

Stanley, T.D. and S.B. Jarrell (1989), 'Meta-regression analysis: A quantitative method of literature surveys', *Journal of Economic Surveys*, **2**, 161–170.

Transportation Research Board (2003), 'Freight capacity for the 21st century', Transportation Research Board Special Report 271, Washington, DC.

US Government Accountability Office (2006), 'Freight railroads: Industry health has improved but concerns about competition and capacity should be addressed', GAO-07-94, Washington, DC.

Vachal, K., Bitzan, J. and K.J. Button (2007), 'Transportation quality indices for economic analysis of non-metropolitan cities', *European Journal of Transport and Infrastructure Research*, **7**, 129–143.

Weigmans, B.W. and A.R.T. Donders (2007), 'Benchmarking European rail freight transport companies', *Transportation Journal*, **46**, 19–34.

Wilson, W.W. (1997), 'Cost savings and productivity gains in the railroad industry', *Journal of Regulatory Economics*, **11**, 21–41.

Wilson, W.W. and W.W Wilson (2001), 'Deregulation, rate incentives, and efficiency in railroad shipping of agricultural commodities', *Research in Transportation Economics*, **6**, 1–24.

Winston, C., Maheshri, V. and S.M. Dennis (2011), 'Long run effects of mergers: The case of US western railroads', *Journal of Law and Economics*, **54**, 275–304.

PART V

Accessibility evaluation and appraisal

10. The value of bicycle trail access in home purchases

Paul Mogush, Kevin J. Krizek and David Levinson

10.1 INTRODUCTION

Many cities, through public dialogues, community initiatives and other land use and transportation policies, are striving to enhance their 'livability'. While 'livability' is a relatively ambiguous term, there is emerging consensus on the following: the ease by which residents can travel by foot or bicycle represents a critical component of this goal. Communities with well-developed non-motorized infrastructure, in the form of sidewalks, bicycle paths, or compact and mixed land uses, are hypothesized to be more 'livable' than those without. This argument is often relied upon by advocates of bicycle paths or sidewalks.

If livability is cherished among residents, and one important component of livability includes bicycle paths, then it follows that living close to bicycle paths should be capitalized into home prices. Documenting this relationship would provide good news for advocates who often seek ways of monetizing the value of these public goods; bicycle facilities are non-market goods, making it difficult to attach an economic value to them.

Social or economic benefits can be measured either through stated preferences, in which users are asked to attach a value to non-market goods, or through revealed preferences. The revealed preference approach measures individuals' actual behavior. This study measures homebuyers' revealed preferences in the form of hedonic modeling to assess proximity to types of bicycle paths, in particular. Section 10.2 reviews previous literature on hedonic modeling, focusing primarily on the dimension of open space and trails. Section 10.3 describes the setting for this work and our data; section 10.4 explains the methodological approach. Section 10.5 describes the results of a hedonic regression model; and section 10.6 reports on the policy implications and relevant conclusions.

10.2   REVIEW OF RELEVANT LITERATURE AND CONCEPTS

Discerning the relative value of non-market goods using hedonic modeling techniques is a method with a long history. Taylor (1916) used what are now called hedonic techniques to explain the price of cotton with its internal qualities, and later applications by Lancaster (1966) and Rosen (1974) standardized the method for consumer products such as houses. An extensive review of this literature (Sirmans and Macpherson 2003) documents nearly 200 applications that have examined home purchases to estimate values of several home attributes including structural features (for example, lot size, a home's finished size in square feet, and number of bedrooms), internal and external features (for example, fireplaces, air conditioning, garage spaces and porches), natural environment features (for example, scenic views), attributes of the neighborhood and location (for example, crime, golf courses and trees), public services (for example, school and infrastructure quality), marketing, and financing.

As the literature describes various methods to assign value to housing characteristics, there are opportunities to increase the explanatory power of hedonic models. Recent contributions to the literature include more robust measures of accessibility, perceived school quality and measures of environmental amenities. For example, Franklin and Waddell (2003) used a hedonic model to predict home prices in King County, Washington as a function of accessibility to four types of activities (commercial, university, K-12 schools and industrial). In assessing the relationship between public school quality and housing prices, Brasington (1999) found that proficiency tests, per-pupil spending and student–teacher ratios most consistently capitalize into the housing market. Earnhart (2001) combined discrete-choice hedonic analysis with choice-based conjoint analysis to place a value on adjacent environmental amenities such as lakes and forests.

Our application here focuses on the relative impact of bicycle lanes and trails. To the casual observer, bicycle lanes and trails may be considered a single facility, where any type of bicycle trail would have the same attraction. A more detailed approach, however, suggests otherwise because of the possible effect of different types of bicycle facilities. Three different types of trails and lanes are examined: (1) trails on existing streets, demarcated by paint striping (hereafter referred to as 'on-street lanes'); (2) trails adjacent to existing roadways (hereafter 'roadside trails') but separated by curbs or mild landscaping (these facilities are sometimes referred to as 'black sidewalks' in the local lexicon because they are nothing more than blacktop in the usual location of sidewalks); (3) other trails clearly separated from traffic and often within open spaces (hereafter 'non-roadside trails'). For the latter category, it is important to explain and control for the degree to which open space, versus the bike trail contained within the open space, contribute to a home's value. In many metropolitan areas in the US, bike trails and open space share a spatial location and at minimum exhibit similar recreational qualities. On-street lanes or roadside trails are often on or near roads. In some cases they will be on well-used collector streets or trunk highways; in others they may be on neighborhood arterial streets. While infrastructure usually has an attraction element, homebuyers tend to be repelled by immediate proximity to busy roadways. Any attraction of bicycle facilities therefore depends on the design speed of the roadway facility and the average daily traffic. Any research failing to account for any of these factors will misestimate the independent value of bicycle trails.

It is therefore important to consider relevant literature estimating the value of open space and its context. For example, Quang Do and Grudnitski (1995) found that homes abutting golf courses sell for a 7.6 percent premium over others. Other studies interact measures of both proximity and size of various open spaces (Mahan et al. 2000; Lutzenhiser and Netusil 2001). Geoghegan (2002) compared the price effects of the amount of permanent and developable open space within a 1 mile radius. Smith et al. (2002) examined the fixed and adjustable open spaces along a new interstate highway corridor. Other approaches further disaggregate developable and non-developable open space in terms of ownership type and land cover (Irwin 2002). Some studies seek to attach values to views of open space. Benson et al. (1998) created a series of dummy variables for four different qualities of ocean views, as well as lake and mountain views. Luttik (2000) combined the vicinity and view approaches, dividing the geography into three levels of proximity.

Anderson and West's work (2004) is particularly relevant. They modeled both proximity and size of six specific open space categories, comparing effects on home prices between the city and the suburbs. They found that proximity to golf courses, large parks and lakes has a positive effect on home prices in the city, with no significant results in the suburbs. The effects of open space on home prices also increased with the size of the open space. Proximity to small parks and cemeteries tended to reduce sale prices. To our knowledge, only one application focuses on proximity to bicycle trails. Lindsey et al. (2003) performed a hedonic analysis of 9348 home sales, identifying properties falling inside or outside a 0.5 mile buffer around 14 greenways in Marion County, Indiana. This research found that some greenways have a positive, significant effect on property values while others have no significant effect. A survey in Vancouver found that the majority of realtors perceive little effect of bicycle trails on home values, either positive or negative (City of Vancouver 1999). However, two-thirds of respondents also indicated that they would use bicycle trail proximity as a selling point.

Given the novelty of our application, theory is derived from a combination of sources, including existing published work (described in part above), consumer theory and anecdotal evidence. Our first underpinning is derived from a local county commissioner who claims that bike facilities, like libraries, are goods that everyone appreciates (McLaughlin 2003). Such a claim comports with the frequent assertions from bicycle trail advocates. Assuming an ability to account for the possible disutility of living on a busy arterial road, bicycle facilities – no matter their type – positively contribute to home value. However, this hypothesis needs to be tempered based on the findings of Anderson and West. Their analysis suggests that open spaces, and by association bicycle facilities, may be perceived and valued differently depending on whether they are located in the city or the suburbs.

Unlike other attributes, which tend to be more universally valued (for example, home size, number of bathrooms), we hypothesize that trails may be more appreciated by subsets of the population. Households residing in cities have higher rates of walking or cycling, particularly for work purposes (Barnes 2004; Krizek and Johnson 2004). Owing to the increased cycling use, city residents are thus hypothesized to attach a higher value to the three types of bicycle facilities.

10.3   SETTING AND DATA

Our investigation is based in the Twin Cities (Minnesota) Metropolitan Area which proves to be an almost ideal laboratory for a variety of reasons. First, the Twin Cities boasts a system of off-street bike paths almost unparalleled for any major metropolitan area in the US, totaling more than 2722 km (1692 miles). While not nearly as extensive, striped on-street bike lanes are common as well. The network of on- and off-street trails is accessible to most Twin Citians, with 90 percent of homes within 1600 meters (1 mile) of an off-street trail. In fact, in many communities within the metropolitan area more than 90 percent of the homes have some form of facility within 400 meters (0.25 mile).

Second, several municipalities and county governments pursue an active role in constructing and maintaining these facilities. The Grand Rounds Parkway in Minneapolis, considered by many to be the crown jewel of parks and recreational trails in Minnesota, consists of more than 70 km (43 miles) of off-street paved trails along the city's chain of lakes, the Mississippi River and Minnehaha Creek. Hennepin County, which includes the city of Minneapolis and many of its suburbs, works in cooperation with the Three Rivers Park District to build and maintain the largest network of off-street trails in the metro area (Jackson and Newsome 2000). Many off-street trails in Hennepin and other counties are located on former railroad rights of way, for the dual purposes of recreation and preservation of the land for future transit corridors. Other off-street trails in the Twin Cities follow arterial and collector streets. The cities of Chanhassen, Eden Prairie and Plymouth have extensive networks of these roadside trails, with somewhat smaller networks in Maple Grove, Roseville, Eagan and Apple Valley. Roseville is the only inner-ring suburb with a substantial network of off-street trails. Third, Twin Citians as a population appear to cherish such trails, particularly in the summer months. For example, Minneapolis ranks among the top in the United States in the percentage of workers (2.63 percent) who self-report as being a regular bicycle commuter (Dill and Carr 2003).

Consistent with the prevailing literature, our hedonic model assumes a competitive market in which homebuyers are seeking a set of home attributes that can be tied to a location. Locations are defined by structural attributes (S) (including internal and external attributes), neighborhood characteristics (N), location and accessibility (L) and environmental amenities (A). We build an equilibrium hedonic price function on these assumptions, where the market price of a home (P_h) depends on the quantities of its various attributes:

$$P_h = P(S, N, L, A).$$

The Regional Multiple Listing Services of Minnesota, Inc. (RMLS) maintains home sale data from major real estate brokers in Minnesota. This database includes all home sales in Anoka, Carver, Dakota, Hennepin, Ramsey, Scott and Washington Counties in 2001, totaling 35002[1] home sale purchases, including structural attributes of each home. Each home's address was mapped and married with geographic information system (GIS) features for spatial analysis using ArcGIS.

Table 10.1 lists each variable, its definition and descriptive statistics. We measure location attributes through simple calculations of linear distance to the nearest central business district (either Minneapolis or St Paul) (*cbdnear*) and the nearest major highway (*hwynear*). A third location variable (*busy*) indicates the presence of an arterial street fronting the home.

Neighborhood attributes include school district and demographic variables; while severely affected by residential sorting and considered to be endogenous (thereby affecting the bias of the results) they were included

Table 10.1   Descriptive statistics of sample

	Variable name	Description	Mean	Standard deviation	Median
Environmental Amenities (A)	contrnr	CITY: distance to nearest on-street bicycle lane (meters)	1276.31	947.90	1023.55
	cnrtrnr	CITY: distance to nearest non-roadside bicycle trail (meters)	799.42	517.82	711.29
	crstrnr	CITY: distance to nearest roadside bicycle trail (meters)	1293.81	716.20	1219.16
	sontrnr	SUBURBS: distance to nearest on-street bicycle lane (meters)	1580.51	2240.18	979.82
	snrtrnr	SUBURBS: distance to nearest non-roadside bicycle trail (meters)	1099.89	1732.29	602.92
	srstrnr	SUBURBS: distance to nearest roadside bicycle trail (meters)	1359.35	1728.01	911.83
	cactive	CITY: distance to nearest active open space (meters)	340.15	203.41	315.35
	cpassive	CITY: distance to nearest passive open space (meters)	683.10	396.64	633.76
	cactive	SUBURB: distance to nearest active open space (meters)	569.92	1176.45	290.07
	spassive	SUBURB: distance to nearest passive open space (meters)	760.73	641.12	613.09
Structural Attributes (S)	bedrooms	Number of bedrooms	3.12	0.91	3.00
	bathroom	Number of bathrooms	2.14	0.88	2.00
	homestea	Homestead status	0.86	0.34	1.00
	age	Age of house	35.88	28.97	27.00
	lotsize	Size of lot (square meters)	2097.98	8053.17	968.00
	finished	Finished square feet of floor space	1871.01	908.66	1708.00
	firepls	Number of fireplaces	0.70	0.76	1.00
	garagest	Number of garage stalls	1.72	1.02	2.00
Location (L)	hwynear	Distance to nearest major highway (meters)	1672.32	1821.44	1149.58

Table 10.1 (continued)

	Variable name	Description	Mean	Standard deviation	Median
	cbdnear	Distance to nearest central business district (meters)	17558.59	10409.61	16374.75
	busy	Home is on a busy street	0.05	0.21	0.00
Neighborhood attributes (N)	*mca5_att*	Standardized test score in school district	4760.46	276.78	4836.10
	pctnonwt	Percent nonwhite in census tract	12.51	14.02	7.82
	avghhsiz	Persons per household in census tract	2.67	0.40	2.66

because of the explanatory power they contribute. Standardized test scores capitalize into home sale prices and are an effective measure of perceived school quality (Brasington 1999). The variable *mca5_att* represents the sum of the average math and reading scores achieved by fifth-grade students taking the Minnesota Comprehensive Assessment. Scores associated with suburban homes are measured at the school district level, while Minneapolis and St Paul scores are assigned to elementary school attendance areas. Demographic variables are derived from the 2000 United States Census. We include the percentage of people in the census tract who do not classify themselves as Caucasian (*pctnonwt*) and the average number of people in each household in the census tract (*avghhsiz*).

10.4 MEASURES OF INTEREST AND METHODOLOGY

10.4.1 Measures of Distance to Bicycle Facility

Our application focuses on bicycle facilities and to a certain extent, open space. Examples of the facilities and trails in this setting are shown in Figure 10.1. Detailed GIS data allowed us to discern all bike trails in the region, separately identifying on- and off-street facilities which are distributed across both major open space corridors (for example, railway lines, rivers and lakes) and other roadways. We marry the MLS data for every home sale in the seven-county study area from 2001 with the location of these trails.

Some on-street and off-street trails are located alongside busy trafficked streets, which is presumably a propelling characteristic for home locations.

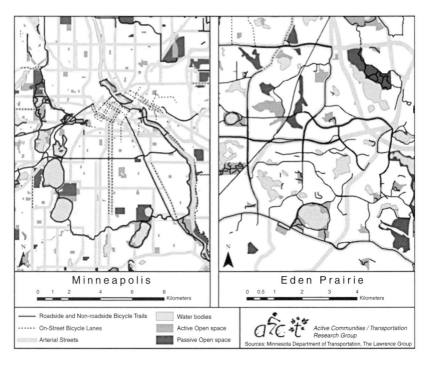

*Figure 10.1   Examples of off-street bicycle trails, on-street bicycle lanes
and open space*

We therefore divide the off-street layer into roadside and non-roadside
trails based on proximity to busy streets. We then calculate distance to the
nearest roadside trail, non-roadside trail and on-street bicycle lane for each
home. As previously mentioned, we also measure distance to open space as
a central variable, classifying such areas by type: active or passive.[2]

10.4.2   Measures of Density of Bicycle Facilities

Motivated by Anderson and West's (2004) findings that proximity and
size of open space matters, we also theorize it to be important to consider
not only the distance to facilities but also the density of trails around a
particular home. The overall density (length) of different facilities within
a buffer area may also be appreciated by homebuyers. They might value
a well-connected system of trails, which are prevalent in many areas
throughout the Twin Cities metropolitan area. We therefore calculate
the kilometers of trails within buffer distance. See Figure 10.2, showing
an example home in Minneapolis and how we measured open space and

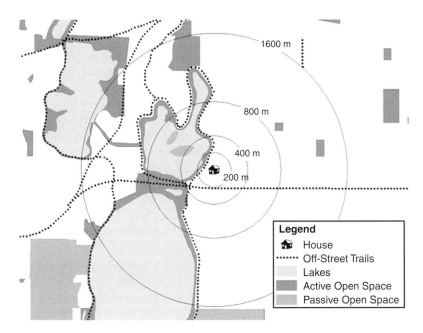

Figure 10.2   Off-street trails and open space within 200, 400, 800 and 1600 meters of a Minneapolis house

density of bicycle facilities by differing radii of 10, 20, 50, 100, 200, 400, 800 and 1600 meters.

10.4.3   Interaction Terms

Many of the structural attributes used in this application tend to be universally valued (for example, home size, number of bathrooms). Several of the spatial attributes employed, however, are hypothesized to vary by segments of the population; that is, urbanites versus suburbanites sort themselves differently according to dimensions of open space and its type. Again, this distinction was found by the application in Anderson and West for the same region. We therefore generate interaction terms (for example, city multiplied by independent variable) to measure the attributes that may vary spatially. Doing so allows us to pool the sample of urban and suburban homes, but still allows us to parsimoniously estimate a single model that preserves the integrity of the differing preferences. This single model provides coefficients that describe the effect of common attributes while producing different coefficients for the spatial attributes that may vary across suburbanites and urbanites.[3]

10.4.4   Fixed Effects

As with any analysis of this type, there are omitted attributes to consider. When estimating phenomena associated with the real estate market this dimension is particularly important. There are likely spatial attributes, not captured by any of our measures, which invariably affect home value. These attributes may include but are not limited to general housing stock of neighboring homes, the reputation effects of different neighborhoods or unobserved characteristics of the neighborhood.

Lacking fixed effects, variation across all observations in all neighborhoods is used to identify the effect of interest. However, given the spatial correlation that is likely between proximity to bicycle facility with other variables, this effect is susceptible to omitted variable bias. We control for bias introduced by potential omitted variables by using local fixed effects, a dummy variable for each RMLS-defined market area (104 areas in our region). These boundaries mostly follow city limits in suburban areas and divide the central cities into several neighborhoods that closely follow similarly natured real estate markets. By controlling for fixed effects we are estimating the effect of proximity to a bicycle trail, assuming a household has already decided to locate in one of the 104 MLS areas in the region. While more accurate, this process makes it difficult to identify the impact of bicycle trail proximity because it in effect reduces the variation of the variables of interest. Michaels and Smith (1990) support this claim, showing that dividing a market into sub-markets results in less robust estimates of the effects of hazardous waste site proximity.

10.5   RESULTS AND DISCUSSION

Our final model (shown in Table 10.2) is an ordinary least squares (OLS) regression to predict the effect of bicycle trail proximity on home sale prices. We employ a logged dependent variable and also log transformations of several continuous independent variables, indicated by 'ln' following the variable name. All structural and location variables are statistically significant and have the expected signs. Home values increase with number of bedrooms, bathrooms, lot size, finished square feet, fireplaces, garage spaces, proximity to a central business district, and school quality. Home values decrease with age and percent non-white in the census tract. Similarly, proximity to a freeway has a negative effect on home value, which implies that the disamenity effects of freeways (for example, noise, pollution) likely outweigh any accessibility benefits within particular neighborhoods. Looking at some of the location and amenity variables

Table 10.2   Regression results

Variable name	Description	Coefficient	Standard error	t-statistic	Effect of 400m closer
contrln	CITY: distance to nearest on-street bicycle lane (ln)	0.003950	0.002689	1.47	
cnrtrln	CITY: distance to nearest non-roadside bicycle trail (ln)	−0.007851	0.003732	−2.1*	$ 509.85
crstrln	CITY: distance to nearest roadside bicycle trail (ln)	0.022772	0.003777	6.03**	$ (2,271.63)
sontrln	SUBURBS: distance to nearest on-street bicycle lane (ln)	0.003334	0.001272	2.62**	$ (364.02)
snrtrln	SUBURBS: distance to nearest non-roadside bicycle trail (ln)	0.003858	0.001325	2.91**	$ (239.65)
srstrln	SUBURBS: distance to nearest roadside bicycle trail (ln)	0.010230	0.001419	7.21**	$ (1,058.73)
cactive	CITY: distance to nearest active open space (meters)	−0.000024	0.000012	−1.96*	$ 1,425.36
cpassive	CITY: distance to nearest passive open space (meters)	−0.000065	0.000007	−9.08**	$ 3,860.35
cactive	SUBURB: distance to nearest active open space (meters)	0.000006	0.000001	3.88**	$ (442.80)
spassive	SUBURB: distance to nearest passive open space (meters)	−0.000028	0.000002	−12.86**	$ 2,066.40
bedrooms	Number of bedrooms	0.033037	0.001570	21.05**	
bathroom	Number of bathrooms	0.079976	0.002018	39.63**	
homestea	Homestead status	−0.027259	0.003481	−7.83**	
ageln	Age of house (ln)	−0.092578	0.001759	−52.65**	
lotsize	Size of lot (square meters)	0.000003	0.000000	21.68**	
finished	Finished square feet of floor space	0.000168	0.000002	82.14**	
firepls	Number of fireplaces	0.068749	0.001768	38.89**	
garagest	Number of garage stalls	0.075257	0.001268	59.37**	
hwynear	Distance to nearest major highway (meters)	0.000009	0.000001	10.35**	$ (637.20)

Table 10.2 (continued)

Variable name	Description	Coefficient	Standard error	t-statistic	Effect of 400m closer
cbdnrln	Distance to nearest central business district (ln)	−0.056065	0.006926	−8.09**	$ 9,861.10
busy	Home is on a busy street	−0.033351	0.005096	−6.54**	
mca5_att	Standardized test score in school district	0.000160	0.000010	15.34**	
pctnonwt	Percent non-white in census tract	−0.004014	0.000183	−21.99**	
avghhsiz	Persons per household in census tract	0.038961	0.004481	8.7**	
	Constant	11.314800	0.079957	141.51**	
	Number of observations: 35 002	** Significant at p < 0.01			
	Adjusted R-squared: 0.7920	* Significant at p < 0.05			

Note: Figures in parenthesis are minus values.

reveals a different story. Open space coefficients are generally consistent with Anderson and West's (2004) findings. Suburbanites value passive open space over active recreational areas. City residents also value lakes and golf courses, but active open space does not affect sale price.

Examining the effect of bicycle facilities reveals a complex story; results are different because we measure three types of facilities for two different populations (urban and suburban). Our discussion separates the findings for city and suburban residents, a matter that is also addressed by using the interaction terms. First, city residents clearly value proximity to non-roadside trails (after controlling for open space). As Minneapolis is well endowed with many off-road facilities and appears to exhibit a relatively high cycling population, this comes as little surprise. The opposite is true for trails alongside busy streets, however, even when controlling for adjacency to the streets themselves. On-street bicycle lanes have no significant effect in the city. The possible reason for this is that, in general, the nature of on-street facilities differs considerably between Minneapolis and St Paul.[4]

As in the city, suburban homes near roadside trails sell for less than those further away, even when controlling for busy streets. The same is true for on-street bicycle lanes, for which there was no statistically significant effect in the city. Suburban off-street trails appear to negatively influence home prices, unlike in the city. We suggest several reasons for this. First, it may be the case that because of decreased cycling use, suburbanites simply do not value access to trails. Such proximity may not even factor into their use or option value of their home purchase locations. Second, counteracting phenomena may be taking place. Some suburbanites may indeed value such trails. However, their preferences may be overshadowed by a combination of the following factors. Some of the suburban trails are along former railway beds. If these property values were formally depressed because of such an externality, such a legacy effect may likely still be in effect. Uncertainty surrounding future uses of such corridors, such as commuter rail, could compound any legacy affect. Snowmobiling introduces additional externalities common to exurban trails. Most notable, many suburbanites simply appreciate the seclusion of their settings. Proximity to trails – no matter their character – may be an indication of unwanted people passing by or other symptoms that run counter to factors that prompted their decision. Similar analysis employing measures of the density of bicycle facilities did not reveal statistically significant findings in any of the models estimated.

Because the policy variables of interest and the dependent variable are logged, the coefficients can be directly interpreted as elasticities. However, we provide the results of an effect analysis to more concretely estimate values. In Table 10.2 the last two columns present the effect of moving a median-priced home 400 meters closer to each facility than the median distance, all else constant.[5] We find that in the city, the effect of moving a median-priced home 400 meters closer to a roadside bicycle trail reduces the sale price by $2272. Assuming a home is 400 meters closer to a non-roadside trail nets $510. While all relationships between bicycle facility proximity and home sale prices are negative in the suburbs, the effect analysis shows significant variation in the magnitude of those relationships. The effect of moving a home 400 meters closer to a roadside bicycle trail is −$1059, compared to only −$240 for a non-roadside trail.

10.6   CONCLUSIONS AND FUTURE RESEARCH

There are several important implications for our results, which confirm our hypothesis that the three types of trails influence home sale prices in different ways. They demonstrate the importance of controlling for bias induced by omitted spatial variables. Such bias is especially relevant for large complex and polycentric housing markets (such as in the Twin Cities, with two central business districts) and in areas where factors that influence home price differ tremendously by neighborhood. We use local neighborhood fixed effects to reduce spatial autocorrelation and also lead to more robust coefficient estimates. Of course using this methodology, while technically sound and robust, also makes it more difficult to detect the effects of such proximity because we are now comparing homes within MLS areas. Furthermore, it is unclear how the values of these results might be affected by omitted variable bias.

Our results also robustly test whether urbanites and suburbanites perceive and value bicycle facilities differently. The use of interaction terms between city and suburb reveals this difference in preferences between city dwellers and suburbanites. We measure bicycle facilities in different ways. Distance to nearest facility is the measure discussed in detail above. Models that were estimated to examine the role of trail density did not produce statistically significant findings. The comprehensiveness of the Twin Cities bicycle trails may contribute to a lack in variation among trail densities near homes. Left unknown in this application is how different types of facilities might be valued according to different cycling trip purposes, for either urbanites or suburbanites.

Other refinements would enhance the approach used here to estimate the value of bicycle facilities. Introducing a stated preference element akin to Earnhart's (2001) application could yield more robust estimates. Additional stratification of variables would also augment our understanding. We divided bicycle trails into on-street, roadside and non-roadside facilities in the city and suburbs. Further data collection efforts aimed at identifying other differentiating characteristics among facilities, such as trail width and adjacent land cover, would allow the implementation of a hedonic travel cost model to place a value on such characteristics (Smith and Kaoru 1987).

Assigning future benefits based on a hedonic model presents complications, as new environmental amenities can take years to capitalize into housing prices. Riddel (2001) shows that cross-sectional studies may underestimate the benefits of these goods, and provides an approach for capturing delayed benefits. In addition to delayed benefits, future benefits also present an opportunity for refining model specification. Shonkweiler and Reynolds's (1986) methodology accounts for the potential conversion of rural land to urban uses, revealing that this qualitative consideration reduces estimation error. More generally, there is value with repeated sales modelling. Cross-sectional hedonic pricing studies may lead to upward-biased estimates. An outstanding question lies in the degree to which changes in bicycle infrastructure lead to changes in housing prices. Repeated sales models do not suffer from the same problems of omitted variable bias, and as a result may find smaller effects than cross-section effects.

From a policy perspective, this research produces three important insights (which are likely peculiar to the US context of the application). First, type of trail matters. On-street trails and roadside trails may not be as appreciated as much as many city planners or policy officials think. Second, city residents have different preferences than suburban residents. Third, and as suspected, larger and more pressing factors are likely influencing residential location decisions. Using fixed effects detects such considerations in terms of neighborhood quality and character. Overall, our results suggest that off-street bicycle trails add value to home sale prices in the city, implying a contribution to social livability. No positive and significant relationship, however, is found for other types of facilities in either the city or the suburbs. In fact, bicycle trails exhibit a disutility in suburban settings. Our results suggest that the consequences of providing for bicycle facilities are context-dependent; the change in welfare is not necessarily positive for all homeowners.

ACKNOWLEDGEMENTS

The authors thank the following individuals for their useful comments and suggestions: Sarah West, Ragui Assaad and Gary Barnes. Conversations with each individual helped considerably to strengthen this work. Katherine Reilly diligently collected and compiled the bicycle facility GIS layers used in the analysis. Jenny Shillcox prepared a pilot study for Hennepin County, procuring the MLS data used in this application.

NOTES

1. Our sample began with 42 750 records. Geocoding and removing records with missing data or unreasonable or incorrect data (for example, homes recorded as having zero bathrooms, zero square feet, or built before 1800) reduced our sample to 35 002. The relatively small number of records removed still provided an even distribution of home sales across the metro area.
2. Active open spaces are primarily used for recreation, and are comprised of neighborhood parks and some regional parks. Passive open spaces are less accessible on foot. They include areas such as golf courses, cemeteries, and large regional parks that are accessible only through designated entrance points and often only by car.
3. Open space and bicycle variable names are prefixed by c for city and s for suburb.
4. In Minneapolis, several of the streets in the downtown core have bicycle lanes (although there are few home sales downtown). Most other on-street bicycle lanes are on busy commuting arterials or around the University of Minnesota commercial district. On-street lanes in St Paul are a different story. They tend to be along a well-maintained boulevard-type corridor (Summit Avenue) and the Mississippi River corridor. These counteracting effects between Minneapolis and St Paul may possibly cancel one other out.
5. The median sale prices in the city and suburbs for 2001 were $148 475 and $184 500, respectively. No significant relationship was found between home prices in the city and proximity to on-street bicycle lanes, so no effect is estimated in Table 10.2.

REFERENCES

Anderson, S.T. and S.E. West (2004), 'The value of open space proximity and size: City versus suburbs', Macalester College, Department of Economics, working paper.

Barnes, G. (2004), 'Understanding bicycling demand', Minneapolis, MN: University of Minnesota, Active Communities Transportation Research Group.

Benson, E.D., Hansen, J.L, Jr, Schwartz, A.L. and G.T. Smersh (1998), 'Pricing residential amenities: The value of a view', *Journal of Real Estate Finance and Economics*, **16** (1), 55–73.

Brasington, D.M. (1999), 'Which measures of school quality does the housing market value?', *Journal of Real Estate Research*, **18** (3), 395–413.

City of Vancouver (1999), 'Bicycle Plan 1999: Reviewing the past, planning the future'.

Dill, J. and T. Carr (2003), 'Bicycle commuting and facilities in major US cities: If you build them, commuters will use them', *Transportation Research Record*, **1828**, 116–123.

Earnhart, D. (2001), 'Combining revealed and stated preference methods to value environmental amenities at residential locations', *Land Economics*, **77** (1), 12–29.

Franklin, J.P. and P. Waddell (2003), 'A hedonic regression of home prices in King County, Washington, using activity-specific accessibility measures', Transportation Research Board, Washington, DC: National Academy of Sciences.

Geoghegan, J. (2002), 'The value of open spaces in residential land use', *Land Use Policy*, **19** (1), 91–98.

Irwin, E.G. (2002), 'The effects of open space on residential property values', *Land Economics*, **78** (4), 465–480.

Jackson, M.E. and P. Newsome (2000), 'A guide to bicycle transportation in the Twin Cities Metropolitan Area: The processes, the players, the potential', St Paul, Minnesota Department of Transportation.

Krizek, K.J. and P.J. Johnson (2004), 'The effect of facility access on bicycling behavior', University of Minnesota, Active Communities Transportation (ACT) Research Group.

Lancaster, K.J. (1966), 'A new approach to consumer theory', *Journal of Political Economy*, **74** (2), 132–157.

Lindsey, G., Man, J., Payton, S. and K. Dickson (2003), 'Amenity and recreation values of urban greenways', Association of European Schools of Planning Congress, Leuven, Belgium.

Luttik, J. (2000), 'The value of trees, water and open space as reflected by house prices in the Netherlands', *Landscape and Urban Planning*, **48**, 161–167.

Lutzenhiser, M. and N.R. Netusil (2001), 'The effect of open spaces on a home's sale price', *Contemporary Economic Policy*, **19** (3), 291–298.

Mahan, B.L., Polasky, S. and R.M. Adams (2000), 'Valuing urban wetlands: A property price approach', *Land Economics*, **76** (1), 100–113.

McLaughlin, P. (2003), Hennepin County Commissioner, Minneapolis, MN, personal communication.

Michaels, R.G. and V.K. Smith (1990), 'Market segmentation and valuing amenities with hedonic models: The case of hazardous waste sites', *Journal of Urban Economics*, **28**, 223–242.

Quang Do, A. and G. Grudnitski (1995), 'Golf courses and residential house prices: An empirical examination', *Journal of Real Estate Finance and Economics*, **10**, 261–270.

Riddel, M. (2001), 'A dynamic approach to estimating hedonic prices for environmental goods: An application to open space purchase', *Land Economics*, **77** (4), 494–512.

Rosen, S. (1974), 'Hedonic prices and implicit markets: Product differentiation in pure competition', *Journal of Political Economy*, **82** (1), 34–55.

Shonkweiler, J.S. and J.E. Reynolds (1986), 'A note on the use of hedonic price models in the analysis of land prices at the urban fringe', *Land Economics*, **62** (1), 58–63.

Sirmans, G.S. and D.A. Macpherson (2003), 'The composition of hedonic pricing models: A review of the literature', National Association of Realtors.

Smith, V.K. and Y. Kaoru (1987), 'The hedonic travel cost model: A view from the trenches', *Land Economics*, **63** (2), 179–192.

Smith, V.K., Paulos, C. and H. Kim (2002), 'Treating open space as an urban amenity', *Resource and Energy Economics*, **24**, 107–129.

Taylor, F. (1916), 'Relation between primary market prices and qualities of cotton', US Department of Agriculture.

11. Accessibility and territorial cohesion: *ex post* analysis of Cohesion Fund infrastructure projects

Mert Kompil[1], Hande Demirel and Panayotis Christidis

11.1 INTRODUCTION

Socio-economic disparities within Europe are expected to be reduced partly with proper transport investments. Several European Union (EU)-level policy frameworks (for example, the Treaty of Lisbon, the Europe 2020 Strategy) and the recently published White Paper on Transport (European Commission 2011b) emphasize the relationship between territorial cohesion and transportation investments. Deficiencies in transport accessibility of regions are seen as an obstacle for harmonious economic development within these frameworks. Therefore, many transport infrastructure projects are being funded or co-funded to improve connectivity of peripheral countries and to remove gaps between less and more developed parts of Europe. One of the most important efforts to achieve this goal has been the Cohesion Fund and the European Regional Development Fund (ERDF) infrastructure projects in the past decades. However, it is not easy to assess impacts of such efforts thoroughly. A common framework for *ex ante* and *ex post* analysis of transport projects and policies in terms of monitoring change in accessibility and regional disparities is still lacking. Hence, an adequate framework should be developed in order to quantify to what extent the projects serve to increase transport accessibility and diminish regional disparities.

Within this context, the aim of this chapter is to develop a framework to assess impacts of various policy options and transport infrastructure investments on accessibility at European level. In order to test the developed framework, impacts of transport infrastructure projects co-funded by the Cohesion Fund and ERDF between 2000 and 2006 were analysed in terms of accessibility and territorial cohesion. These projects aimed at improving road and rail transport networks in the peripheral and/or enlargement countries while connecting them to the core network. Their impact on accessibility of regions was evaluated for passenger transport using an appropriate combination of various accessibility indicators. At first, the travel costs with and without the improved infrastructure were estimated using the TRANS-TOOLS model (Tools for Transport Forecasting and Scenario Testing; the Europe-wide transport network model used as one of the main reference tools for impact assessments by the European Commission); then, the output of the model was used to compute regional accessibilities at NUTS 3 level in Europe. Finally, several statistical techniques were introduced to detect changes in the accessibility pattern of Europe and to assess similarity /dissimilarity of regions.

In the next section, a brief review on accessibility measures at European level is provided. In section 11.3, Cohesion Fund and ERDF projects to improve transport infrastructure are discussed and elaborated in the context of European transport policy. The relationship between accessibility, territorial cohesion and regional economic development is then discussed. The proposed accessibility indicators with their selection criteria are introduced in section 11.4. The methodology of the study and data are presented in section 11.5 together with the description of transport model and the assumptions applied. The results are presented in section 11.6, and the concluding remarks in section 11.7.

11.2 AN OVERVIEW OF ACCESSIBILITY MEASURES AT EUROPEAN LEVEL

Accessibility refers to people's ability to reach goods, services and activities as an ultimate goal of transport activity. It is the ease with which activities can be reached from a certain place and with a certain system of transport (Morris et al. 1979), or in other words, a measure of proximate opportunities available to individuals or users. From the economic point of view, transport infrastructure and accessibility play a vital role for economic development of a region. It is evident that an area is more attractive and competitive by being accessible. Accessibility indicators are useful in order to identify regional differences and can to a certain extent explain inequalities of regions. As indicated in Gutiérrez (2009), the spatial distribution of accessibility mainly depends on geographical locations (for example, being central or peripheral) and transport networks. In transportation policy, transport networks have particular importance since they serve to reduce the gap between central and peripheral regions while increasing the attractiveness or competitiveness of remote regions.

The quantitative methodology of measuring accessibility is performed by a broad range of indicators. They are in general a combination of two functions, one representing the activities or opportunities to be reached, and the other representing the effort or cost spent to reach them. Since the purpose may vary with the spatial scale, socio-economic dimension and scope of the analysis, there exist several accessibility measures. The classification by Curtis and Scheurer (2010) divides accessibility measures into seven categories: spatial separation measures, contour measures, gravity-based measures, competition measures, time–space measures, utility-based measures and network measures. In order to measure accessibility in this chapter, mainly the gravity-based measures were used. The accessibility concepts based on the contour and the competition measures were also applied. However, person-based and utility-based measures were ignored since they are not suitable for zone-based aggregate analysis. The accessibility indicators used for the analysis are described in section 11.4 with the selection criteria. Further information on various accessibility measures can be acquired from comprehensive reviews by Geurs and van Wee (2004), Gutiérrez (2009), Curtis and Scheurer (2010) and Páez et al. (2012).

Many studies investigated changes in accessibility of regions at the European level and tested likely impacts of improvements in transport infrastructure and shifts in transport policy. See the extensive reviews included in Rietveld and Bruinsma (1998), Wegener et al. (2001) and Spiekermann et al. (2011) for information on accessibility studies at the European level. This section lists only a limited number of European studies (Table 11.1) having similar characteristics to current analysis, and tries to identify common methodological areas.

Considering the above-mentioned studies and the wider list of studies presented in Spiekermann et al. (2011, pp. 21–22), some common characteristics of European level accessibility studies can be defined as follows:

- The gravity type of potential accessibility measure is the most widely applied accessibility measure in European-level studies. It is followed by the spatial separation and daily accessibility measures, generally with travel distance and travel time as the travel impedance.
- The destination activities are usually represented with population or gross domestic product (GDP) for potential type of accessibility indicators.
- Monetary travel costs or generalized travel costs are rarely used, and fewer studies are available for freight transport.

Table 11.1 Accessibility studies at European level

Name and year of the study	Aim of the study	Accessibility Indicators	Geographical Scale	Impedance Factor	Transport Mode and Type
TRACC – 2011 (Spiekermann et al. 2011)	to analyse territorial cohesion and regional accessibility pattern at the European scale	Potential accessibility Daily accessibility	NUTS-3 regions Other specific origins/destinations	Travel time Travel distance	Multi-modal Passenger/Freight
White Paper on Transport – 2011 (European Commission 2011a; Christidis and Rivas 2012)	accessibility analysis of various policy scenarios during the preparation of the latest White Paper on Transport	Travel cost indicator Potential accessibility	NUTS-3 regions	Generalized travel cost	Multi-modal Passenger/Freight
SASI 2000 – (SASI 2000; Wegener 2008)	to identify the way transport infrastructure contributes to economic development in different regional contexts	Travel cost indicator Potential and Daily accessibility	NUTS-3 regions	Travel time Generalized travel cost	Multi-modal Passenger/Freight
ESPON – 2006 (Spiekermann and Wegener 2006)	to analyse territorial trends and basic supply of transport infrastructure for territorial cohesion	Travel cost indicator Potential and Daily accessibility	NUTS-3 regions	Travel time Travel distance	Road and Rail Passenger/Freight
ASSESS – 2005 (Transport & Mobility Leuven 2005)	assessment of the contribution of the TEN and other transport policies to the midterm implementation of the Transport White Paper	Travel cost indicator	NUTS-2003 regions	Travel time	Multi-modal Passenger/Freight

- Different modes of transport have rarely been considered, and multimodal travel times are generally not included.
- Generally NUTS 2 and NUTS 3 regions are used as origin–destination pairs for Europe-wide studies.
- The majority of the studies do not use a transport model to estimate changes in travel costs, modal shift or travel demand. Impacts of change in the key transport components on accessibility are estimated directly, without taking mode choice and traffic assignment into account.

One of the most important findings of the Europe-wide studies is that Europe has a strong core–periphery accessibility pattern. It is possible to see this pattern in almost all types of analyses with various accessibility indicators. More importantly, as stated in several longitudinal or before-and-after analyses with respect to transport accessibility (Wegener et al. 2001; Gløersen et al. 2006; European Parliament 2007; European Commission 2010), the gap between the core and the peripheral regions of Europe could not be reduced as much as was expected in the past decades. This also constitutes one of the important reasons for putting more balanced and more integrated approaches and policies into practice lately, to ensure the territorial cohesion of Europe and to convert existing territorial diversities into strengths for Europe (e.g., European Commission 2008; European Union 2007a, 2011a).

11.3 EUROPEAN TRANSPORT POLICY, ACCESSIBILITY AND TERRITORIAL COHESION

11.3.1 Cohesion Fund and ERDF Projects for Transport Infrastructure

The main emphasis of the European transport policy is to use less and cleaner energy and make better use of transport infrastructure, allowing basic access to users, providing them high-quality mobility services. Within this policy framework, improving transport infrastructure and providing alternatives to the core transport network has always played an important role in European policy. In particular, it was aimed to put in place an efficient transport network across the member states to promote growth and competitiveness, mainly with the Trans-European Transport Networks (TEN-T) and the Transport Infrastructure Needs Assessment (TINA) projects. With the progressive enlargement of the EU in recent decades, accessibility and cohesion aspects of transport investments gained importance.

Within this context, European regional assistance has been supporting the member states through the Cohesion Fund since 1994 in order to speed up economic, social and territorial convergence within the EU. The Cohesion Fund financed up to 85 per cent of eligible expenditure of major projects in the areas of transport and environment. Eligible countries were the least prosperous member states of the Union whose gross national product (GNP) per capita was below 90 per cent of the EU average (European Union 2011b, 2013). According to the *Fifth Report on Economic, Social and Territorial Cohesion* (European Commission 2010, p. 182), since 1996 the cohesion policy has invested some €400 billion in the transport network. Almost a third came from different EU sources, much of it from the Cohesion Fund, which is confined to financing investment in member states with relatively low income levels.

Most of the investments have centred on completing the TEN-T to ensure that the internal market functions smoothly and that the main centres of population and economic activity are reasonably well connected. The focus of the TEN-T policy, however, has been on strengthening links across the EU rather than on improving the accessibility of lagging regions, though it has undoubtedly contributed to this (European Commission, 2010). The European Union provided more than €28 billion (in 2004 prices) to the Cohesion Fund for the period of 2000–2006 (European Union 2011b), and €66 billion for the 2007–2013 period (European Commission 2013). This was used for transport activities (mainly the priority projects) and the environment. As a result of infrastructure projects subsidized not only by the Cohesion Fund but also by the ERDF (aiming to compensate main regional imbalances in the EU), national rail and road networks in several member states have been improved and are better interconnected to the rest of Europe.

11.3.2 Accessibility and Territorial Cohesion

With the Lisbon Treaty (European Union 2007b), territorial cohesion has become one of the three main goals of the EU, along with economic and social cohesion. Since then, EU policies that contain territorial aspects including the transport sector have been updated with the new objectives. Although many definitions exist, territorial cohesion can be defined as 'a set of principles for harmonious, balanced, efficient sustainable territorial development ... the principle of solidarity to promote convergence between the economies of better-off territories and those whose development is lagging behind' (European Union 2011a, p. 4). It has three main goals: (1) overcoming differences in density; (2) connecting territories by overcoming distance; and (3) cooperation by overcoming division

(European Commission 2008, pp. 5–8). Territorial cohesion especially reinforces the importance of access to services, sustainable development, functional geographies and territorial analysis; whereas economic and social cohesion focus on regional disparities in competitiveness and well-being (European Commission 2010, p. 24).

In order to reduce territorial imbalances in the socio-economic domain, access to infrastructure and knowledge have to be secured. This requires coherent, integrated efforts to improve territorial connectivity and cooperation. Hence, transport infrastructure and the transport sector plays a vital role. Improvement in the connectivity of regions, increasing access to economic activities and reducing travelling time, will certainly increase the size of the market and the competitiveness of regions. For instance, the importance of transport networks for regional development is indicated by a territorial impact assessment of ESPON (2010) which shows evidence for a general economic benefit for the EU as a whole, and a much greater one for the EU-12, through increasing market potential, regional competitiveness and gross domestic product (GDP) per head (European Commission 2010, p. 57).

However, efforts to reduce territorial disparities via improved infrastructure could bring negative economic impacts for some certain regions as well. For instance, in some European-level studies (ECORYS 2006; Spiekermann and Wegener 2006), it was argued that many of the new network connections do not link peripheral countries to the core, but strengthen the ties between central countries and so reinforce their advantage in accessibility and competitiveness. Impacts depend also on the local characteristics of regions including their initial level of infrastructure and competitiveness. Hence, the relationship between transport infrastructure and economic development has complex, multiple dimensions. As indicated in Rietveld (1994) and Vickerman et al. (1999), although they are highly correlated, there is no direct causal relationship between accessibility and economic development.

It is obvious that in order to monitor territorial cohesion and identify the efficiency of the applied transport policies, well-established and quantitative and qualitative information is required. As emphasized in several other studies (Wegener et al. 2001; López et al. 2008; Spiekermann et al. 2011), accessibility measures are useful to identify regional disparities and can help in assessing regional cohesion effects of transport investments. Ideally, results should be obtained for two different periods to present the territorial trends on cohesion; however data and tailored indicators are usually lacking. In this respect, well-developed, mature indicators to measure transport accessibility could better serve for evidence-based policy-making.

11.4 INDICATORS PROPOSED TO MEASURE EUROPEAN TRANSPORT ACCESSIBILITY

11.4.1 The Criteria for Selection of Accessibility Indicators

Selection of appropriate accessibility indicators depends strongly upon the purpose, scale and scope of the analysis. According to Morris et al. (1979), the level of disaggregation of the population and activities, and the weight given to ease of operation and interpretation of measure, constitute the principal difference in choosing appropriate accessibility measures. Apart from this, accessibility indicators should: (1) incorporate an element of spatial separation and react to changes in the performance of transport system; (2) have sound behavioural foundations; (3) be technically feasible and operationally simple; and (4) be easy to interpret and preferably understandable for everyone (Morris et al. 1979, p. 94). In addition to this, suitable accessibility indicators should respond in the same direction to changing numbers of available opportunities, and should take into account the capacity restrictions of available opportunities and the temporal and personal constraints of individuals (Geurs and van Wee 2004).

Considering these principles, several accessibility indicators were initially tested for the proposed framework. Among them, an appropriate combination was chosen based on predefined criteria for selection. According to these criteria, any measure proposed to be used at European level should be sensitive to: (1) network improvements; (2) modal and technological shifts; (3) demand- and supply-side changes; and (4) changes in socio-economic and demographic characteristics, that is, in the GDP and population of regions.

The indicators should also be suitable for zone-based aggregate measures and efficient in monitoring and evaluating European accessibility patterns. Eventually, six accessibility indicators were selected, having diverse properties: (1) potential accessibility; (2) potential-demand accessibility; (3) inverse balancing accessibility; (4) location accessibility; (5) daily accessibility; and (6) modified daily accessibility indicators. They are described briefly in the subsequent section. For further information on similar indicators, it is recommended to refer to the review articles cited in section 11.2 above.

11.4.2 Description of Selected Accessibility Indicators

Potential accessibility (*Ind. A*)
Accessibility measure for zone *i* based on the cumulative economic potential (represented by total GDP) of destination zones and the travel time between zone pairs with a distance decay parameter:

$$Ind.A_i = \sum_j \frac{W_j}{(c_{ij})^\beta}.$$ (11.1)

Potential-demand accessibility (*Ind. B*)
Accessibility measure for zone *i* based on the cumulative economic potential (represented by total GDP) of destination zones divided by the overall demand (represented by total population) and the travel time between zone pairs with a distance decay parameter:

$$Ind.B_i = \sum_j \frac{W_j/(c_{ij})^\beta}{D_j}, \; D_j = \sum_i \frac{P_i}{(c_{ij})^\beta}.$$ (11.2)

Inverse balancing accessibility (*Ind. C*)
Accessibility measure for zone *i* based on the cumulative economic potential (represented by total GDP) of destination zones and the travel time between zone pairs with a distance decay parameter. The indicator is balanced iteratively by demand (represented by total population) of origin zones incorporating competition between demand and supply:

$$Ind.C_i = 1/A_i, \text{ where } A_i = 1/\sum_j B_j W_j (c_{ij})^{-\beta}, B_j = 1/\sum_i C_i P_i (c_{ij})^{-\beta}.$$

Iteratively, and $\sum_{ij} I_{ij} = \sum_i P_i = \sum_j W_j$ and $\sum_i I_{ij} = W_j$ and $\sum_j I_{ij} = P_i$ (11.3)

Location accessibility (*Ind. D*)
Accessibility measure for zone *i* based on the cumulative economic potential (represented by total GDP) of destinations and the travel time between zone pairs which excludes location effects of the impact of distance decay parameter:

$$Ind.D_i = \frac{1}{\sum_j \dfrac{W_j * c_{ij}}{\sum_j W_j}}.$$ (11.4)

Daily accessibility (*Ind. E*)
Accessibility measure for zone *i* based on the cumulative economic potential (represented by total GDP) of destination zones which are accessible on a daily basis, and the travel time between zone pairs with a distance decay parameter. The maximum one-way travel time was set to five hours and the activities above the maximum limit were assumed to be non-accessible on a daily basis:

$$Ind.E_i = \sum_j \frac{W_j.\delta_{ij}}{(c_{ij})^\beta}. \tag{11.5}$$

Modified daily accessibility (*Ind. F*)

Accessibility measure for zone i based on the cumulative economic potential (represented by total GDP) of destinations, and the travel time between zone pairs with a distance decay parameter. It is a combination of daily and potential accessibility indicators which gives more weight to the destinations accessed on a daily basis. In its formula, the weight for destination potentials which are accessible daily was set to 1 and the weight for destination potentials which are non-accessible on a daily basis was set to 0.25:

$$Ind.F_i = \sum_j \left[\left(\frac{W_j \cdot \delta_{ij}}{(c_{ij})^\beta} \right) + \left(\frac{W_j \cdot \theta_{ij}}{(c_{ij})^\beta} * \frac{1}{4} \right) \right]. \tag{11.6}$$

Description of notations

(c_{ij}): Travel time between zone i and zone j, β: distance decay parameter, W_j: economic potential (total GDP) of zone j, P_i: propulsion potential of (total population) of zone i, I_{ij}: interactions between zone i and zone j, δ_{ij}: binary variable for daily accessibility measure, 1 if $c_{ij} \leq c_{max}$ and 0 if $c_{ij} > c_{max}$, θ_{ij}: binary variable for modified daily accessibility, 0 if $c_{ij} \leq c_{max}$ and 1 if $c_{ij} > c_{max}$, c_{max}: daily accessibility threshold, usually 4–6 hours.

11.5 DESCRIPTION OF DATA AND METHODOLOGY

11.5.1 Description of Data and the Transport Model

The subject of this analysis covers road and rail network improvements co-funded by (mostly) the Cohesion Fund and the European Regional Development Fund in 2000–2006. The countries in which the network improvements took place were Bulgaria, the Czech Republic, Estonia, Greece, Hungary, Ireland, Latvia, Lithuania, Poland, Portugal, Romania, the Slovak Republic, Slovenia and Spain. Within these countries the number of road and rail links built or (mostly) improved was 457 and 356, respectively. The total length of road and railways constructed or improved were 8.115 and 11.074 km which constitute, respectively, 1.6 per cent and 6.1 per cent of total network lengths in existing transport (TRANS-TOOLS) networks. Figure 11.1 shows the spatial distribution of infrastructure projects for road and rail transport, where the majority

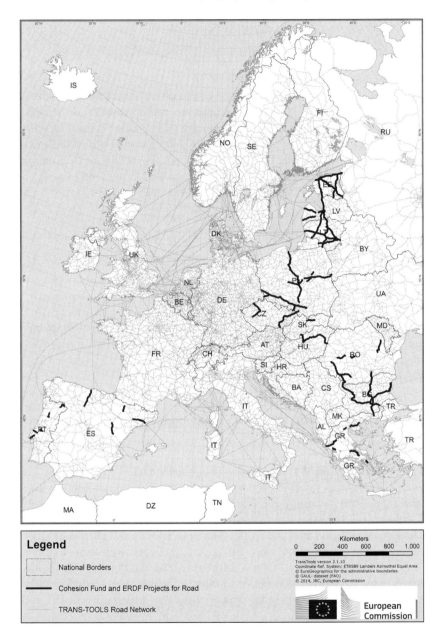

*Figure 11.1   Road and rail infrastructure projects supported by the
             Cohesion Fund and ERDF*

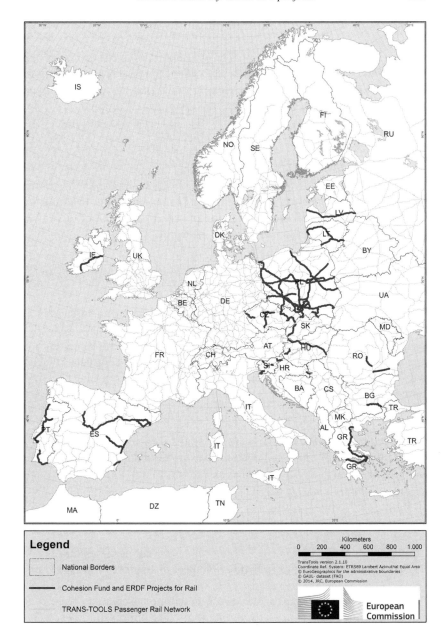

Figure 11.1 (continued)

of them were located in the peripheral and/or enlargement countries of Europe.

In order to analyse likely impacts of network improvements of the investments on accessibility, the TRANS-TOOLS model is used. TRANS-TOOLS is a European transport network model that has been developed in collaborative projects funded by the European Commission's Joint Research Centre Institute for Prospective Technological Studies (JRC-IPTS) and Directorate-General for Mobility and Transport (DG MOVE) (TRANS-TOOLS 2008b). It is used by several services of the Commission as one of the main models for transport policy analysis. It combines a conventional four-step transport modelling approach with economic activity, trade, logistics and environmental outputs. The model covers 42 countries, 1441 NUTS 3 zones and the network for all main transport modes. It gives results both for passenger and freight transport at NUTS 3 level. It is mainly used to measure changes in transport networks, especially TEN-T; changes in transport demand and its distribution; changes in logistics and distribution systems; and impacts of pricing and taxation policies (Kompil et al. 2013).

The first version of TRANS-TOOLS was operational in June 2007 at the end of the (Sixth Framework Programme-founded) TRANS-TOOLS project. TRANS-TOOLS v2, which was used also for this analysis, was finalized in 2009 as a result of the TENConnect project conducted by DG MOVE (Hansen 2011). The base year for NUTS 3 regions and network-based data in this version is 2005. Further information on TRANS-TOOLS can be obtained through the documentation available on its website (TRANS-TOOLS 2008a).

The main advantage of using such a model for accessibility analysis is that it allows use of enhanced options to estimate changes in travel cost or impedance. Apart from the detailed expression of network attributes and origin–destination characteristics, the modules that compute transport demand, mode choice and traffic assignment bring significant advantages in estimating changes in travel costs correctly when testing likely impacts of specific shifts in transport system characteristics.

11.5.2 Main Assumptions to Estimate Impact of Improved Infrastructure

The indicators proposed to measure accessibility of regions use GDP, population and travel time as the main inputs. The improved or new infrastructures for road and rail are expected to reduce existing travel times between regions. Therefore, the following main assumptions were made to estimate the likely changes in travel times between regions. First, the data that show improved network links in the form of spatial vectors were matched with the TRANS-TOOLS network. Then the free flow speed attribute of the improved road and rail network links in TRANS-TOOLS increased by 25 per cent to be able to estimate likely impacts of improved infrastructure on travel times between regions. The amount of increase rate was decided with a heuristic approach. With and without the changed free flow speed attributes of the network links, two separate simulations were produced using TRANS-TOOLS. The average travel times between regions were computed after a mode choice and a traffic assignment with the modified network, including congestion times for road transport. The results on travel time with the baseline and the cohesion infrastructure were than analysed separately in order to measure changes in accessibility of regions.

Apart from this, another important assumption was made in identifying the type of infrastructure investments co-funded by the EU. Detailed information on quantity and quality of network improvements and differentiation on the newly built or improved infrastructures was not available through the database provided by DG REGIO. It included only information on coordinates and the transport mode of the co-funded transport projects. Therefore, within the analysis, all network links built or improved for rail and road transport are assumed to be improved homogeneously up to a certain amount, that is, a 25 per cent increase in free flow speeds of all improved network links.

Finally, in order to measure accessibility of regions, the distance decay parameters for road and rail were calibrated based on Wilson's (1967, 1970) doubly constrained gravity model and using the maximum likelihood parameter estimation technique with TRANS-TOOLS data. The values of beta parameters were calibrated as 2.75 for road and 2.5 for rail passenger transport using a power cost function. Initially, the results on accessibility measures were evaluated with and without the calibrated distance decay parameters. However, it was decided not to use the calibrated distance decay parameters for the analysis due to some inconsistencies and biases they create in the distribution of accessibility results, because of the heterogeneous, non-uniform NUTS 3 zone sizes and unrealistic intra-zonal travel times.

11.6   RESULTS

Similar to the several other studies mentioned above, overall results indicate that the existing accessibility pattern in Europe for road and rail passenger transport follows a core–periphery pattern. For road transport accessibility, the distinction is especially evident. Apart from this, a distinction between different groups of regions with different accessibility levels can

Table 11.2   A classification of the European accessibility pattern for road and rail transport

Description of different groups	Level of accessibility
Very remote, peripheral regions with sparse economic activity and low urbanization (e.g., parts of Norway, Sweden and Finland)	Lowest regional accessibility
Remote, peripheral regions with sparse economic activity and low urbanization (e.g., parts of Estonia, Romania and Bulgaria)	Lower regional accessibility
Semi-peripheral regions with moderate economic activity and low urbanization (e.g., parts of Poland, Slovak Republic and Hungary)	Low regional accessibility
Peripheral regions with very dense economic activity, high urbanization and dense transport network (e.g., Athens, Istanbul and Stockholm)	Moderate regional accessibility
Semi-central regions with very dense economic activity, high urbanization and dense transport network (e.g., Madrid, Barcelona and Rome)	
Central regions with moderate economic activity, high urbanization and dense transport network (e.g., parts of France and Germany)	High regional accessibility
Central regions with dense economic activity, high urbanization and dense transport network (e.g., Benelux countries and Germany)	Higher regional accessibility
Very central regions with very dense economic activity, very high urbanization and dense transport network (e.g., Paris and Brussels)	Highest regional accessibility

be made, according to their pattern of economic activity, geographical location and urbanization level. A description of these distinctions and the accessibility of these regions, from lowest to highest, is provided in Table 11.2. Additionally, the spatial distribution of accessibility for road and rail transport is presented in Figures 11.2 and 11.3.[2]

This classification is applicable to accessibility measures which consider the economic potential of all other regions in the system. For the daily accessibility measure, the main distinction should be made between the regions with very dense economic activity, very high urbanization and dense transport networks, and the regions with sparse economic activity and low urbanization. Apart from this, an important distinction to this classification can be made in terms of rail transport accessibility. Since the density of the rail network and the level of its services (for example, speed and frequency) is less homogeneous than for the road network, the regions

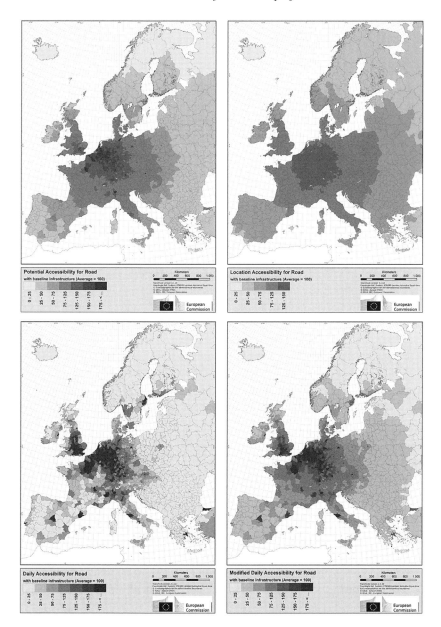

Figure 11.2   Accessibility pattern in Europe for road transport

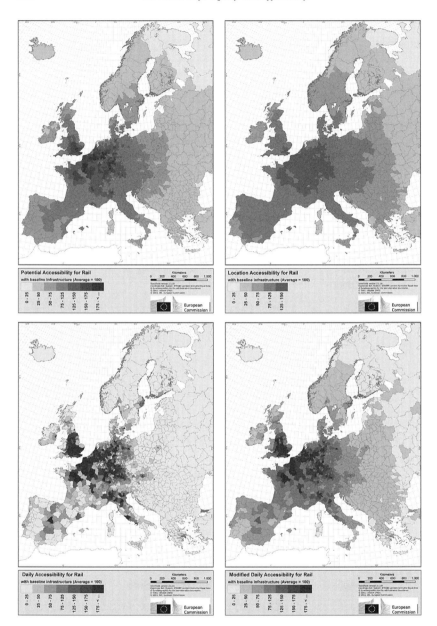

Figure 11.3   Accessibility pattern in Europe for rail transport

having denser rail networks and a better level of services achieve higher accessibility levels than their geographical locations suggest (for example, in some parts of the United Kingdom, Spain and Sweden).

In order to analyse impacts of the co-funded transport infrastructure projects on the European accessibility pattern, two different cases with and without the improved infrastructures were compared. Table 11.3 shows the mean percentage changes in accessibility of regions after the improved road transport network. The results are given for all types of accessibility indicators under three main groups: for all Europe (1441 zones), for the countries with improved road infrastructure (311 zones), and for the zones (103 zones) where the improved road infrastructure took place. It was also statistically tested whether the mean percentage changes significantly differ from zero. For all of the cases the mean percentage changes significantly differ from zero, at a 95 per cent confidence interval.

Considering the whole Europe, the majority of the accessibility indicators show that the road accessibility increases slightly with the cohesion infrastructure; the increase changes on average from 0.34 per cent to 0.43 per cent. The outliers, among others, are the daily and the potential-demand accessibility measures which respectively show a 1.34 per cent and 0.04 per cent change on average. Naturally, the average amount of change increases when only the 12 countries with the improved infrastructure are taken into consideration; that is, the mean percentage change for the potential accessibility rises to 1.12 per cent, and for the daily accessibility to 5.92 per cent. Finally, the positive impact is more remarkable at a regional scale when it is concentrated only on the zones with the improved infrastructure. In 103 peripheral regions where the investments took place, the cohesion infrastructure leads to a 16.9 per cent average increase in daily road accessibility, which is a considerably high increase, and important for reducing disparities among the regions. The highest relative increases in daily road accessibility of regions were recorded in Poland, Estonia, Lithuania, Bulgaria and Romania, as indicated in Figure 11.4.

The mean percentage change for rail accessibility shows a similar pattern among different indicators. However, the amount of positive change is significantly higher than for road accessibility, since the total length of improved rail infrastructure (6.1 per cent of the total rail network) has a higher share in the entire network compared to the improved road infrastructure (1.6 per cent of the total road network). The results provided in Table 11.4 mainly indicate that the rail transport accessibility at European level increases on average 1.1–1.5 per cent with the improved infrastructure. It is around 3 per cent on average, if measured with the daily accessibility indicator. Considering the 14 countries (331 zones) where the rail investments took place, the change in the accessibility of regions is around

Table 11.3   Comparison of the baseline and the cohesion.infrastructure: change in percentages for road transport accessibility

All Europe (1441 zones)

Pairs of indicators Number of observations = 1441	Mean percentage change (%)	Standard deviation	95% confidence int. for mean		t-statistic	p-value
			Lower bound	Upper bound		
A cohesion – A baseline	0.36	0.74	0.33	0.40	18.71	$p < 0.01$
B cohesion – B baseline	0.04	0.61	0.01	0.07	2.36	$p < 0.05$
C cohesion – C baseline	0.34	0.65	0.31	0.37	19.66	$p < 0.01$
D cohesion – D baseline	0.44	0.50	0.42	0.47	33.41	$p < 0.01$
E cohesion – E baseline	1.34	8.27	0.91	1.77	6.15	$p < 0.01$
F cohesion – F baseline	0.43	1.15	0.38	0.50	14.38	$p < 0.01$

Countries with the improved road infrastructure (12 countries, 311 zones)

Pairs of indicators Number of observations = 311	Mean percentage change (%)	Standard deviation	95% confidence int. for mean		t-statistic	p-value
			Lower bound	Upper bound		
A cohesion – A baseline	1.12	1.21	0.99	1.26	16.42	$p < 0.01$
B cohesion – B baseline	0.54	1.04	0.43	0.66	9.20	$p < 0.01$
C cohesion – C baseline	1.01	1.04	0.89	1.12	17.09	$p < 0.01$
D cohesion – D baseline	0.75	0.75	0.66	0.83	17.62	$p < 0.01$
E cohesion – E baseline	5.92	16.96	4.03	7.81	6.16	$p < 0.01$
F cohesion – F baseline	1.52	2.03	1.30	1.75	13.25	$p < 0.01$

Regions with the improved road infrastructure (103 zones)						
Pairs of indicators Number of observations = 103	Mean percentage change (%)	Standard deviation	95% confidence int. for mean		t-statistic	p-value
			Lower bound	Upper bound		
A cohesion – A baseline	2.06	1.47	1.77	2.34	14.16	$p < 0.01$
B cohesion – B baseline	1.36	1.31	1.10	1.61	10.50	$p < 0.01$
C cohesion – C baseline	1.79	1.28	1.54	2.04	14.22	$p < 0.01$
D cohesion – D baseline	1.10	0.90	0.92	1.27	12.40	$p < 0.01$
E cohesion – E baseline	16.93	26.20	11.81	22.05	6.56	$p < 0.01$
F cohesion – F baseline	3.27	2.63	2.75	3.78	12.59	$p < 0.01$

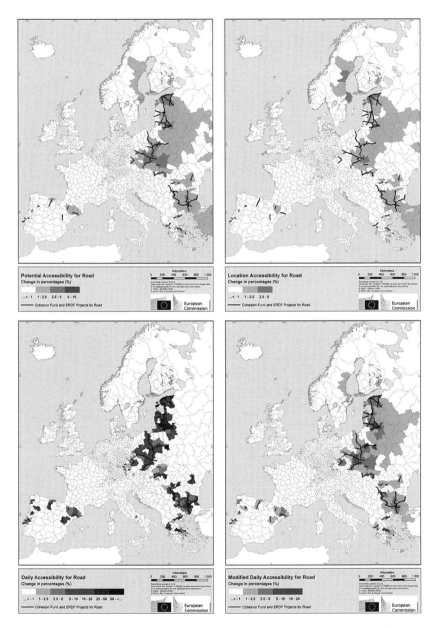

*Figure 11.4   Change in road transport accessibility of regions after the
               Cohesion Fund and the ERDF projects*

Table 11.4 Comparison of the baseline and the cohesion infrastructure: change in percentages for rail transport accessibility

All Europe (1441 zones)

Pairs of indicators Number of observations = 1441	Mean percentage change (%)	Standard deviation	95% confidence int. for mean		t-statistic	p-value
			Lower bound	Upper bound		
A cohesion – A baseline	1.16	1.75	1.07	1.25	25.18	p < 0.01
B cohesion – B baseline	0.04	1.36	−0.03	0.11	1.20	p < 0.05
C cohesion – C baseline	1.18	1.59	1.10	1.26	28.20	p < 0.01
D cohesion – D baseline	1.53	1.20	1.47	1.59	48.47	p < 0.01
E cohesion – E baseline	3.09	21.70	1.97	4.21	5.41	p < 0.01
F cohesion – F baseline	1.31	2.50	1.18	1.43	19.80	p < 0.01

Countries with the improved rail infrastructure (14 countries, 331 zones)

Pairs of indicators Number of observations = 311	Mean percentage change (%)	Standard deviation	95% confidence int. for mean		t-statistic	p-value
			Lower bound	Upper bound		
A cohesion – A baseline	3.29	2.20	3.05	3.53	27.15	p < 0.01
B cohesion – B baseline	1.51	1.82	1.32	1.71	15.17	p < 0.01
C cohesion – C baseline	3.11	1.97	2.89	3.32	28.71	p < 0.01
D cohesion – D baseline	2.74	1.65	2.57	2.92	30.23	p < 0.01
E cohesion – E baseline	13.28	43.79	8.54	18.01	5.51	p < 0.01
F cohesion – F baseline	4.13	3.78	3.73	4.54	19.90	p < 0.01

Table 11.4 (continued)

All Europe (1441 zones)

Regions with the improved road infrastructure (103 zones)

Pairs of indicators Number of observations = 113	Mean percentage change (%)	Standard deviation	95% confidence int. for mean		t-statistic	p-value
			Lower bound	Upper bound		
A cohesion – A baseline	4.49	2.74	3.98	5.00	17.33	p < 0.01
B cohesion – B baseline	2.67	2.19	2.26	3.08	12.90	p < 0.01
C cohesion – C baseline	4.20	2.42	3.74	4.65	18.35	p < 0.01
D cohesion – D baseline	3.26	2.02	2.88	3.64	17.08	p < 0.01
E cohesion – E baseline	20.77	23.51	16.37	25.17	9.35	p < 0.01
F cohesion – F baseline	6.15	3.76	5.45	6.86	17.34	p < 0.01

3–4 per cent on average. Daily accessibility in these countries increased on average by 13.28 per cent, and Poland, Greece, Portugal and Czech Republic were the countries having the highest increases, as shown in Figure 11.5. Finally, in 113 peripheral regions with the improved transport network, the cohesion infrastructure leads to a 20.77 per cent average increase in daily rail accessibility, which is higher than the increase in road transport. All these considerably high increases in accessibility of regions, especially in the peripheral regions, are supposed to reduce disparities in accessibility among regions and contribute to territorial cohesion across Europe. One of the ways to measure the amount of change in the disparities is to use cohesion indicators.

Cohesion indicators, or indicators to measure dispersion, describe the distribution of accessibility across regions. They summarize several individual measures into one single measure of spatial concentration. Differences in these indicators reveal whether one distribution is more equitable or more polarized than another. Changes in cohesion indicators over time, after certain infrastructure improvements for instance, indicate whether the existing disparities in accessibility of regions increased or decreased (Wegener et al. 2001). In order to evaluate disparities in accessibility of regions, whether they are diverged or converged, two well-known cohesion indicators were used: the coefficient of variance and the Gini coefficient. Rising values for both of the indicators indicate that the inequality in accessibility between areas is increasing or diverging. The results for the cohesion indicators are presented in Table 11.5. Additionally, the measure of dispersion in accessibility of regions is illustrated with the Lorenz curves in Figure 11.6. According to the results in Table 11.5, and the distribution of accessibility measures presented earlier with the figures:

- For the potential, potential-demand and the inverse balancing accessibility measures, the coefficient of variation lies between 0.39 and 0.47, and the Gini coefficient lies between 0.22 and 0.27 for both the road and rail transport. These values imply a medium-sized dispersion among accessibility of regions in Europe. If we classify regions as metropolitan, rural, central, semi-central and remote/peripheral, the main source of dispersion for the existing accessibility pattern is the huge differences among these groups, rather than the differences within the groups. While the dense urban areas with central locations are accessible at higher levels, the remote areas with sparse economic activity have lower accessibility values.
- Among the all accessibility indicators, the location accessibility indicator shows the lowest dispersion among regions. The coefficient of variation is around 0.33 and the Gini coefficient is

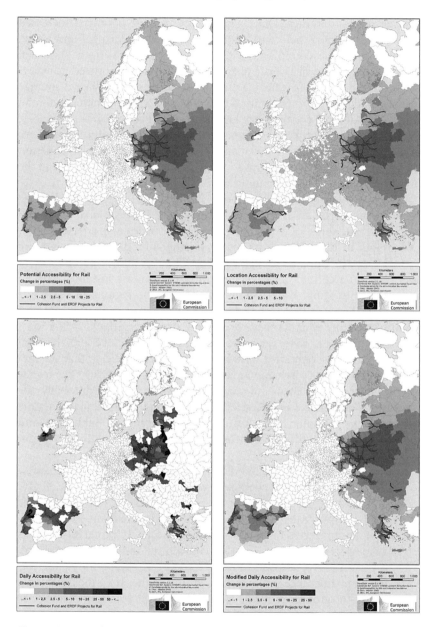

*Figure 11.5   Change in rail transport accessibility of regions after the
Cohesion Fund and the ERDF projects*

Table 11.5 Measure of dispersion in accessibility of regions

Measure of dispersion for road transport accessibility

Name of accessibility indicator	Coefficient of variance		Change in coefficient of variance (%)	Gini coefficient		Change in Gini coefficient (%)
	Baseline	Cohesion		Baseline	Cohesion	
Potential accessibility (*Ind. A*)	0.4726	0.4707	−0.394	0.2704	0.2693	−0.402
Potential-demand accessibility (*Ind. B*)	0.3888	0.3873	−0.377	0.2226	0.2217	−0.387
Inverse balancing accessibility (*Ind. C*)	0.4361	0.4343	−0.410	0.2496	0.2485	−0.420
Location accessibility (*Ind. D*)	0.3306	0.3302	−0.128	0.1870	0.1867	−0.125
Daily accessibility (*Ind. E*)	1.1074	1.1045	−0.262	0.5559	0.5545	−0.246
Modified daily accessibility (*Ind. F*)	0.6786	0.6763	−0.339	0.3688	0.3675	−0.341
Average change			−0.318			−0.320

Measure of dispersion for rail transport accessibility

Name of accessibility indicator	Coefficient of variance		Change in coefficient of variance (%)	Gini coefficient		Change in Gini coefficient (%)
	Baseline	Cohesion		Baseline	Cohesion	
Potential accessibility (*Ind. A*)	0.4708	0.4643	−1.389	0.270	0.266	−1.408
Potential-demand accessibility (*Ind. B*)	0.4021	0.3973	−1.193	0.230	0.228	−1.226
Inverse balancing accessibility (*Ind. C*)	0.4402	0.4342	−1.371	0.252	0.249	−1.398
Location accessibility (*Ind. D*)	0.3350	0.3313	−1.094	0.190	0.188	−1.100
Daily accessibility (*Ind. E*)	1.2607	1.2533	−0.593	0.615	0.612	−0.529
Modified daily accessibility (*Ind. F*)	0.6877	0.6807	−1.024	0.373	0.369	−1.066
Average change			−1.111			−1.121

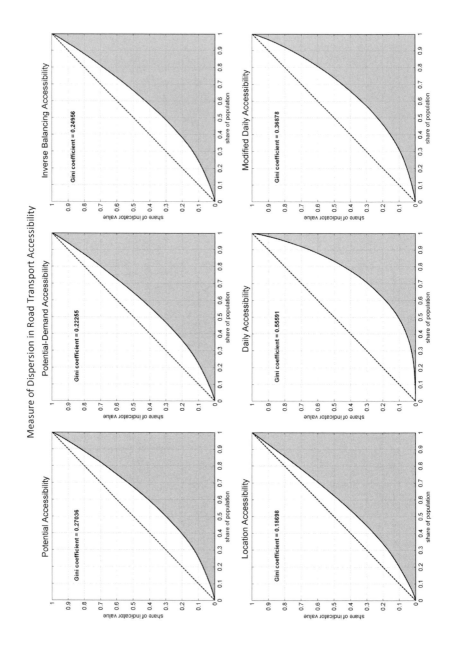

Measure of Dispersion in Road Transport Accessibility

Potential Accessibility — Gini coefficient = 0.27036

Potential-Demand Accessibility — Gini coefficient = 0.22255

Inverse Balancing Accessibility — Gini coefficient = 0.24956

Location Accessibility — Gini coefficient = 0.18698

Daily Accessibility — Gini coefficient = 0.55591

Modified Daily Accessibility — Gini coefficient = 0.36878

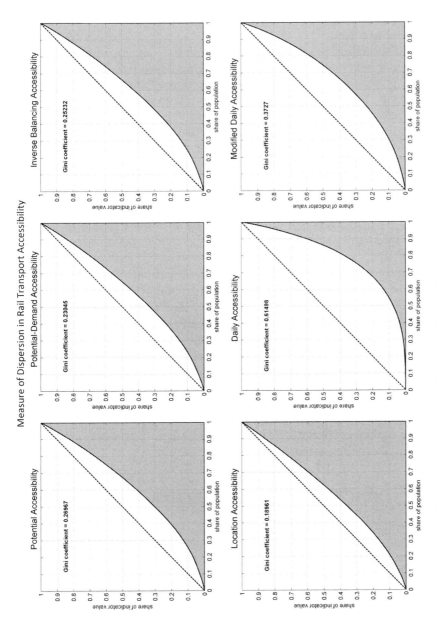

Figure 11.6   Measure of dispersion in accessibility with Gini coefficient

237

around 0.19 for the location accessibility indicator of road and rail transport. The location accessibility measure indicates less dispersion among regions due to the reduced impact of geographical advantages.

- The highest polarization in accessibility of regions is observed in daily and modified daily accessibility measures. For daily accessibility, the coefficient of variation is 1.1 for road and 1.2 for rail transport. For modified daily accessibility it is around 0.67 for both road and rail transport. The Gini coefficient for daily accessibility is also higher than the others: it is 0.55 for road and 0.61 for rail transport. Although the daily accessibility does not constitute high inequalities for the majority of regions, the extreme examples raise disparities and increase polarization between the regions. For instance, daily accessibility for big metropolitan areas such as Paris, Brussels, Milan and Amsterdam and most of the regions in western Germany such as Essen and Duisburg is more or less 5–10 times greater than the European average.

The results indicate that the disparities between regions are slightly reduced with the improved transport infrastructure. On average, the road and rail transport investments co-funded by the European Union reduced the existing disparities in accessibility of regions by 0.32 per cent for road and 1.12 per cent for rail. Considering that these investments constitute only a small part of the entire network (1.6 per cent of the total road network, and 6.1 per cent of the total rail network), these slight reductions in the inequalities of regions could be seen as an important achievement. It should also be taken into account that the impact of infrastructure improvements and decreasing dissimilarity in accessibility of regions may have a multiplier effect on the social and economic instruments aiming at territorial cohesion within Europe.

11.7   CONCLUSIONS AND FURTHER RESEARCH

This chapter proposed a framework to assess impacts of various policy options and transport infrastructure investments on accessibility at European level. It was tested by measuring the impacts of road and rail transport infrastructure investments co-funded by the Cohesion Fund and ERDF between 2000 and 2006, mainly in the European peripheral and enlargement countries. Considering the proposed methodology for measuring accessibility, the following points must first be underlined:

- With the analysis, the likely impacts of the improved infrastructure were analysed with several accessibility indicators which are sensitive to any: (1) network improvements; (2) modal and technological shifts; (3) demand- and supply-side changes; and (4) changes in socio-economic and demographic characteristics.

- Among them, daily accessibility was found to be the most suitable and effective measure for this type of analysis. It is superior in highlighting relative changes in the investment regions and in their neighbours. Modified daily accessibility was also proved to be a useful and an efficient measure since it highlights grey areas between the daily and the potential accessibility indicators.

- Other proposed accessibility measures (for example, potential demand and inverse balancing indicators) are especially sensitive to the changes in GDP and population, and could be utilized for future-oriented scenarios with changing demand factors.

Apart from this, with the analysis of the spatial distribution of accessibility, it was shown that the existing accessibility pattern in Europe follows a core–periphery pattern for both road and rail passenger transport. Accessibility of regions is higher at the centre and lower at the periphery. The distinction is less evident for rail accessibility, in that the regions with dense rail networks and a better level of services have higher accessibility than their geographical locations suggest. The overall results indicate that the transport infrastructure investments in the European peripheral countries co-funded by the Cohesion Fund and the ERDF have significantly improved the accessibility of regions in these countries, and slightly reduced the dissimilarities between regions within Europe.

The amount of increase is rather small if the whole of Europe is taken into consideration. However, if the increase in daily accessibility of regions where the network improvements took place is taken into account, the impact is much higher. The average increase is 16.9 per cent for daily road and 20.77 per cent for daily rail accessibility in these regions. Although the accessibility of peripheral regions increased significantly, the disparities between accessibility of regions converged only slightly with the improved transport infrastructure. The road and rail transport investments co-funded by the Cohesion Fund and ERDF reduced the existing disparities in accessibility of regions by 0.32 per cent for road and 1.12 per cent for rail passenger transport on average. The co-funded transport investments constitute only a small part of the entire transport network (1.6 per cent of the total road network, and 6.1 per cent of the total rail network). Therefore, these slight reductions in the inequalities of regions should be seen as key achievements that need to be supported with other social and economic instruments aiming at territorial cohesion in the EU. It should also be noted that the transport infrastructure investment is only one of the several important macro factors that shape accessibility, and it is more effective in the long term.

Finally, further work in the same direction may include testing these accessibility indicators for future-oriented scenarios and elaborating the analysis in monitoring change in regional disparities to include the welfare effects. Overall, the accessibility measures demonstrate that the disparities between regions are slightly reduced with the improved transport infrastructure within Europe. However, as the daily accessibility and the modified daily accessibility measures indicate, polarization within any single country is sometimes much higher and the new infrastructure may have the effect of increasing polarization within a country. So other further work could analyse the impact of these infrastructure improvements on local accessibility and polarization levels within a country using higher spatial resolution or smaller origin–destination zones.

NOTES

1. The views expressed are purely those of the authors and may not in any circumstances be regarded as stating an official position of the European Commission.
2. The spatial pattern for the potential-demand accessibility and the inverse balancing accessibility indicators are only slightly different from the potential accessibility indicator. Therefore, they are not included within the figures that map accessibility patterns. The results on these two indicators are elaborated through the tables.

REFERENCES

Christidis, P. and N.I. Rivas (2012), 'European transport policy: Methodology to assess accessibility impacts', in K. Geurs, K. Krizek and A. Reggiani (eds), *Accessibility Analysis and Transport Planning: Challenges for Europe and North America*, Cheltenham, UK and Northampton, MA, USA: Edward Elgar Publishing.

Curtis, C. and J. Scheurer (2010), 'Planning for sustainable accessibility: Developing tools to aid discussion and decision-making', *Progress in Planning*, **74** (2), 53–106.

ECORYS Nederland BV. (2006), 'Strategic evaluation on transport investment priorities under structural and cohesion funds for the programming – period 2007–2013', No 2005.CE.16.AT.014, Rotterdam.

ESPON (2010), 'TIPTAP: Territorial Impact Package for Transport and Agricultural Policies', Applied Research Project 2013/1/6, Final Report – Part C, ESPON 2013 Programme.

European Commission (2008), *Green Paper on Territorial Cohesion: Turning Territorial Diversity into Strength*, COM (2008) 616 final, Brussels.

European Commission (2010), *Investing in Europe's Future: The Fifth Report on Economic, Social and Territorial Cohesion*, Luxembourg: Publications Office of the European Union.

European Commission (2011a), *Impact Assessment Accompanying Document to the White Paper: Roadmap to a Single European Transport Area – Towards a Competitive and Resource Efficient Transport System*, SEC (2011) 358 final, Brussels.

European Commission (2011b), *White Paper: Roadmap to a Single European Transport Area – Towards a Competitive and Resource Efficient Transport System*, COM (2011) 144 final, Brussels.

European Commission (2013), 'Regional policy – inforegio: Cohesion Fund', available at http://ec.europa.eu/regional_policy/thefunds/cohesion/index_en.cfm (accessed 1 November 2013).

European Parliament (2007), 'Regional disparities and cohesion: What strategies for the future?', IP/B/REGI/IC/2006_201, Directorate General Internal Policies of the Union, Brussels.

European Union (2007a), 'Territorial agenda of the European Union: Towards a more competitive and sustainable Europe of diverse regions', Agreement of the ministerial meeting on urban development and territorial cohesion, 24–25 May, Leipzig, available at http://www.eu-territorial-agenda.eu/Reference Documents/Territorial-Agenda-of-the-European-Union-Agreed-on-25-May-2007.pdf (accessed 11 November 2013).

European Union (2007b), 'Treaty of Lisbon amending the Treaty on European Union and the Treaty establishing the European Community', 2007/C 306/01, *Official Journal of the European Union*, C 306.

European Union (2011a), 'Territorial agenda of the European Union 2020: Towards an inclusive, smart and sustainable Europe of diverse regions', Agreement of the informal ministerial meeting of ministers responsible for spatial planning and territorial development, 19 May, Gödöllő, Hungary, available at http://www.eu2011.hu/files/bveu/documents/TA2020.pdf (accessed 11 November 2013).

European Union (2011b), 'The Cohesion Fund at a glance (archive)', available at http://ec.europa.eu/regional_policy/archive/funds/procf/cf_en.htm (accessed 1 November 2013).

European Union (2013), 'Glossary: Structural Funds and Cohesion Fund', available at http://europa.eu/legislation_summaries/glossary/structural_cohesion_fund_en.htm (accessed 1 November 2013).

Geurs, K.T. and B. van Wee (2004), 'Accessibility evaluation of land-use and transport strategies: review and research directions', *Journal of Transport Geography*, **12** (2), 127–140.

Gløersen, E., Dubois, A., Copus, A. and C. Schürmann (2006), 'Northern peripheral, sparsely populated regions in the European Union and in Norway', Nordregio Report 2006: 2, Stockholm: Nordregio.

Gutiérrez, J. (2009), 'Transport and accessibility', in R. Kitchin and N. Thrift (eds), *International Encyclopedia of Human Geography*, Oxford: Elsevier.

Hansen, S. (2011), 'TRANS-TOOLS user guide. Project: TRANS-TOOLS v2.0 Documentation', Copenhagen: Rapidis.

Kompil, M., Christidis, P., Lopez-Ruiz, H.G., Maerivoet, S., Purwanto, J. and M.V.

Salucci (2013), 'Modelling future mobility – scenario simulation at macro level', Luxembourg: JRC Technical Reports, DOI: 10.2791/29292.

López, E., Gutiérrez, J. and G. Gómez (2008), 'Measuring regional cohesion effects of large-scale transport infrastructure investments: An accessibility approach', *European Planning Studies*, **16** (2), 277–301.

Morris, J.M., Dumble, P.L. and Wigan, M.R. (1979), 'Accessibility indicators for transport planning', *Transportation Research Part A*, **13** (2), 91–109.

Páez, A., Scott, D.M. and C. Morency (2012), 'Measuring accessibility: Positive and normative implementations of various accessibility indicators', *Journal of Transport Geography*, **25**, 141–153.

Rietveld, P. (1994), 'Spatial-economic impacts of transport infrastructure supply', *Transportation Research Part A: Policy and Practice*, **28** (4), 239–341.

Rietveld, P. and F. Bruinsma (1998), *Is Transport Infrastructure Effective? Transport Infrastructure and Accessibility: Impacts on the Space Economy*, Berlin: Springer-Verlag.

SASI (2000), 'Socio-economic and spatial impacts of transport infrastructure investments and transport systems improvements', available at http://www.srf. tuwien.ac.at/Projekte/sasi/sasi.htm (accessed 1 November 2013).

Spiekermann, K. and M. Wegener (2006), 'Accessibility and spatial development in Europe', *Scienze Regionali*, **5** (2), 15–46.

Spiekermann, K., Wegener, M., Kveton, V., Marada, M., Schürmann, C., Biosca, O., Ulied Segui, A., Antikainen, H., Kotavaara, O., Rusanen, J., Bielanska, D., Fiorello, D., Komornicki, T. and P. Rosik (2011), 'Transport accessibility at regional/local scale and patterns in Europe', Interim Report of ESPON TRACC, Dortmund: Spiekermann & Wegener Urban and Regional Research.

Transport & Mobility Leuven (2005), 'ASSESS final report: Assessment of the contribution of the TEN and other transport policy measures to the mid-term implementation of the White Paper on the European Transport Policy for 2010', DG TREN, European Commission.

TRANS-TOOLS (2008a), 'TRANS-TOOLS Documentation', European Commission, JRC-IPTS, available at http://energy.jrc.ec.europa.eu/transtools/ documentation.html (accessed 1 October 2013).

TRANS-TOOLS (2008b), 'TRANS-TOOLS Home', European Commission, JRC-IPTS, available at http://energy.jrc.ec.europa.eu/transtools/index.html (accessed 1 October 2013).

Vickerman, R., Spikermann, K. and M. Wegener (1999), 'Accessibility and economic development in Europe', *Regional Studies*, **33** (1), 1–15.

Wegener, M. (2008), 'SASI model description', Working Paper 08/01, Dortmund: Spiekermann & Wegener, Urban and Regional Research, available at http://www. spiekermann-wegener.de/mod/pdf/AP_0801.pdf (accessed 1 November 2013).

Wegener, M., Eskelinnen, H., Fürst, F., Schürmann, C. and K. Spiekermann (2001), 'Criteria for the spatial differentiation of the EU territory: Geographical position', Forschungen 102.2, Bundesamt für Bauwesen und Raumordnung, Bonn.

Wilson, A.G. (1967), 'A statistical theory of spatial distributions', *Transportation Research*, **1**, 253–269.

Wilson, A.G. (1970), Entropy in Urban and Regional Modelling, London: Pion.

Index

access
  to train stations
    population distribution and access to stations 132–4
  time
  modes
accessibility
  basic level of 4–5
  definitions 3, 211
  criteria for selection of indicators 217
  description of selected indicators 217–19
  in European road and rail transport 210–40
  Hansen-style measure of 60
  high-speed rail networks, levels of 125–40
  impact of mobility costs on, in Munich 83–106
  indicator, potential accessibility 217–18, 227–9, 231–2, 235–7, 239
  indicator, potential-demand accessibility 218, 227–9, 231–3, 235–7, 239–40
  industrial 167–84
  justice-oriented 5
  labour market, 64–6, 77
  link to efficiency and equity 4–5
  measures of
    calculations 129–30, 134–5
    European transport 211–14, 217–19, 223–40
    simple vs. complex 36
    types 29
    uses 216
    see also Gini coefficient for accessibility; Gini index for accessibility, public transport accessibility

population
  depopulation in Norway 55–78
  in Huambo, Angola 112–13, 116–18
  in Madrid-Levante HSR corridor 132–4, 137–8
  in Portuguese interior 33–52
  in Swiss municipalities 11–29
public transport
  factors, improvements dependent on 33
  HSR 139–40
  time constraints 37
  weakening over time 12, 23–8
rail transport, Europe
  existing patterns of 223–4, 239
  increasing with cohesion infrastructure 227, 231–3, 239
  indicator results 233, 238
  measure of dispersion in 235, 237
  spatial distribution of 224, 226–7
road transport, Europe
  existing patterns of 223–4, 239
  increasing with cohesion infrastructure 227–30, 239
  indicator results 233, 238
  measure of dispersion in 235–6
  spatial distribution of 224–5, 227
shrinking services 37–8
train station access and train use in Netherlands 144–6
use, and costs, in Munich 85–106
Adamos, G. 127, 140
Anderson, S.T. 195–6, 200–201, 204
Axhausen, K.W. 13, 15, 29

Banister, D. 3, 11, 15, 125–8, 139
Ben-Akiva, M.E. 15, 146
Berechman, J. 3, 15, 125

.